God and Community Organizing

God and Community Organizing

A Covenantal Approach

Hak Joon Lee

BAYLOR UNIVERSITY PRESS

Cover and book design by Kasey McBeath, typesetting by Scribe Inc.
Cover art: Shutterstock/VasilkovS

Library of Congress Cataloging-in-Publication Data
Names: Lee, Hak Joon, 1958- author.
Title: God and community organizing : a covenantal approach / Hak Joon Lee.
Description: Waco : Baylor University Press, 2020. | Includes
  bibliographical references and index. | Summary: "Brings covenantal
  theology into conversation with the community organizing theory of Saul
  Alinsky to model a Christian communal response to contemporary societal
  challenges"-- Provided by publisher.
Identifiers: LCCN 2020021999 (print) | LCCN 2020022000 (ebook) | ISBN
  9781481313155 (hardcover) | ISBN 9781481313810 (pdf) | ISBN
  9781481313803 (mobi) | ISBN 9781481313179 (epub)
Subjects: LCSH: Community organization--United States. | Community power. |
  Church and social problems. | Covenants--Biblical teaching.
Classification: LCC HN90.C64 L44 2020 (print) | LCC HN90.C64 (ebook) |
  DDC 303.30973--dc23
LC record available at https://lccn.loc.gov/2020021999
LC ebook record available at https://lccn.loc.gov/2020022000

NATIONAL
ENDOWMENT
FOR THE
HUMANITIES

God and Community Organizing has been made possible in part by a major grant from the National Endowment for the Humanities: NEH CARES. Any views, findings, conclusions, or recommendations expressed in this book do not necessarily represent those of the National Endowment for the Humanities.

To
my teachers, Peter J. Paris and the late Max L. Stackhouse,
and
my students

Contents

Foreword

With *God and Community Organizing: A Covenantal Approach* Hak Joon Lee has met the moment.

Hak Joon Lee completed his manuscript before the pandemic. The pandemic has, however, underscored and intensified what he describes at the very outset of this book: the longing of people for a new direction and a moral vision, together with a framework for meeting the overwhelming challenges we confront. Lee's work could not have been more timely, nor more constructive.

Yearning and expectation are in the air. So are instances of uncommon civil solidarity. "We're all in this together" and "Together, we're stronger" are heard everywhere.

To be sure, many ache for a return to "normal." Yet most know that is not possible. Nor is it desirable. "Normal" is unconscionable inequality and injustices that fall disproportionately on poor, black, Native, brown, Asian, and migratory peoples. "Normal" is government that prioritizes the least vulnerable—big corporations and the ranks of wealth—over protection of the most vulnerable. "Normal" is the lot of those we have come to call "essential workers," as the lot of the lowest paid and least respected, while less-than-essential workers—hedge fund owners, corporate lawyers, hotel and golf course moguls—have power and standing and take home millions. Neoliberal capitalism as "normal" shreds our common bonds and has little interest in the common good.

If we return to normal in the way Washington asks, we only exacerbate the underlying and preexisting conditions that render us all highly vulnerable not only to future pandemics, climate rupture, and the social injustice Hak Joon Lee exposes so clearly, but it also renders us highly vulnerable to further degradation of the very economy upon which we're wholly and forever dependent—nature's.

At the same time that we ache for the stability and security that "normal" is supposed to bring but does not, a sound moral vision, even a decent moral compass, has gone missing at the highest levels of government. So has a coherent strategy for addressing the fissures and fault lines of modernity, fissures and fault lines that existed long before pandemic X-rays exposed them. Some of them, like endemic and institutional racism trailing in the wake of slavery, and settler takeover of Native American lands, are three and four centuries old.

Over a century old is the kind of analysis that has provoked Hak Joon Lee's passion for social justice. One voice was Ernst Troeltsch's. Addressing "the modern social question" or modern "social problem," Troeltsch wrote in 1911:

> This social problem is vast and complicated. It includes the problem of the capitalist economic period and of the industrial proletariat created by it; and of the growth of militaristic and bureaucratic giant states; of the enormous increase in population, which affects colonial and world policy; of the mechanical technique, which produces enormous masses of materials and links up and mobilizes the whole world for purposes of trade, but which also treats men and labour like machines. (Ernst Troeltsch, *The Social Teaching of the Christian Churches* [Chicago: University of Chicago Press, 1981], 2:1010)

This, then, is the charged moment in which we find ourselves, and the moment *God and Community Organizing* addresses. On the one hand, we likely have the best chance in a long while to address modernity's centuries-old fault lines and fissures. The desire for systemic and structural reform runs deep and is palpable. On the other hand, sound method and strategy, together with a theological-ethical vision and framework (or its secular parallel), do not stand at the ready. However present and palpable the desire for reform is, vision, method, and strategy are not clearly in view.

No single volume can do all that we must collectively undertake for much-needed systemic and structural reform today at many levels, conceptual, tactical, and otherwise. But this remarkable work fits the needs and circumstances of our moment as few others do, by zooming in on key elements that the author weaves together as "covenantal organizing."

For good reason he leads with biblical and theological-ethical substance. Choosing the prominent theme of covenant, Lee makes the case that covenant and organizing are inseparable in Scripture—not only inseparable but foremost; covenant is God's "primary method of organizing a new just community."

Organizing from a covenant base has distinctive stages. These, too, are drawn from Scripture: judgment (deliverance/liberation from chaos and injustice), formal consent and commitment, and building an alternative community.

Covenantal organizing shows a unique capacity to be creatively adapted for use in widely varied contexts and cultures. Lee studies these in depth. He exposits Hebrew Bible texts (the exodus story and its centrality) and Christian New Testament texts (Jesus and the kingdom of God), then selects postbiblical instances—the Puritans, Martin Luther King Jr. and the Civil Rights Movement, and Saul Alinsky and the community organizing of recent decades, right up to the present. In all of this, human beings are coworkers with God in effecting covenant as "the most politically effective and morally appropriate way to organize community."

The theological-ethical substance and framework do not stand alone. Their power arises from the way in which they are joined to our social and environmental reality (those fissures and fault lines of modernity) and the way in which they give us a way to undertake structural reform. Lee incisively analyzes and responds to four interlocking crises that expose the lack of a viable social philosophy for a world careening hither and yon without direction or purpose. The crises are the crises of depleted community and civic institutions, the erosion of sound moral formation and agency, the erosion as well of democratic polity and of civil society itself, and the presence of a global economic order that had made market logic the logic of society itself and the logic of collective action that diminishes and degrades the planet. Hak Joon Lee's analysis of our lived world and its crises may well be the best I've seen. It would be an outstanding work in its own right.

This opus does not stop there, however. The contextual analysis and the theo-ethical treatment of covenant join a third element, a study of community organizing, to arrive at the constructive presentation of covenantal organizing. Covenantal organizing is then directed to our pressing needs. The outcome is a vision with legs, so to speak. The outcome is vibrant grassroots democracy in and for global community on a small, endangered planet.

We should not ask for more than *God and Community Organizing* provides, a public theology of community and organizing that yields a vision, strategy, and method. In profound ways it meets the historical moment that is ours.

Heartening, too, is that a sequel is already in view. Covenantal organizing will be brought to bear on constructive ecclesiology and pastoral leadership. Hints are already part of the final chapter of this volume.

—*Larry Rasmussen, Reinhold Niebuhr Professor Emeritus of Social Ethics, Union Theological Seminary, New York City, June 2020*

Preface

The 9/11 attacks, the 2008 financial crisis (the Great Recession), Brexit, the Trump election, the acceleration of global warming with burning forests and dying corals, the stagnation of employment and wages, the uptick in depression and suicide rates, the prevalence of opioid addiction, the rise of white nationalism and illiberal democracy in the West . . .

It seems that we are living in a runaway world without direction or purpose; the ground is shifting, and the social fabric is unraveling. The COVID-19 crisis has ruthlessly exposed deep flaws within the governing system of the most powerful nation in dealing with the trying challenge of a pandemic, which required swift, rational responses and highly sophisticated coordination among governmental institutions and citizens. The complexity and magnitude of our social problems are staggering, overwhelming for any one nation to fix, although these are all human-made problems. The instinctive human response to a threat—fight or flight—has taken new forms of expression. Many today desensitize themselves from pain and suffering with self-medication, consciously shut down their emotions and sensibilities, and choose a path of flight to indulgence, entertainment, personal comfort, careerism, or substance abuse and addiction, because fighting is too overwhelming, exhausting, and distressing. People are longing for a new direction, moral vision, and framework for addressing the opportunities and challenges posed by such massive changes.

This book is a theological-ethical response to the current malaise of our society, born in particular from concerns about Christian responses to the situation. The past several decades have borne painful witness that the voices of Christians have been relatively silent about, embarrassingly irrelevant to, or downright destructive for contemporary social-political realities. This has in large part been the result of a deficiency of a coherent social philosophy. Hence, many Christians simply react to the events taking place around them or uncritically adopt and assimilate to secular political ideologies of partisan politics.

This book proposes covenant organizing as a way to address our crisis. The readers may be familiar with covenant or community organizing, but perhaps not with their convergence in covenantal organizing. This book presents covenant as the primary method of God's organizing of a new just community. The idea offers us a lens to understand God's reign and God's dealing with humanity. I claim that covenantal organizing constitutes God's reign and the human ethical response to it. God's reign unfolds through covenant, and its purpose is to build a just, righteous, and loving community. Through God's liberating work of deliverance and salvation, God frees humans from the bondage of sin, evil, and oppression, and invites them to a new community where God reigns. By entering God's covenant, humans become God's coworkers in building a new community.

The core claim of this book is that covenant and organizing are inseparable in the Bible. Covenant can be best understood in terms of the organizing of a social relationship and a community, and the Bible presents covenant as the most politically effective and morally appropriate way to organize a community.

The Exodus story forms the heart of the biblical imagination for organizing of a new just community: the mighty God fought against a superpower for the liberation of Hebrew slaves, and promised them land under the condition that they form a new, just, moral community that lived out their memory of enslavement and liberation for the benefit of all humanity. The Sinai Covenant was the organizing principle of their community at the intersection of past liberation and future hope. Capturing the yearning and desire of all oppressed peoples, the Exodus story has injected new meanings into the common life of humanity and transformed human moral imaginations and values in the West.

Because of this insight, the Exodus and the biblical idea of covenant were the source of the sociological imagination and passion of ancient Israel and Jesus, of Jews and Christians. In more recent centuries, it has inspired Puritans, African Americans, and many others. The Exodus and the Sinai Covenant carry the memory of liberation and the hope of restoration, and were eschatologically renewed in Jesus' liberative ministry, death, and resurrection. Covenant was a major impetus for the birth of constitutionalism, democracy, human rights, associational pluralism, and vocation. And in the twentieth century, the Exodus vision guided Martin Luther King Jr.'s audacious dream to "redeem the soul of America" and the movement to deepen and expand democracy.

As a member of a marginalized group, justice is dear to my social existence and professional activities. I have learned that organizing is, pragmatically, at the heart of achieving justice. Organizing begins with the assumption that power comes from organizing, and organizing is the best weapon of the have-nots for their survival, protection, and well-being. Saul Alinsky's insight was based on the observation that injustices, either small or great, are typically the result of power imbalances in social relationships. That is, the sources of injustices are not just the absence of good policy ideas, or a lack of knowledge by politicians or elite decision makers (in fact, there are already many good ideas placed in the Constitution, the law, and public policies). Rather, the problem lies in those who have positions of power, but who, due to their self-interest and their social location in the center, refuse to protect and promote those in the periphery. Consequently, those most hurt by the system are those who do not have organized power to resist those in the position of power and the system run by them.

Why do we need organizing today? Many of our problems have to do with the difficulty of organizing our society afresh according to principles of justice. This difficulty is due to the complexity and radical speed and scope that globalization and new technologies create for our social life. The US is especially culpable; instead of using its superpower status to assist the organization of the globalizing world into a just political and legal community that matches with economic globalization, it has usurped its power and resources for its imperial and hegemonic ambition to protect its rich people and corporations. The result is chaotic unraveling in many parts of the world: treacherous global warming, competition for natural resources, a pervasive refugee/migrant crisis, as well as racial-ethnic and religious conflicts.

The crisis is also related to the growing concentration of power and wealth in the hands of several rich corporations and individuals. With this increasing concentration, democracy is now turning into oligarchy, and the sufferings of people born without resources are exacerbated. More and more people are upset with the current neoliberal arrangement and domination over other spheres of social and political life. In the angry reaction to neoliberal oligarchy, we see the rise of populist politics in the West—the collective assertion of the ordinary people to take back their power from power elites and the wealthy class. However, populism is often emotionally driven, politically volatile, and morally ambiguous. In particular, it is vulnerable to demagogic manipulations when it lacks a moral center, focus, and purpose. Manipulated by demagogues, populism can easily devolve into the vulgar racism, nativism, and enthocentrism exhibited today in sweeping sentiments of Islamophobia, anti-immigration, and racism.

The current status quo is intolerable. We cannot just sit around and assume that things will get better. If these trends continue, and if we do not take any major action, the crisis will metastasize, and we may never fully recover.

It is time for Christians to retell the liberating stories of the Exodus and of Jesus. We need more than prophetic criticism and populist anger. Going one step further than criticism, we need to do grassroots organizing to reverse the decay of our democratic system. Jeffrey Stout observes:

> Loosely grouped liberals are doing some good. They express their qualms about the status quo mainly by casting votes, attending occasional rallies, signing petitions, and donating money to agencies like Oxfam and Amnesty International. Such acts have good effect. But they will never succeed in overturning plutocracy and militarism. The liberals' aversion for strong ties hampers them.[1]

Only massive public pressure can force politicians to listen to the voice of Main Street over Wall Street. We need democratic renewal and a reweaving of civil society. We need democracy in the economic realm as well as in politics.

A change begins with local grassroots organizing. Only through organizing can we build up energies and resources for a new God-movement in our time. Major social movements, such as the movements of Martin Luther King Jr., César Chávez, and Nelson Mandela and Desmond Tutu, began with local grassroots organizing. Rooted in strong local organizations, they were able to change the course of history.

The future of humanity and the earth depends on how we organize ourselves and our society now. Will we do so on the basis of justice? God is organizing people for a God-inspired movement. No one knows when the next movement will be; however, if we do not prepare ourselves through organizing, we may miss the opportunity. We neither create nor determine *kairos*, but we may contribute to its advance and fulfillment.

For this task, the biblical idea of covenant offers to us the way of organizing with moral integrity and political effectiveness.

Acknowledgments

There are a number of people who were indispensable to the completion of this book.

I am deeply grateful to those who assisted me in the various stages of writing this book. In particular, I thank Joshua Beckett and Jae Yang, who have generously helped me with their careful proofreading of the manuscript.

Special thanks go to my wife, Jackie, and my two sons, Jon and David, who have supported me with their generous prayer and encouragement in every step of my intellectual journey. Especially, Jackie's keen sense of organizing in household and business matters and her aesthetic sensibilities helped me to see God's work from the angle of organizing for beauty and harmony.

I appreciate Cade Jarrell of Baylor University Press for trusting in the value of this work and faithfully guiding me throughout the entire process of publication.

In particular, I want to express my sincere thanks to my two dear mentors: Peter Paris, who deepened my sense of justice and the indispensability of organized resistance to achieve justice, and the late Max Stackhouse, who taught me about the value of covenant and its public theological significance. This book owes so much to their contributions and mentorship, although all of its mistakes and flaws are mine.

My gratitude also goes to my students at New Brunswick Theological Seminary and Fuller Theological Seminary. They have morally supported my scholarship through their excitement about my teaching, and they have been willing to hang out with me over meals and coffee. I am overjoyed to relate the good news that some of them have become my dear friends and colleagues.

Through this work I want to pass on the prophetic tradition and public theology that I have learned from my mentors to the next generation of young Christians who deeply care for the future of Christianity and the future of the planet.

I hope that this book offers a biblically informed moral vision and ground of a Christian grassroots organizing—to help them rediscover a lost (or at best fading) biblical vision of covenant and strengthen the habit of grassroots organizing.

So, I dedicate this book to my mentors and my students.

Introduction

Our society is fraught with unparalleled changes and disruptions. Of course, changes and disruptions are not new; they have occurred through all times of human history. The changes we're experiencing today, however, are noticeably different from those of previous eras, not only in speed and scope, but also in depth and permanency. From globalization to mass migration, from urbanization to the digitization of our culture, the changes are profound and touch almost every aspect of our lives. The world is being integrated through the spread of the free market economy and the advancement of communication and transportation technologies. As a result, people's experiences of space and time have dramatically changed. The idea of a closed society is increasingly obsolete; people can freely move around and interact with each other without the mediation of states, either actually or virtually via the Internet. Human relationships are no longer attached to a particular time or a particular space, and people are increasingly disembedded from face-to-face relationships and communities. This increased mobility has altered people's experiences and habits, as well as their sense of identity.

At the same time, over the last several decades, defying national boundaries and transcending religious-cultural differences, the neoliberal economic system has globally expanded its reign with the lone goal of turning the world into a single market. In terms of its policy, it advocates smaller government; a flexible labor market; the dismantling of the welfare state; the free movement of capital, goods, and services; the privatization of public enterprise (e.g., social housing, prison); and tax reductions for the rich. Indeed, it claims to "stimulate economic growth" by lowering tax barriers and environmental regulations to induce the free flow of foreign investment.

The combined forces of globalization, technological advances, and neoliberal capitalism are transforming the very fabric of our society, altering the underlying moral assumptions of social institutions, undermining the legitimacy of democracy and social arrangements, and fragmenting the resultant social interactions. The current crises are far bigger than isolated policy issues or corporate scandals involving greedy CEOs. They are structural: the interlocking forces of neoliberal economy (that concentrates inordinate power to the extraordinarily wealthy), globalization (that precipitates radical pluralism and identity politics), and the advance of communication technology (that facilitates both) undermine the organizing and governing capabilities of society. The depletion of communities and civic institutions, the erosion of moral agency and character, and the demise of democracy and civil society in the West are the symptoms of this structural crisis, and the COVID-19 pandemic has disclosed the depth of this structural crisis and the depleting organizing and governing capabilities of the West.

Community

As market values and contractual forms of relationships are spreading through global capitalism, our society is increasingly organized by the logic of the market. Money now operates as the universal medium of exchange and relationship, dissipating the sense of interdependence and commitment among people. In a society where money reigns, social relationships are based on artificial choices and personal preferences and thus are temporary (as far as they serve individual interests). Under a highly individualistic ethos, even families and religious institutions increasingly acquiesce to the logic of the market and adopt a contractual model of organization and sociality. That is, communities and institutions are increasingly fragmented and depleted as people's commitment to them is fluid and thin, and the experience of a good community is increasingly difficult to find.

Moral Agency

The demise of primary communities has made a profound impact on individual moral formation and identity development. Because much of our identity formation takes place in primary communities such as family, church, and neighborhood, the fragmentation and erosion of these communities lead to the erosion of the very basis of identity. Larry Rasmussen laments, "Our society currently lives from moral fragments and community fragments only, and both are being destroyed faster than they are being replenished. This bodes trouble for basic moral formation and community, not to say for society at large."[1]

The cultural ethos of transience, rapid change, turnover, instant gratification, and anonymous online interactions are inimical to stable human bonds and long-term relationships. Disembedded from a native community or lacking any community at all, individuals are losing their ability to holistically integrate themselves.[2] This erosion of trust and the breakdown of primary communities are socially costly. An increasing number of individuals suffer from personality disorders, depression, addiction, and ADHD, while rates of divorce, loneliness, and suicide remain high. All these symptoms reflect the increasingly unbearable burden and stress of individuals.

Democracy

The erosion of community and moral agency threatens liberal democracy in the United States and other Western countries. Civic participation is a victim of this individualistic and commodified culture. In a society where economic prosperity is the goal, morality and civic responsibility easily become the first collateral damage.[3] It is not easy to mobilize our political will and democratic energy and power.

At the same time, the democratic achievements of the past century—freedom, social equality, social welfare programs, and voting and workers' rights—are being severely undermined as political power and resources are moved to the rich, large corporations and their elites. Simultaneously, jobs are disappearing due to outsourcing and technological advances (robotization and computerization). In the United States, economic inequality has now reached levels parallel to the pre–New Deal era.[4]

While social problems mount, politicians are beholden to corporate powers seeking their own self-interest. Our political system now serves corporate powers. It has resulted in a highly stratified society—an economic caste system where the economic class of one's parents determine the fate of individuals from birth. Over the past several decades, human suffering has been aggravated rather than mitigated. The consequence is that our political and economic system is losing legitimacy and authority among the people.

Although a democratic social system relies on horizontal coordination and mature, well-trained, self-reflective citizens, the cumulative consequences of global mobility, economic competition, and contractual individualism make social coordination and democratic governance difficult and challenging. It is dubious whether liberal democracy will be able to survive in a highly utilitarian culture that lacks public virtues and care for the common good.

Many are angry because their rights and benefits are being compromised and personal dignities are under attack. Their anger is spilling over into the public realm in the form of populist politics, both on the left and right, which demagogues exploit for their own extremist agendas, as we see in the rise of vulgar racism, nativism, ethnocentrism, Islamophobia, and anti-immigrationism, among others. Various social movements, in particular, the Tea Party movement, the Occupy movement, and the election of Obama and Trump to presidency, were the manifestation of this populism—the collective assertion of the ordinary people to take back their power from the elites and the wealthy class.

Global Order

As mentioned in the opening paragraph, globalization poses a serious challenge to the question of governance, both domestic and transnational. There is a significant gap between economic-cultural globalization and political-moral globalization. It is integrated at economic and popular cultural levels, and in market and technological advances, but political, legal, and moral realms are seriously lagging behind. As a result, global governance is still quite nascent while the political and moral vacuum looms large. Multinational corporations and superpowers exploit this vacuum for their own benefits, increasing worldwide risks and dangers, as seen in the financial crisis of 2008.

The global community requires a new moral and legal framework that coordinates the diverse activities of institutions, nation-states, and individuals. Without proper coordination, any structural arrangement of a global society, the competition for limited and depleted natural resources and export markets may escalate tensions and spark new international conflicts and military confrontations.[5]

Search for a Solution?

How do we address the mounting challenges of the four crises: the fragmentation of identity, erosion of community, delegitimization of democracy, and dearth of global governance? How can we deter the spread of aggressive materialism and thin contractualism in order to restore civic virtues and democratic solidarity? How can we put this runaway world back on track? The challenges are massive and quite overwhelming. These questions are related to the survival of civilization. This is a somber moment in human history.

Our social problems cannot be solved by technological improvements and technocratic decisions and policies. Reliance on technocracy actually results in further weakening of democracy and the agency of ordinary citizens. In technocracy, experts set the agenda and make important policy decisions at the exclusion of ordinary citizens, appealing to the increasing complexity of technological problems or circumventing concerns with the technicality of arguments. Even lawsuits become limited in scope to correct structural injustices. While necessary, they seldom change the culture and status quo around unjust power relationships. Similarly, populism is not sufficient. Emotionally driven, populism is usually politically volatile and morally ambiguous, and thus vulnerable to demagogic manipulations, especially when it lacks a moral center, clear focus, and understandable purpose.

Our society requires a major moral and institutional reorganization and renewal of its organizations at both grassroots and governmental levels. For this kind of organizing, we need a new encompassing social vision and new ethics, namely a new social philosophy of organizing that assists and guides a renewal of society. Larry Rasmussen is right in saying that "all that belongs to the present moral life must of needs be engaged anew—cosmology; community reformation of human character and conduct; the understanding of what is morally normative; and the shape, behavior, and outcome of systems, structures, and practices."[6] Without this reorganization, the political system will continue to lose its legitimacy, society will further deteriorate into anomie, and more conflicts will arise as people grow more confused, angry, and desperate.

Also, given growing inequality and the concentration of power into corporations and their power elites, such a structural reorganization is

not possible without the grassroots organizing of people and the empowerment of their democratic agency to build a massive social movement
that dismantles neoliberal oligarchy and its legal arrangements, the totalizing power of administrative technocracy, and the ongoing fetishization
of culture. In short, we need organizing at personal, grassroots, institutional, and government levels.

This is not a small task, and there is no guarantee for success in the
short term. What we need is a practical political-social philosophy of
organizing whose sociological imagination is comprehensive and capacious in coordinating the multiple levels of needed organization and
capable to address the current crises. We need such a philosophy because,
as Eric Voeglin maintains, the sustenance of a political community ultimately depends on people's self-definition, their interpretation of who
they are, how they are related to each other, and what values, goals,
interests, and ideas they share.

> Essentially a people share symbols and myths that provide meaning
> to their existence together and link them to some transcendent order.
> They can thus act together and answer the basic political questions:
> Through what procedures do we reach collective decisions? By what
> standards do we judge our actions? What qualities or characteristics
> do we strive to maintain among ourselves? What kind of people do we
> wish to become? What qualities or characteristics do we see or require
> in those who lead us?[7]

Voeglin's point is that forming a new political community is not only
a matter of the law, but also of the vision, culture, and agency of the
people. In this regard, a religious worldview or a social philosophy matters for our common life because it constitutes the way we see ourselves
and neighbors, as well as our past, present, and future. The claim that
a good theory is the best solution to a problem is not a far-fetched idea.
Like a roadmap, a good religious worldview or a social philosophy offers
the first important step toward a solution. Christians need a good public
theology (that functions as a social philosophy). Due to the deficiency
or lack of a coherent public theology, I have found that many Christians simply react to political events or incidents or uncritically adopt
and assimilate to secular political ideologies of partisan politics. I believe
that covenant, a prominent symbol of the Bible and modern democracy,
serves this purpose well as a capacious and plausible public theology of
organizing.

Thesis

This book studies the biblical idea of covenant as a public theology (social philosophy) of community organizing that addresses the four crises described above: concerns of community, agency, democracy, and global order. At the heart of the biblical narrative of covenant (as attested by the Sinai Covenant and the New Covenant of Jesus) is the attempt of God and God's people to organize a wholesome, just, egalitarian community on the basis of fairness, trust, and care. Covenantal organizing offers the vision, norms, values, and practices that are necessary for a major moral reconstitution of society, one that can assist in the restoration of people's democratic agency and social power to reweave civil society.

What Is Covenant?

In a popular culture, usually indistinct from contract, *covenant* describes a mechanism of reaching an agreement through the exchange of promises and stipulation of respective rights and obligations. However, in the Bible, covenant means more than mutual agreement. It denotes an encompassing method of community organizing—humanity as well as the creation—by specifying the terms of mutual cooperation, sharing, and fighting against injustices. Covenant was the birthplace of the people of God, both Israel and the Church; God used covenant to organize (establish and build) His people into an alternative community of love, justice, and trust to replace those that were unjust and exploitative. Community formation, organizing, and renewal are directly associated with covenant.

Furthermore, covenant carries in it a liberative impulse and an aspiration for a just, fully liberated society, as it poses itself as an alternative to the oppressive, hierarchal society. Covenant is critical of the monopoly of the powerful few. To enter covenant means to commit to free, egalitarian, reciprocal fellowship and to accept the moral obligations of mutual aid and care in a shared life.

As a mechanism of God's organizing work in history, covenant empowers marginalized people. Covenant protects each person's basic rights of freedom and equality in relationship to others. The very fact that humans are invited to a reciprocal relationship of covenant with God, as God's moral partners, is itself an empowering message. Through shared worship and communal practices, covenant forms and nurtures people to work for justice and the beloved community. The support, care, and trust in a new community have the effect of alleviating emotional and economic insecurity and anxiety.

A covenantal way of organizing a community is distinct from hierarchal, contractual, or organicist forms. A covenant community is not hierarchal because it is based on the freedom, equality, and reciprocity of all people, not coercion. It is not completely natural or biological (purely based on race, gender, or blood) but intentional. It dreams of a moral community built upon mutual trust, voluntary commitment, and the consent of the members. Thanks to this liberative motif, grassroots orientation, and egalitarian thrust, covenantal theology has played a crucial role in the rise of modern democracy, human rights, civil society, and their renewals, as we will discuss extensively in chapters 4 and 5.

The organizing vision and power of covenant is sociologically comprehensive; it helps to horizontally organize human life in its different spheres such as family, church, work, neighborhood, and school, and vertically organize different levels—interpersonal, institutional, and societal.

Structure

This book has three major parts: first, it presents covenant as a public theology of community organizing (chapters 1 through 5); second, it demonstrates its public nature by critically engaging covenant with Saul Alinsky's community organizing (chapters 6 and 7); and third, it tests its practicality of covenant as an organizing principle in our current social context by examining how it helps to fight against neoliberal oligarchy and cope with the four crises, which are closely associated with neoliberal oligarchy.

(1) Covenantal Organizing

Chapter 1 examines the motifs of organizing in the actional ontology of the Trinity and God's communication. It presents God as the Master Organizer and explores the Trinity as the identity and impetus of God's self-organizing in history. Thus it offers a theological justification for community organizing in the very being and doing of the triune God. Chapters 2–5 examine the organizing nature and power of covenant through the study of two biblical examples and two historical examples within Christianity: the Exodus-Sinai event, Jesus' Kingdom Movement, the Puritan Movement, and Martin Luther King Jr.'s Civil Rights Movement.

In studying different examples of covenant-based organizing, my approach is typological. I use the biblical idea of covenant, especially the Exodus-Sinai Covenant, as a prototype of a covenantal organizing and examine how later generations of Jews and Christians (Jesus and the early Christians, the Puritans, and Martin Luther King Jr.) reactualized, recontextualized, and interpreted the Exodus-Sinai story and the idea of covenant as a model of organizing in their own contexts when they were fighting for justice and the renewal of their communities.

Why is Sinai (inextricably linked with the Exodus event, the wilderness, and the promised land) the prototype of covenantal organizing? Typically framed as the Exodus motif or narrative, it repeatedly appears throughout the Bible.

> The lexical, conceptual, and influential allusions to this founding event of the ancient Hebrew nation resonate throughout the Bible: in the Psalms, Prophets, and the postexilic literature. Yet these ripples do not stop in the Hebrew Bible. The New Testament literature appeals to the exodus event as well. . . . It serves as the organizing paradigm for several of the Gospels and influences the book of Acts. Paul's two most doctrinal letters, Romans and Galatians, lean heavily on the exodus for their theology. The apostle Peter puts an ecclesiastical spin on the exodus, and Revelation ties all the threads together in John's tapestry of consummation.[8]

In the process of recontextualization, the motif itself, without losing its core identity and constitutive pattern, experiences considerable theological transformations and adjustments in response to new and changing situations. That is, the reactualization or recontextualization of the motif is neither a mere mechanical repetition nor a wooden application; rather, the motif is "taken up, transformed, [sometimes] 'eschatologized,' and ultimately repackaged into a tapestry that mesmerizes readers and draws them into the drama of salvation."[9] In other words, guided by the Spirit, the Exodus paradigm is reperformed by God's people in different social contexts.

Throughout the Bible and Christian history, the Exodus-Sinai motif has been continuously reworked as an integral part of the unfolding pattern of God's redemptive work. The Exodus-Sinai event has exercised a revelatory power. Its revelation has never been exhausted or treated as complete, but rather continually applied in new contexts with passion and vigor.[10] In this vein and in this spirit, a critical engagement with Alinsky is another attempt to expand, recontextualize, and revitalize the

Exodus-Covenant motif in today's context when covenant is losing its liberative spirit, grassroots orientation, and transformative edges.

Taking the Exodus motif as the springboard of God's organizing, I want to make one clarification. The Exodus, the Sinai Covenant, and the vision of the promised land are inextricably tied together in the biblical narrative constituting the overarching structure of God's organizing work. God's judgment against evil, the formation of God's people, and the vision for a just and righteous society are seamlessly connected as these four integral components of God's organizing work. One cannot think of one without the others. Christian scholars often do not treat the Exodus (deliverance from Egypt), the Sinai Covenant, and the promised land as one unified, coherent narrative that describes God's organizing work, but instead focus on only one or two dimensions of them to the marginalization of the others. For example, Latin American or black liberation theologians tend to focus on the event of the Exodus and the vision of the promised land, disregarding the Sinai Covenant, while Reformed theologians emphasize the Sinai Covenant and its laws, often at the expense of the Exodus and the promised land. However, the book of Exodus as the grand narrative of God's organizing is not only the story of liberation or striving toward an ideal society, but also the story of the covenantal formation of a people. In fact, covenant is central to God's organizing work that mediates liberation and a new society. Hence it is my premise that missing any one of these aspects inevitably results in a misunderstanding of God's redemptive, organizing work, and thus of Christian ethics.

Through the study, this book demonstrates the capaciousness and adaptability of covenant as an organizing principle of a community in diverse contexts. Covenant is not static, but an evolving and adapting mechanism of community organizing. This means that its organizing method is still open and relevant to a new social context. At the same time, the idea of covenant has a self-corrective capability even after the initial transformative liberative ethos is corrupted or substantially dissipated. Because of its liberative impetus and self-corrective capability, covenant has been appealed to again and again by political and religious reformers (e.g., prophets, exiles, reformers, social activists) throughout history in their attempts to restore or renew a society into a more righteous, caring, and just one.

(2) Conversation with Saul Alinsky

Chapters 6 and 7 explore how to reactualize covenantal organizing in our own social-political contexts by taking Saul Alinsky's community organizing as a conversational partner. Chapter 6 introduces Saul Alinsky's community organizing as a method of grassroots political engagement, with a particular focus on its historical origin, social background, distinctive characteristics, core values, strategies, and tactics, while Chapter 7 examines the similarities and differences in covenantal organizing and Saul Alinsky's community organizing. I claim that covenantal organizing and Alinsky's method are compatible and complementary.

A critical engagement with Saul Alinsky is important for a few reasons. First, Alinsky's community organizing is a modern form of grassroots organizing in a democratic society. Designed to be a mechanism of political activism and democratic intervention to resist injustice, it has proven to be a practical and effective tool for social change, and a worthy partner for critical dialogue and comparison with covenantal organizing. Alinsky is worthwhile for an academic study of community organizing as well as collaboration between community organizers (participants) and Christians.

Attracted to its political effectiveness, a large number of Christians, both left and right, have become involved in community organizing or adopted some of its methods (techniques) in their political activism. Inspired by Alinsky's work, many Christians are working at a local grassroots level to address the many social issues that affect the lives of ordinary citizens. Furthermore, his method is now internationalized. More and more young people in the United States, United Kingdom, South Africa, and other countries are interested in community organizing in the wake of the failure of the Occupy movement. They strongly feel the importance of patient, long-term grassroots organizing for major social change, such as economic reform and ecological justice, as more powerful with lasting repercussions than one-day mass protests or voting.

Second, the dialogue with Alinsky is important to prove the capaciousness of public nature and pertinence of covenantal organizing even today beyond its religious boundary. Through the study, I demonstrate the deep (methodological) affinity between the two, and trace the source of the affinity to the influence of the commonwealth tradition in American democracy. I claim that Saul Alinsky's community organizing is a secular expression of covenantal tradition in the United States. The US democratic tradition is deeply tied to covenantalism, and covenant was America's founding fabric for better and worse—for better democracy, for worse racism. Covenant also inspired the formation of numerous civic organizations and major social movements. Given its enormous historical effectiveness, the covenantal tradition is still alive in civil society, if not necessarily in a religious form, and one of its expressions is community organizing.

Hence a critical engagement with Alinsky is an attempt to recontextualize covenantal organizing (the Exodus-Sinai motif) in our current political context. I believe that a covenantal organizing, in particular its political praxis, would be benefited by incorporating Alinsky's pragmatic strategies and tactics of trust building, co-deliberation, and agitation and confrontation.

(3) Application and Implications for Our Own Era: The Four Crises

The final part (chapter 8 and conclusion) wraps up these discussions and explores the significance and distinctive contributions of covenantal organizing for both Christian ministry and the renewal of democracy and ordering of a global society in the twenty-first century. Chapter 8 examines the meaning, significance, and implications of our study of covenantal organizing for our own political and social situations—how covenantal organizing helps us to fight against the oppressive and fragmenting power of neoliberalism and the four crises associated with it. In addition to the discussion of how covenantal organizing addresses the concerns and challenges of eroding agency and community, and worsening inequality and injustices under neoliberalism, the chapter briefly discusses how covenantal organizing offers new insights and directions in organizing the rising global society, specifically how its federalist model of society would be helpful in connecting the local with the global and coordinating various levels and sectors.

I conclude with the claim that covenant offers a coherent social vision and method, both theory and practice of organizing for institutions, a society, and a global community, by comparing its plausibility and relevance with several reigning social philosophies in the West: liberal democracy, communitarianism, identity politics, and postmodernism.

Method

As indicated above, this book relies on the method of public theology in studying covenantal organizing. Now well known among religious scholars, as a distinctive genre (method) of Christian theology, "public theology advocates for a constructive public role for religious discourse in a pluralistic society, neither suppressing religious expressions nor dismissing democratic values such as human rights, tolerance, and equality."[11] Public theology is ethical in nature as it is concerned with the wellbeing of a society; it is communicative as it seeks "the discovery and communication of the public meaning and import of religious symbols and creeds" through dialogue with others in search for truth and justice.[12] Hence it is willing to validate its truth and moral claims embedded in religious canons, symbols, and rituals to its members or outsiders with warrants and evidences. Public theology is religious in its nature, but its political expression is ethical in nature and democratic in its core ethos.[13]

In this book, I show that covenantal organizing, despite its religious nature, is ethical and democratic, inclusive in its orientation. The public (and inclusive) nature of covenant has not been equally embodied or manifested in the organizing process in these four historical examples that we study, but it has never disappeared or dissipated; it always existed in a latent form due to the moral nature of God's character and God's economy in the Bible. The public nature and inclusive vision of covenant has been consistently proclaimed and advocated since the time of Hebrew prophets. More specifically, the ideas of natural law, common grace, compact, coalition building, and the common good demonstrate the capability of covenantal organizing to embrace the public nature of politics and morality without compromising its particular religious identity.

Grounded in the doctrines of creation (the Creation Covenant and the Noahic Covenant), the ideas of natural law (or natural rights) and common grace offer a common moral ground for humanity. Jesus' kingdom message and eschatological vision of the restored creation also embody the universal scope and encompassing nature of covenant. More evidence is the Puritan creative adoption and use of the idea of compacting as a public form of organizing for a society which is compatible and congruent with covenantal organizing.[14] Similarly, Martin Luther King Jr.'s embrace of associational and cultural pluralism and practice of coalition building with non-Christians displays the public competence and moral capaciousness of covenantal organizing.

Scope and Limitation

While the Bible includes many different forms of covenant, this book focuses on its collective form, that is, the covenants used to organize God's people rather than those that describe interpersonal relationships, the Sinai Covenant and the New Covenant of Jesus. Also, in studying covenant as a biblical method of community organizing, I will attend to the following characteristics in particular: its grassroots orientation; overarching narrative pattern of liberation and restoration (resistance-alternative); constitutive principle of unity in diversity (in close association with the dynamic composite of love, justice, power); democratic or quasi-democratic motifs and principles (free consent, equality, communicative reciprocity); and rule of law.

Even while I fully recognize the interest of scholars and activists in practical applications of covenantal organizing to congregational ministries, local communities, and grassroots organizations, such inquiry does not fall within the bounds of the current work. I reserve this for my next project. My focus and interest here are intentionally more theological (in the realm of public and political theology) than practical, in order to complement rich and growing literature on community organizing that is mostly practical or sociological. However, the final chapter does offer a brief test case to display the practical relevance of covenantal organizing in coping with the threat of neoliberal capitalism.

Contribution

The public theology of community organizing makes several distinctive contributions. It helps to redeem and renew the idea of covenant by identifying its radical liberative impetus. The redemption of covenant is important because the idea of covenant has been gravely misused in Western history. For some young Christians, the word is the symbol of intolerance and exclusion as we see in the idea of Manifest Destiny, a redeemer nation, and the apartheid system of South Africa. However, a racist exclusionary practice is not intrinsic to the biblical covenant, but a Western (white) distortion of it for political economic interest through a poor, selective, and skewed interpretation of the Bible. Despite its past misuses and distortions, I do not believe that we should forfeit the idea; to do so is to throw away a baby with its bath water. This book, contrary to the abuses, shows that the biblical idea of covenant symbolizes a liberative political practice that aims at the formation of a free, just, egalitarian community.

The redemption of covenant is important, especially for the United States, because the idea of covenant is a symbolic anchor of the nation, serving as the source of shared memory and aspirations of the nation and its people. Constituting its religious and moral self-understanding, covenant has shaped the collective identity and democratic project of the United States. However, over the last several decades, covenanta-lism has dramatically dissipated and been depleted in the political life of the United States, increasingly replaced by utilitarian individualism, contractualism, postmodernism, or racial and gender identity politics. Today our nation has forgotten about the covenant. Our young people are unfamiliar with this symbol (and its good and bad effects).

Without knowing the idea of covenant, however, one cannot prop-erly understand the origin, history, and identity of America as a political community—both its positive accomplishments and its wrongdoings. In any society, a key symbolic word, such as covenant, helps to better comprehend the deep structures of a society and relationships between its members and institutions.[15] This means that without a key symbol, people lose their sense of collective identity and purpose; accordingly, social cohesion is eroded, social coordination is difficult, and charting the future together gets challenging. The increasingly litigious, conflic-tual, and divisive nature of our social life, the spread of fake news, and unbounded individualism in US society are the evidence of this loss of collective memory, hope, and identity.

Covenantal organizing invites and empowers Christians to critically and constructively engage with the American democratic tradition in a global and pluralistic social context. This engagement is important for the future of American democracy because the Puritan idea of covenant has left deep imprints on the American democratic tradition (especially consti-tutionalism, human rights, civil society, and associational pluralism), and community organizing itself is rooted in this radical democratic tradition inspired by covenant. Hence, a renewed idea of covenantal organizing could help to reconnect covenant, democracy, and grassroots organizing in a new theological framework. As such, it may very well contribute to the reconstitution and revitalization of civil society and democracy in a highly divided nation that is in desperate need of a major social transformation.

Through its roots in the triune God and covenant, community orga-nizing obtains a new scope, direction, and content. Covenantal practices help to ground community organizing in a richer, deeper, and more theo-logical basis by making it more resilient, enduring, and capacious than its current form and practices. The deep theological insights of covenant help to refine, strengthen, and expand various moral values, practices, and strategies (including liberation, democracy, moral formation, politi-cal advocacy, and trust building) of community organizing in a critical and constructive manner.

1

God

The Maestro of Organizing

In studying a biblical and theological basis of community organizing, one cannot but ask: who is God and how is God related to community organizing? The God of Christianity is the protagonist of the Scripture and the center of the Christian faith, a monotheistic religion based on God's initiating self-disclosure. Without demonstrating how God is related to community organizing, any assertion of a theological justification of community organizing would not be sufficient enough. In exploring a theological ground of community organizing, I introduce God as the organizing God—a grand, masterful organizer—who organizes his creation into shalom community. Scripture describes God's action in many different ways: God is ruling, God is communicating, God is healing, God is liberating, God is reconciling, etc. But I present "organizing" as a key motif that describes God's being and action with the focus on the doctrines of the Trinity and covenant as a distinctive biblical ground of community organizing;[1] that is, the doctrine of the Trinity describes God's self-organizing as the Father, Son, and Spirit, while covenant denotes God's method of organizing of humanity/the world in history.

The Bible describes God's organizing work as the central narrative of the Scriptures. God organizes the world according to His will, and through organizing, God actualizes God's intention. Shalom is the goal of God's organizing, and the universe is God's organized community. The biblical ideas of God's order, reconciliation, atonement, and redemption are closely associated with God's organizing. God organizes chaos into cosmos in justice and peace (Ps 47:9; 95–99). God's organizing is comprehensive, encompassing both human and biotic world.[2] The well-being of the cosmos depends on God's ongoing organizing work.

Organizing is a community-building and renewing work. Organizing is essentially ethical in nature because it pertains to the process to create a new community or renew the existing community according to moral rules and principles that contribute to God's purpose. God's organizing has to do with God's *oikonomia*. Organizing involves the use of God's power (to fulfill intention), God's justice (to put things right), and God's love (to bind the creation in unity and harmony). God organizes things toward shalom. God's organizing, regardless of its religious and liturgical manifestations, takes a political nature because of shalom as its ultimate horizon and telos. It is also economic because it pertains to production, accumulation, processing, and distribution of power and resources.

God's reign refers to this constant organizing work of God that aims at shalom. Generally speaking, there is no meaningful reign without organizing, because reign indicates "organizing" (and ordering) of territory, people, animals, artifacts, and resources within it. In the Bible, God's reign is always associated with the organizing (formation) of God's people in Eden, Israel (Canaan), and church (new creation).

The Trinity and Organizing

Then why does organizing play such a central role in God's economy? What does this biblical narrative of God's actions reveal about God's being and person? The origin of this impetus of divine organizing is the Trinity.[3] The triune God eternally organizes Himself—the three in one, one in three—as Father, Son, and Spirit, through constant ecstasy of communication among them. The term Trinity describes the rich, organic, complex, dynamic, mysterious, and highly differentiated nature of God's being and God's interaction with the world.

Trinity is the most distinctive and encompassing Christian description of the biblical God who is living, relational, and dynamic (both transcendental and immanent). The Trinity describes the interpersonal nature of God. Each person of the Trinity is never isolated or independent from the other persons. In the Trinity, identity and relationship go together; the trinitarian persons are unique by virtue of their relationship to two other persons. Their personal identity is constituted in their relationships. From a trinitarian theological perspective, to be is to be in relationship and to be a person is to be a unique distinct person in relationship with others. Various prepositions describing the trinitarian economy, such as "through," "with," "in," "to," "for," "toward," show the intrinsically relational nature of the triune God.[4]

The triune God exists in unity in diversity, diversity in unity. That is, God is the one only in the unity of the three persons as the Father, the Son, and the Spirit. In the Trinity, there exists "a reality of communion in which each particular is affirmed as unique and irreplaceable by the others."[5] An ancient theological term, perichoresis, describes this dynamic, constant, ecstatic nature of communion among the three persons.[6] Perichoresis is characterized by the triune life of the eternal self-giving and receiving. In their perichoretic communion, the three trinitarian persons constantly give and receive themselves from one another, and love denotes the unceasing, delightful, and self-giving communication among the three persons. At the same time, the term perichoresis explains how the three trinitarian persons are self-organizing through constant coinherence (mutual interpenetration) among themselves. That is, God eternally organizes Godself as the communion (love) through unceasing, dynamic, and self-giving communication.

God's organizing in history is the work of the Trinitarian perichoresis *ad extra*: "trinity *ad intra* leads to organism *ad extra*."[7] The triune God, by virtue of God's very overflowing nature of perichoretic love, has a disposition (habit) for communication and community. God is inwardly and outwardly self-communicating,[8] and God's communication with humanity is the expression of God's being as the Trinity. "God is eternally disposed to create, to give and share life with others. The welcome to others that is rooted in the triune life of God spills over, so to speak, in the act of creation."[9]

The creation of the world and humanity was the result of a free and natural overflow of a rich perichoretic life of the triune God.[10] Out of overflowing, kenotic love, the triune God graciously allowed the creation to exist alongside Godself.[11] In particular, God created humans in God's image (as communicative beings), and invited them to loving fellowship—to know and enter a relationship with God. This is substantiated in 1 John 1:3: "We declare to you what we have seen and heard so that you also may have fellowship with us; and truly our fellowship is with the Father and with his Son Jesus Christ."

Reflecting and displaying the fullness of life in the triune God, creation is in a sense a dynamically organized community of all creatures in the power of the triune God. Reflecting the triune life of God as the communion, it is intended by God to be the life in full communion (shalom), that is, to be with others in love.

The Organizing Work of the Trinity

The work of the triune God in history is the organizing work of God's reign. Existing as the communion of the three persons constantly communicating with each other, God's reign is never static. As Jesus said, "My Father is still working, and I also am working" (John 5:17).[12]

The trinitarian persons collaborate in their economy in perfect communication and unity. While the Father is the source (font) and the goal, the Son and the Spirit are the two hands of the Father God in achieving the goal. Father works through the Son and the Spirit; the Son and the Spirit witness the Father; the Son embodies God's will for humanity through his incarnation; the Spirit draws people to the Son; the Spirit fulfills the Father's intent; the Son's work is completed and perfected through the Spirit.[13]

As the "anchor" person in the Trinity, the Father is the one "who gives order and direction to the Trinity as a whole."[14] The Son, called Logos, indicates "God as form, or order." Jesus Christ, the incarnate Logos, is the mediator between God and the creation, God and humanity as he is fully God and fully human.[15] The Spirit denotes "God as act" or God as effect (power).[16] The orienting work of the Father and the ordering work of the Son are actualized through the empowering and contextualizing work of the Spirit. In His own way, the Spirit is also an organizing power. As He unites the Son and the Father in Godhead (as "the bond of love"), the Spirit also unites the Father and the creatures in Jesus Christ while keeping their distinctiveness. The work of the Spirit is unique in uniting and differentiating different persons simultaneously: "The Spirit makes possible of the crossing of boundaries and the preservation of particularity 'in relationship.'"[17]

Trinity and Covenant

This reciprocal, communicative pattern of the self-organizing God as the Trinity is expressed in God's economy in history, in particular, through the covenant. The Bible identifies God as a covenantal God. Walter Brueggemann notes:

Even if it is not lexically explicit, that capacity and willingness of God to enter into enduring, risky solidarity are what we meant by covenant. The God of the Bible is a God who makes covenant.[18]

Covenant reflects the life of the triune God who eternally organizes Himself as the Father, Son, and Spirit—the three in one, one in three.

If the triune God is self-giving love that liberates life and creates new and inclusive community, then there is no salvation for the creature apart from sharing in God's agapic way of life in solidarity and hope for the whole creation (cf. Rom. 8:18-39).[19]

Covenant displays an active, historical, and relational nature of God as the triune God. The core values of covenant—freedom, equality, and reciprocity, and covenant's communicative structure are congruent to the values embedded in the perichoretic life of the triune God. God uses covenant for the original organizing of God's creation as well as reorganizing of it after the Fall. As the primary means of God's organizing, covenant shows that God's reign is also not impassive, immutable, mystical, but concrete, relational, historical, and political.

Covenant as the Storyline of the Bible

The basic storyline of Scripture, one that maintains unity between the Old Testament and the New Testament, is God's covenantal action in history.[20] Kevin Vanhoozer comments, "The covenantal shape of the biblical *mythos* is arguably the architectonic scheme of the entire theodrama, not simply one biblical or theological theme among others. The God/world distinction and relation alike is ultimately a matter of covenantal drama."[21] Major biblical events and historical turning points, and every critical moment of God's dispensation, for that matter, can be interpreted as a covenant or covenant-related.

Covenant constitutes the narrative plot of the Bible and is an architectonic structure of redemptive history. But beyond just history, it also holds the seemingly disparate contents of Scripture, along with their associated doctrines, together. Crucial biblical ideas, norms, and practices cluster and converge around the idea of covenant. In terms of its contemporary relevance, covenant has been constructively used to better understand modern institutions—their structures and patterns—and social issues associated with them (e.g., family, business, politics, congregation, medicine, law, education). Covenant's inherent theological potency and ethical capaciousness sets it apart from other biblical metaphors or concepts. Max Stackhouse notes that "the sociotheological idea of covenant is so rich with ethical content that it gives moral meaning to all it touches."[22]

Covenant is the *modus operandi* that God takes in interacting with humanity and the world. God fulfills God's purpose for humanity and creation through covenant. Christian moral obligations are primarily informed and structured by covenant, under the premise that obligation arises in particular relationships. Hence, many organic or ordering motifs in the Bible, such as trust, reciprocity, dialogue, atonement, reconciliation, restoration, and law are clustered around covenant. Similarly, God's moral attributes—trustworthiness, faithfulness, love (*hesed*), justice, and forgiveness—are covenantally grounded.

Covenant as the Paradigm of God's Organizing

Covenant is indispensable to the understanding of God's kingship and interaction with the world.[23] In the Bible, God's reign is intimately tied with organizing as it occurs through covenant. The idea of covenant answers the questions regarding God's reign: What are its moral natures and characteristics? How does God exercise the reign? What is the goal of the reign? How does it manifest, unfold, and actualize itself? How is it experienced in our lives? As it is central to God's reign, God responds with a covenant or a covenant plan whenever there is major chaos and confusion in history.[24] In fact, covenant was at the center of Israel's and the church's understanding of God's reign and right ordering (shalom). God relies on covenant as a primary means of God's organizing and management of the world. The mantra of God's community organizing is: "I shall be your God, you shall be my people."

Importantly, in the Bible, the coming of God's reign is inextricably tied with the organizing of people: the formation of peoplehood. God's organizing has two-fold dimensions: 1) liberation from sin, evil, and death and 2) establishing a new, wholesome, egalitarian community. Inseparable from one another, God accomplishes them through the covenantal organizing of God's people. Accordingly, God's reign cannot be separated from the gathering of people because God's reign is actualized in a community through his people. "The rule of God presupposes a people of God, in whom it can become established and from whom it can shine forth."[25] In the Bible, covenant is the metaphor of a newly organized society with a radical egalitarian vision. Covenant is instrumental in building a community. Brueggemann's remark confirms the organizing role (function) of covenant in the Bible: "All the 'torah-law' of the Old Testament, in one way or another, is an attempt to organize concrete social relations around this radical theological vision."[26]

God's reign means God's Lordship as the creator and ruler of heaven and earth, and affects every aspect of human life. As the principle of God's reign, covenant is a comprehensive mechanism of organizing and ordering. Covenant applies to every relationship under God's reign: God-human, human-human, human-other-species relationship. God's organizing includes organizing of a person (through the formation of identity and virtues) and an organization (such as family, church, or school) as well as a society, and the universe, thus all levels of a social life—interpersonal, institutional, international.

Covenant—the Composite of Love, Justice, and Power

Covenant is the organic composite of love, justice, and power—a creative, constructive mechanism that manages power through justice toward a loving fellowship. It adequately portrays what God's reign is like morally.

Generally speaking, the idea of kingship (reign) is inseparable from power. Synonymous with governance, rule, or dominion, it describes the exercise of the authority and power of a king in pursuing the goal of governance. It is a general expectation that the principles of justice should guide and regulate the exercise of power.

The Bible declares God as the King of kings, the Lord of lords. The basis of this declaration is that God is the creator—the maker of heaven and earth. God's kingship indicates that God is the source of all powers and authorities, and that human kings and political leaders are only God's deputies. While the supreme King, however, God does not rule the cosmos arbitrarily, but always according to God's righteousness and justice that reflects God's own character and intention.

Covenant describes how God's reign takes place and what it looks like in history. David Novak says, "In covenant, justice is not only what God has decreed for the world, it is what God does in the world as well."[27] Justice is integral to covenant because covenanting itself denotes righting of relationships—"putting things right"—through free exchange of commitments and a fair distribution of power and resources. Covenant presupposes that each person is endowed with certain inalienable rights, and everyone has a responsibility to respect them.

While denoting a structure of just and righteous relationship, covenant has a communal intent—the building of the beloved community.

Justice is indispensable in covenant but not the ultimate goal of God. God's goal is a loving communion, which Daniel Migliore describes:

> From the foundation of the world, the purpose of the triune God has been to share life with others, to create a community of love in which all are united without loss of enriching differences.[28]

Covenant constitutes a structure (organization) of relationship where the exercise of power is justly and fairly organized in advancing mutual interest, trust seeking fellowship, and a deeper union. In the covenant, love describes this richness and ecstasy and joy of this organized life while justice delineates its structure and form, and power is the energy and capability given to every living creature to pursue its fulfillment in the justly organized life. Once formed, covenant serves as the structure of a community that preserves basic just order (from the chaotic power of violence, injustice, immorality) that maximizes the potentials of each person while striving toward perfected fellowship (shalom) among the members.

In summary, one may say that covenant is the dialectic composite of love, justice, and power. This organic and dialectic nature of covenant is what distinguishes covenantal organizing from Alinsky's community organizing.

God's Organizing as the Christian Redemptive Narrative

Christian redemptive history is framed in terms of God's organizing, with covenant as a central method of this organizing. The following section briefly discusses how the motif of covenantal organizing is pervasive in the Bible and Christian theology.

Creation

Scripture presents creation as the fruit of God's organizing act. Creation was a story of God's covenantal organizing of the disordered chaos into a harmonious community. Through organizing, God provides the condition for flourishing of every creature. God organized the world because God desires the flourishing of every life. One characteristic of covenantal organizing is unity in diversity.

Establishing order through differentiating and fettering (unity in diversity) is a typical covenantal motif.[29] Creation is organized in a way that respects differences and diversities within the matrix of delicate interdependence, exchanges, and mutual communication.

> Despite the mystery and virility, Genesis 1 is really about order. Chaos is untangled into light and darkness, inchoate ground is divided into water and land, and a firmament is erected to hold the rainstorms above at safe distance from the ground water below. Most of the language is about separating and dividing, like the task of one doing laundry. Order governs the six-day work week as well. Days forge perfect parallels between habitats and creatures. It takes three days to create earth's spaces and three days to fill them with correlating animate and inanimate creatures. For example, on the second day, God creates the dome of heaven in the midst of the waters (v. 6-8), and then, on the fifth day, he fills the sky and the water with birds and fish (v. 20-23). Every day fits the scheme. And poetic repetition of phrases like, "It was good" infuse Genesis 1's spatial proportion with a moral aesthetic.[30]

Creation echoes the Trinitarian life and its principle of unity in diversity. In the triune God, creation is destined toward a community in freedom, mutuality, and interdependence.

> Creation itself intimates an ultimate power that fosters openness and spontaneity among creatures. It is also a realm where reciprocal relationships can be enacted on a finite level and where the Trinity can be reflected in the communion of social creatures. These image-bearers can mirror God's image in the sphere of nondivine reality and reproduce the filial relationship that the Son enjoys with the Father. From this world the Father longs to hear the very *yes* from the creature that he hears eternally from his beloved Son.[31]

God's creation is an organic body where creatures live in a symbiotic association with each other. It constitutes an intricate web of the incredibly dynamic but harmonious community where each member is in a covenantal relationship with the others. Each creature is interdependent with others while keeping its own distinctive pattern, rhythm, and boundary of life. The creation consists in delicate, complex, evolving, ceaseless exchange and communication among its members, including not only living organisms but also natural cycles of the earth that are constantly evolving and changing. God's intention for creation was the flourishing of all lives in the fellowship with God and others. God blessed all creatures: "Be fruitful and multiply" (Gen 1:28).

Just as God organized the creation out of chaos, the Genesis story also portrays the relationship between Adam and Eve in a typically covenantal framework. God created them as differentiated persons (male and female) in unity, whose relationship was characterized by freedom, equality, reciprocity, and fellowship (Gen 2:23)—unity in diversity and diversity in unity, reflecting the life of the triune God.

Genesis 1–3 serves as a classic, covenantally oriented typology of salvation history. As much as the positive metaphors associated with covenant—such as sonship (kingship) and blessings—are present, the negative metaphors—such as temptation, disobedience, broken relationship, and expulsion from the Garden—are also found there. These are repeated throughout the OT in the apostasy, disobedience, disloyalty, and exile of Israel.[32]

Sin: De-organizing of the Good Creation

While creation shows the beauty of God's organizing in its cosmic scope and microscopic details, then sin is disruption of God's organization and frustration of His plan to organize the world into shalom. Sin indicates the breaking of the covenant with God and others. It threatens the integrity and harmony of creation and a community that God has created. Genesis 3 shows how beautiful harmony and solidarity and intimacy are suddenly lost with human sin; alienation, evil, death, and distortion of communication are the results of sin. Sin is now disintegrating God's creation and depriving the Sabbath and disrupting shalom.

Sin is a chaotic power that deorganizes the covenant by undercutting the justice and rightness of relationships and violating the necessary rights and boundaries of others. The idea of sin and injustice are interrelated; sin is a distortion of the rightly organized relationship designed and intended by God, such as God-human, (e.g., idolatry, blasphemy), parents-children (e.g., disobedience or misuse of authority), wife-husband (e.g., adultery), neighbor-neighbor (dishonesty), human-nature (e.g., waste and exploitation). Sin perverts unity and diversity into uniformity and division (disagreement). Uniformity is a sinful parody of God's glorious unity,[33] which is typically maintained by coercion, while division, I would say, is another sinful parody of God's rich and brilliant diversity, which leads to disorder and conflicts.

Redemption

With the sin of humans, the creation threatened to disintegrate into chaos. In response to the power of sin that frustrates, God takes a new initiative through covenant. After the Fall, God's organizing has become intentional to restore the beauty and blessings of the creation. After the Fall, covenant has become the means that God uses to reverse the effects of sin and death in order to put all things right again.[34] As was the case with the creation, God's redemption takes place through God's covenantal organizing work of Israel and then later the Church. The incarnation of the Son and the outpouring of the Spirit are the final decisive actions that fulfill God's covenantal organizing of humanity and the creation.

God's organizing work has culminated in the life, death, and resurrection of Jesus, who delivered humanity from the power of sin, evil, and death, and heralded the advance of a new creation. Specifically, the New Covenant of Jesus offers the necessary ground of reconciliation, of the eternal divine-human, human-human fellowship. The Christian idea of salvation is covenantal in nature. Reconciliation, a synonym of salvation, explains it well: reconciliation denotes the restoration of broken or damaged relationships into a new just/righteous community. As Michael Horton observes, "The covenant, not a general metaphysical scheme, specifies what kind of alienation and reconciliation are in view" in Christianity.[35] Outside the framework of covenant, reconciliation tends to lose its dimension of justice or rightness. However, reconciliation without restoration of a just and righteous relationship is not a genuine reconciliation; it is a cheap shot for a sugarcoated relationship.

Church

The Church is the direct fruit of the organizing work of the triune God. It indicates the eschatological formation of God's people. The church is not primarily an institution but a new peoplehood, called and organized by the power of the triune God for His glory—the full organizing of the creation. It is constantly organized and being reorganized in Jesus Christ by the power of the Spirit for the glory of the Father.

As God organized Israelites (former slaves) into God's priestly kingdom, God organizes God's people (both Jews and Gentiles) into one body of Christ. God organizes those called out of the world (ecclesia) through worship, fellowship, mutual instructions, encouragement, and prayer, and uses them to reorganize the world, across the categories of individuals, institutions, and societies (*diaconia*), in love and justice.

Church is a covenantal community.[36] Church is a new Israel, the Exodus people of God. They are "called out for a special task" of resisting sin, evil, and the power of death, and building an alternative community reflecting God's character.[37] Among many metaphors of the church in the Bible, the idea of the church as koinonia describes the intimate covenantal fellowship of love, justice, and mutual care.

Church is a community liberated from the power of sin, evil, and death, while anticipating the redemption of all creation.[38] Church exists as the alternative community to the broken world—a foretaste of shalom. It is a pilgrim community on journey toward God's shalom in the memory of God's liberating power in the life, death, and resurrection of Jesus.

Jesus embodied such a community in his eucharistic body by reconciling all things with God. Christians who participate in his body form an alternative community to the divisive and violent world. Comprising Jews and Gentiles, men and women, slave masters and slaves in freedom, equality, and solidarity in Jesus Christ, the Church is a kingdom-temporarily-organized on earth.

Eschaton

The eschaton indicates the consummation of creation in which the abolition of all deorganizing forces against God's good creation takes place; that is, the victory of justice over injustice, love over hatred, peace over hostility, friendship over alienation. God's organizing work is finally fulfilled in all dimensions (personal, communal, societal, and cosmic) and all realms (family, school, church, government, etc.).[39] Humanity experiences full communion with God and others, and the covenantal mantra ("I will be your God, you shall be my people") is finally actualized in history as God intended at the time of creation. God's reign is established in the world in its fullness and wholeness.

The eschaton is not the cause of fatalism but the source of Christian hope. It serves as the assurance of God's unfailing promise for God's people. It also denotes the scope of God's organizing, which transcends institutional churches and their ministries. The doctrine reminds us that the Church does not exist for itself, but for the organizing of the world under God's reign. In light of the eschatological vision, all of history and the world are the theatre of God's organizing reign, and humans are called to be God's co-agents of the shalom-organizing. The eschaton tells that God's organizing work is not confined to the church but expands to the entire world. Hidden to human eyes, God's organizing is already taking among various people in the world to restore his creation.

The above brief observation shows that the ideas of the triune God as the organizing God (the maestro of organization) and the covenant as God's organizing method have immense explanatory power in understanding Christian redemptive history. Such a comprehension has huge ramifications in understanding God's relationship with the world—God's goal and God's method in achieving the goal. Human history is the history of God's organizing.

Shalom—the Goal of Organizing

The ultimate goal of God's organizing is shalom, which Martin Luther King Jr. called the beloved community—a just, loving, and reciprocal community where every life is respected and interrelated, which reflects the moral nature of the triune life. Covenant strives toward the perfected fellowship among the partners: shalom.

Shalom is the goal of God's organizing and covenant. It refers to the blissful reality where God's love, justice, and power are finally actualized in the flourishing of all creatures. Hence, shalom is characterized by blissful joy, peace, the ecstasy of love that comes from mutual trust, reciprocity, and willing contribution to the excellence of each other and the common good. It is a dynamic, perfectly organized community with harmony, intimacy, vitality, delight, and peace among all creatures in the eternal joyful dance of the triune God. It indicates the perfection of covenant. According to Nicholas Wolterstorff, shalom is a human being dwelling in peace with all of his or her relationships with God, self, fellow human beings, and nature.[40] Shalom is the cosmic beloved community.

The Sabbath is a historical practice, the foretaste of shalom that God intends. The Sabbath is the occasion, the feast of God, where all the guests are free and equal before God and enjoy the rich blessings of God as they are fed by God's gifts. As we discuss in the next chapter, Sabbath has huge implications on the political economy of Israel. Once a week, all the members of a community—men, women, adults, children, human and other species—stop their work and rest in the triune God. They renew and reorient themselves, restoring their mental and physical energies in attunement to God's goal and life in the feast of the triune God. Shalom indicates the longing of the entire creation for perfection and excellence in harmony.

As shalom is the ultimate goal of Christian life, covenant is its historical, penultimate structure (form). Through covenant, God invites humans into the joint task of reorganizing the creation, *tikkun olam*. For Christians, baptism is an initiation process (rite) of covenant through which God and humans become partners on this joint project, while the Eucharist is a nurturing sustaining system of covenantal life in memory of God's deliverance and in the hope of fulfillment.

Covenantal Organizing

Narrative: The Organizing Trajectory of Covenant

When we carefully examine major biblical covenants in their narrative contexts, it is clear that God's organizing work in history unfolds from "liberation" (from chaos, sin, and death) to "restoration" (building of a new community), with covenant mediating the two phases.[41] Constituting the rubric (tenet) of the biblical account of God's covenant, this pattern appears in major biblical covenants: God's deliverance of the universe from chaos to cosmos (the Creation Covenant); Israel from the Pharaoh to the promised land (the Sinai Covenant); and humanity from the power of sin and death to a new creation (the New Covenant of Jesus). In these covenants, Eden, the ancient nation of Israel (the land of Canaan), and the Church (the new creation) respectively indicate the new community of shalom (aspiring to common flourishing) opposed to disorder, confusion, oppression, sin, and death. That is, the biblical idea of covenant is not a mere judicial agreement between two parties, but is grounded in God's deliverance (liberation) while aiming at the building of an alternative community.

In the biblical narratives, God's liberation forms the immediate preceding historical context of covenant; deliverance is not part of covenant, but constitutes its immediate, indispensable background. For example, in the Exodus story, God's liberating work precedes the formal establishment of covenant at Sinai, as a historical prologue of the Ten Commandments states: "I am the LORD who brought you up out of Egypt" (Exod 20:2). Similarly, the New Covenant presupposes Jesus' life, death, and resurrection (defeat of sin and death) as the basis of God's covenant with all of humanity. While it always presupposes God's initiating act of unconditional love, covenant specifically is based on free human agreement to enter this enduring relationship with God and others. In general, there are two types of covenants in the Bible—divine-human and human-human. Among these covenants, divine-human covenant is logically prior to and more authoritative than human-human covenant. The latter is guided and stipulated by the former.

God's covenantal organizing, broadly speaking, includes three stages: judgment (deliverance/liberation from an unjust society), formal consent, and building of an alternative community restoration. All three stages are inextricably interrelated as they constitute the overarching paradigm (pattern) of God's organizing. When God liberates the oppressed, God's intention is to build a new community among them; God does it by inviting them to a covenant relationship with Him and each other. When humans accept the invitation and enter the covenantal relationship, then a new community is formally constituted. The covenant serves a constitutive structure of a new society in contrast to the old one. Covenantal organizing is to bridge the gap between "what it is like" and "what it should be like," and it happens primarily through organizing work for justice. Covenant mediates resistance and alternative—God's liberation and his building of a new society. Let's briefly examine this narrative trajectory in further detail.

Liberation

God's organizing begins with God's judgment against chaos, evil, and injustice, and deliverance of the people from oppression.[42] God's judgment is the exercise of God's kingship—God's triumphant power over the power of chaos, sin, evil, and death. This judgmental dimension is intrinsic to major biblical covenants (Noah, Sinai, Jesus), and it reflects the just and righteous character of God. God judged against the violence and corruption of Noah's contemporaries, the Egyptian subjugation of Israel, and the demonic power of sin and death working through the Jewish religious and the Roman imperial systems. Through the work of liberation, God undoes (deorganizes) the powers of chaos, sin, and oppression that obstruct or impede just and harmonious relationships; therefore, their judgment (removal) is the prerequisite for building a new just society of common flourishing.

God's judgment and justice are inseparable. God's judgment always presupposes God's justice, because God's judgment is enactment of His justice. God's judgment is public; it is typically addressed first toward the rulers and leaders of a society—both religious and sociopolitical, such as king, priests, judges, and the wealthy—while defending the rights of the poor and the marginalized against the rich and oppressors.[43] Public judgment against unjust rulers and their political-economic system is necessary to restore justice and righteousness in society because, as the leaders of a society, they set the moral tone for the society and exercise a huge influence in shaping its cultural ethos and making its policies and laws.

God's judgment is not only external (judging social ethos, laws, and political economic systems) but also internal, calling for the repentance of people from sin, complicity with injustices, and corruptions. In other words, it is not punitive, but restorative, as it aims at forming the collective moral agency of people.

Alternative Society

God's organizing aims at building a new community based on love and justice. God's deliverance does not stop with liberation, but always points toward the alternative form of a society that is organized under freedom, equality, justice, and solidarity. After delivering it, God invites humanity as God's partner in building a new community. An old social order is not overcome simply by liberation (deorganizing it), but by reconstitution into a new community order. It includes renewing, renorming, and restructuring processes, and covenant offers an opportunity for such processes.

A covenantal community embodies a new moral community—a liberated, just, and reconciled form of a communal life. God's people are required to embody God's reign of justice, peace, and love in their personal and social life, as the metaphors of the priestly kingdom (Exod 19:6; 1 Pet 2:9), salt and light (Matt 5:13-16), pearl (Matt 13:45-46), and leaven (Matt 13:33) indicate. Daily spiritual and moral practices in the covenant community are designed to help people to approximate such a new society.

Justice

Reflecting God's judgment against evil powers and structures, covenant takes justice as the basic constitutive (ordering or organizing) structure of a society. Covenant assumes a society that is organized on the basis of justice. As mentioned above, covenant denotes the righting of relationships. The exchanges in covenant are fair exchanges based on free consent. Specifically, a communal life is newly organized in the covenant using God's moral law as the guideline.

Covenant has a leveling effect. Because of this constitutive principle of justice, entering, establishing, or renewing a covenant entails the change of power relationships within a community. The principles of justice serve as a plumb line to morally measure the actions of Israelites, other nations, and God.[44] To be covenanted means to hold each other accountable to justice in God; each person and the entire community are required to implement the requirements of justice prescribed by the covenantal stipulations in an ongoing, faithful manner.

Political Economy

In understanding God's reign and God's design of a new, alternative society, God's organizing is inseparable from the political economy of a society,[45] which pertains to the arrangement of power and authority and distribution of resources.

The political economy of a society does not exhaust God's reign or covenantal organizing, as the latter touches every dimension of human life (personal, interpersonal, and public). However, without addressing political economy (the question of power and resources), God's reign loses its biting edges and focus. Detached from the political economy of a particular society (and faith community), God's reign becomes overly spiritualized and psychologized often at the disregard of structural sins, systematic injustices, and deep cultural corruptions, losing sight of how the powers, principalities, and spirits of the world reign in a society. The powers, principalities, and spirits are the descriptors of this-worldly reign that first and foremost manifests through political economy and supporting a cultural ethos that decisively shapes, controls, and affects people in general. Furthermore, the political economy is theologically important because it is typically the site of idolatry—the worship of power and money disguised in national ideology, civil religion, or popular adoration of materialism. Without a deep knowledge of God's covenant political economy, the church is not able to discern how powers and principalities and spirits of the world operate, and joins their side rather than that of God's kingdom.

God's reign is materialized in the organizing of a new community (people of God) that is committed to a particular form of political economy based on covenantal principles, a community which rejects the concentration of power, protects basic rights of individuals, encourages the sharing of resources through mutual aid and care, and contributes to the commonwealth. Through covenant, "the kingdom of God has remarkably concrete political, social, and economic references."[46]

The two central covenants of the Bible, the Sinai Covenant and the New Covenant, delineate the nature of God's political economy. Both were born out of their critique of the political economy of Pharaoh and Caesar, economies that were hierarchal, imperialistic, exploitative, and violent. Both dreamed of an alternative society based on love and justice. Hence, they carry the revolutionary vision of how power and resources are to be shared among members, and how the members of God's community practice such a lifestyle and vision through their worship, fellowship, and ministry (*diakonia*).

The Organizing Power of Covenant

Externally, the pattern of liberation-reconstruction (a new society) creates the narrative arc for God's organizing work (resisting injustices and building an alternative society), but internally, the principle of unity in diversity (how to bring diverse members into a new community) guides the concrete organizing work of community building. While the former has to do with a telos (dispositional trajectory), the latter is concerned with a constitutive dimension of community organizing.

The Unity-in-Diversity Principle

As the constitutive organizing principle of relationship, covenant indicates a method of bonding people together through mutuality and cooperation and sharing. According to Daniel Elazar, "A covenant establishes a partnership linking diverse entities into a purposeful union of unlimited duration, but one in which the partners maintain their respective integrities throughout."[47] That is, covenant affirms the basic rights (distinctiveness) of each person as well as the unity of humanity in God. Covenant shares the same dynamic mechanism of the unity in diversity of the Trinitarian life.

> [I]t is significant that cutting (dividing) and binding, are the principal elements in terminology and early practice of covenant-making since a covenant both divides and binds, that is to say it clarifies and institutionalizes both the distinction between or separate identities of the partners and their linkage. This is, of course, precisely what covenants are about. In other words, the covenant relationship is to social and political life what Buber's I-Thou relationship is to personal life. Through covenants, humans and their institutions are enabled to enter

into dialogue while maintaining their respective integrities within a shared framework.[48]

God's covenantal organizing rejects all sorts of uniformity (imperialism) and division (chaos), as it respects genuine unity and diversity. In God's redemptive work, God confronts both oppressive/suffocating uniformity (hierarchy) and chaotic selfish diversity (anarchy). Covenant harmonizes the two opposing impulses of unifying and diversifying (particularizing) in a dialectical tension through truthful communication. A good communication (and the rule of law as agreed-upon rules) has a moderating effect for the extreme tendencies toward uniformity and chaos and disorder.

Communication

Communication plays a crucial role in mediating unity and diversity in covenant. Communication is a process through which individual members express and coordinate their views and opinions with others in seeking agreement.[49]

Covenant is communicative in nature. For example, divine-human covenant is built and sustained through a series of communicative actions such as invitation, promise, pledge, and response.[50] Most moral values of covenant (freedom, equality, and reciprocity) are closely associated with covenant's communicative structure. Communication presupposes freedom and equality of each party, and promotes mutual understanding (reconciliation) and friendship between the parties through reciprocal exchanges. Elazar comments:

> Covenant is not a matter of revelation, which essentially is a unilateral act among radical unequals. The conditions of covenant require communication with both sides participating, in which the radical inequality is modified or suspended at least for purposes of the communication.[51]

Good communication has the effect of channeling people's energy and affections toward a shared goal. It also has a relationship-building and sustaining power; trust is built and grows through good communication. Good, truthful communication not only affirms the freedom and equality of each person but also has the effect of deepening the bond among different parties. A covenantal relationship is sustained through ongoing communication among the participants guided by the law as well as the Spirit, who encourages and empowers each party to truthfully and generously interact with each other. In the Christian life, worship, preaching, sacraments, and fellowship—called the means of grace—are the occasions of communication between God and humans, human and human.

Communication not only sustains and strengthens the bond but is also vital for the renewal of a covenant; it helps to readjust the covenantal relationship in response to new and changing social situations. Communication is instrumental in reinterpreting the meaning and spirit of the covenantal relationship through the exchanges of critical and constructive ideas among members. Through ongoing communication with God and others, the members of a covenantal community carefully attune to God's call and changing situations, and collectively discern what covenantal fidelity means and what its requirements are in new situations. Through dynamic and genuine communication, covenant avoids irrelevance and stagnation and renews its relationship without losing its identity.[52]

Law: Covenantal Stipulations

God's covenantal organizing takes place around not only shared goals, but also agreed-upon law. The law has a distinctive organizing function in covenant by bringing stability and predictability to the relationship among participants. As an integral part of covenantal stipulations, it offers guidelines for actions—what is right and wrong, what is good and bad.[53] By doing so, it preserves people from self-destruction, instructs toward holiness, and contributes to virtue formation (transformation of inner dispositions) as they imitate God through the knowledge of the law.[54] The law is not heteronomous in the covenant, because it is the product of communicative consent among the participants. The members of a community are tied (bonded) through the agreed-upon law (stipulations) of the covenant.

As part of the covenantal stipulation, the law is a measurement rod to see whether a covenanted people are faithful to God and others, in particular in their exercise of power, sharing of community resources, and treatment of each other. It delineates the condition of staying in (not entering!) the covenant: its severe violation may lead to the expulsion and excommunication of its members or the nullification of the covenant itself.

Compassion

Compassion (manifested in the form of generosity, forgiveness, and free giving) is another force that builds a community. In response to God's initiating grace, displaying compassion toward others is required for every person who is covenanted with God. To be faithful to God is not to forget God's redemptive grace, but to demonstrate God's generous and gracious acts in one's relationship with others, especially the poor and the downtrodden.[55] Covenanted with God, each person is required to treat others in the way God has treated them. The logic behind human actions is *imitatio Dei*, and there are many motivational clauses in the Bible that demonstrate this logic (e.g., Lev 20:7; 1 Pet 1:16)

In the covenant, the members are expected to voluntarily do for others more than the stipulations legally require. It is the insight of the Bible that this compassionate aspect is important in the building of a good community. In addition, this compassion is necessary because covenant recognizes that the possibility of moral fallout (moral mistakes and failures) always exists in human relationships. Humans are never perfect despite all genuine intentions; hence, forgiveness is necessary, together with moral alertness/warnings.

Out of this awareness, covenant offers a mechanism of restoration, called atonement mechanism, for those who fail to live out their commitments with God. They can be restored to relationship with God when they truthfully confess their mistakes and sins. Restoration typically takes the form of confession and the practice of atonement rituals, and they are communicative (performative) in nature. In comparison to contract and compact, a covenantal relationship is stickier and more solidaric because of its communal, compassionate nature initiated and sustained by God.

Empowerment

The overarching narrative pattern (resistance-alternative) and various mechanisms of covenants (such as the principles of justice, communication, worship, and fellowship) empower human moral agency. As we see in the next four chapters, the story of God's unconditional love (*hesed*) and judgment of injustices emboldens the downtrodden and the marginalized to stand up for their own dignity. It also empowers human agency by stipulating the respect of freedom and basic rights of each person, and applies to God-human relationships as well. By entering a bilateral relationship with God, humans become free, responsible agents. Life in worship and fellowship in a new community also helps to sustain and support the members. Rather than overwhelming or debilitating human agency, God in the covenant empowers humans by treating them as free, responsible agents who collaborate with God to achieve the common goal of shalom.[56]

Renewal of Covenant

Covenant, once established, serves as the formal constitutive basis as well as an ongoing organizing mechanism of a society. Covenant challenges every member and every generation to live faithfully toward God as their deliverer and justly and compassionately toward the poor and the oppressed.

Covenantal renewal is reconstitutive and reactualizing in nature and effect, including the reinterpretation of the law and reorganizing (or reconstitution) of the people and their community.

One finds two different strands in this renewal: moderate (adaptive) and revolutionary. A moderate form of renewal of covenant means rededication and reorienting one's life and values toward God. It intends to renew and reinforce identity and solidarity as one people of God by recommitting to God and one another as the people of God. Through the ceremony, people renew their commitment pledges to live by the high moral principles of justice, mutual care, and trust in God. Israelites were required to participate in a renewal of covenant every seven years (Deut 31:10-13).

A radical covenantal renewal happens when it is necessary to correct unrighteous and unjust relationships and implement justice (do the right things). A radical form of covenant renewal usually repeats a similar pattern of resistance and alternative. It begins with deliverance (resistance), which leads to the renewal of the covenant with the delivered people. Here the renewal of covenant is to reset (renew) the entire relational orientation of a community, worship, and ethics, with God. One finds such examples in the return of the exiles from the Babylonian captivity, which led to the establishment and renewal of the covenant, and Jesus' movement. Following the Exodus-Sinai tradition, major covenant renewals in the Scripture typically entail the readjustment of covenantal stipulations and redistribution of resources (forgiveness of debts) among its members (e.g., Nehemiah; Jesus).

The covenantal renewal exhibits that covenantal ethics is not legalistic; a trusted and faithful relationship is prior to the law, and the legal and ritualistic codes are neither final nor exhaustive, but rather intended to broadly instruct and guide people until more detailed directions are worked out later. Covenant acknowledges that human life cannot be boxed into preconceived legal codes; the demands and requisites of fidelity should be repeatedly discerned according to the nature and spirit of the relationship itself in light of the memory of God's past deliverance and in the hope of future fulfillment.

Conclusion

This chapter has discussed God as the Grand Organizer, demonstrating how organizing is integral to Christian theology, especially God's being and action as the triune God. The triune God is the source, power (efficacy), and goal for the organizing of the world. As an apt descriptor of God's reign, organizing is not an auxiliary but a central motif of the Bible. The biblical narrative is the story of God's organizing from creation (Eden), flood, Israel, and church, to the new creation (the eschaton).

God's organizing in history happens through covenant. Covenant portrays how God's organizing takes place in the creative composite of love, justice, and power. God's covenantal organizing of humanity begins with resistance to evil and injustices, and moves toward building of a new alternative society. The following statement of Brueggemann concisely describes the insoluble tie between covenant and God's organizing work in history.

> To characterize God as the one who makes and keeps covenants has immediate theological implications: (1) It means that issues of human justice and human dignity are always primary and never derivative or optional. (2) It means that this God is best characterized in relational, political categories and not in the conventional theological categories of self-sufficiency, such as omnipotence, omnipresence and omniscience, or in private categories of psychological-spiritual inclination. Neither set of such categories expresses the radical historical, relational character of Yahweh. (3) It means that this God is characterized in profound tension with the other gods, each of which tends to be a legitimator of imperial power of one kind or another. In challenging the gods [in Ps.82], Yahweh also enters into tension with oppressive power in the world. This characterization of God is central and decisive for the Bible.[57]

Brueggemann explains how the particular character of Christian discipleship and ethics derive from God and covenant, and why it cannot avoid being *political* (in a broad sense), and its clash with unjust forms of reign.

The idea of God's covenantal organizing gives us new and rich insights on the biblical idea of God's economy and ethics. Building upon these insights, the following four chapters study how God's covenantal organizing concretely took place in history. God's organizing work is most vividly and dramatically displayed in the Exodus-Sinai story, which serves as a central paradigm of community organizing for the rest of the Bible. In Western history and wherever the gospel is preached, the Exodus-Sinai narrative represents the story of deep human longing and hope for a new, just society. Mediating the two poles of resistance and alternative, covenant carries in it the memory of God's deliverance and hope for a new alternative society where all lives flourish.

2

Exodus

The Biblical Paradigm of Community Organizing

"[I] will be your God, and you shall be my people."

Leviticus 26:12

Our memory of history is marked more by certain dramatic events than specific chronological information. For instance, many may not immediately recognize the significance of November 22, 1963, but would definitely remember the assassination of JFK. In Western history, the Exodus event, in a symbolic sense, is one of the most significant historical events, although we do not know exactly when it happened. Generally speaking, in the Jewish understanding, occupying most of the Pentateuch, it broadly refers to the dramatic events of God's intervention and guidance of the Israelites from their liberation in Egypt to their wilderness journey to Canaan. There are other events in the West that changed the course of history (e.g., the French Revolution, the Russian Revolution, the collapse of the Soviet Union, the September 11 terrorist attacks). However, in terms of their symbolic power and political impact, they do not surpass the Exodus. The Exodus story has generated major social movements and political and economic ideologies in the West. As a symbol of a deep human aspiration for a just society, it has been a never-drying well of inspiration for radical politics and revolutionary struggles.

Never exhausting the human imagination, the Exodus story sets the paradigm for a biblical understanding of God's organizing work for later generations. It constitutes the metanarrative of ancient Israel, setting the tone, offering key theological-ethical parameters, and serving as the frame of reference for the rest of the Bible. Indeed, the Exodus-Sinai story is repeatedly referred to, explicitly and implicitly, throughout the Bible. Furthermore, throughout Western history, the Exodus story has continuously appealed to people under oppression fighting for freedom and searching for an alternative society.[1] Therefore, a biblical understanding of community organizing cannot be imagined without the story of the Exodus.

This chapter examines the Exodus story from the perspective of community organizing. Among many stories of God's organizing work associated with covenant in the Bible, God's most elaborate and systematic discussion is found in the Exodus-Sinai narrative. The Exodus-Sinai narrative, as a drama of God's organizing (starting with Israel's liberation from Egypt, moving to the covenant at Sinai, and journeying through the wilderness before reaching the promised land), displays God's intention and method of organizing in a far more detailed and specific manner than in other stories of the Bible. Hence it is a treasure for studying the theme of God's organizing.

The Exodus Event: Resistance and Liberation

The Exodus-Sinai story, in the most detailed and paradigmatic terms found in the Bible, indicates both resistance to oppression and the search for an alternative society.

The book of Exodus begins with a report indicating the changed social status of the Israelites in Egypt from sojourners into slaves, and it gives an account of their miserable living conditions under a new Pharaoh who saw the flourishing of the Israelites as a threat to himself and his people. Under his iron rule, the Israelites experienced unbearable physical and emotional suffering: "The Egyptians became ruthless in imposing tasks on the Israelites, and made their lives bitter with hard service in mortar and brick and in every kind of field labor. They were ruthless in all the tasks that they imposed on them" (Exod 1:13-14). Even worse, Pharaoh issued the genocidal edict that every newborn Hebrew male child be killed, which would wipe out the Israelites entirely within a few generations.

The story of the dispute among the Hebrews after Moses killed an Egyptian taskmaster reveals the grave distress and disunity of the oppressed people who were unable to build group solidarity and were reduced to desperation for mere individual survival and individual interest. In terms of numbers and military power, the Israelites were no match for the Egyptians; there was no way they could emancipate themselves. However, this did not mean that they were completely despondent. Having no other realistic means of protest, they cried out to their God—the God of Abraham, Isaac, and Jacob—to protest this unjust brutal reality.[2] Their lament had a political meaning. Lament is a form of prayer, which arises on the verge of depression when human pain and suffering reach a breaking point. In the Bible, lament is a moral act emotionally mobilized to force God to address unjust human situations. Lament arises in the perceived abyss between "what should be" and "what is now." Lament is a form of social criticism; indeed, "[b]ringing hurt to public expression is an important first step in the dismantling criticism that permits a new reality, theological and social, to emerge."[3]

In addition, the book of Exodus reports the surreptitious acts of resistance by several Hebrew women, in particular, two midwives engaging in civil disobedience against Pharaoh's edict. There is no reference to God's instigation of this resistance; their resistance was more a natural human response to Pharaoh's genocidal act. The story of the two midwives then leads to the story of Moses' mother—another woman of courage. She protected Moses until she could no longer hide him. Even then, she did not give him up, but placed him in a basket and sent it down the river, entrusting him completely into the hand of God. Moses was providentially redeemed by an Egyptian princess, a compassionate woman, and raised in the Pharaoh's court.

In the opening story of the Exodus, women—relatively powerless and lower in social status in traditional society—work as God's agents to save fragile and vulnerable lives; like many women in poor countries today,[4] these Hebrew women (midwives and Moses' mother and sister) were the last line in defending their family and children against the genocidal force of the Pharaoh, bravely acting to save newborn babies. In the Exodus story, they were the signs and witnesses of God's goodness in the midst of horrendous oppression.[5] Their resistance turned out to be the vehicle of God's deliverance by helping give birth to and nurturing a future leader.[6]

Against this background of suffering people and resistant women, God emerges as the protagonist of freedom and the organizer of an alternative society. Exodus 3:7 reports: "Then the LORD said, 'I have observed the misery of my people who are in Egypt; I have heard their cry on account of their taskmasters. Indeed, I know their sufferings, and I have come down to deliver them from the Egyptians.'"

God's intervention/deliverance was God's act of justice and compassion. God identified Himself with the oppressed. As the story progressed, the image of God gradually emerged as the organizing God. God's organizing work in the Exodus story was first subversive, then later public. God first worked indirectly, subversively working behind the scenes through the hands of women (midwives, Moses' mother and sister, and an Egyptian princess). Starting with the calling of Moses (Exod 3:1-10), however, God's work became public. God recruited Moses, with Aaron as his spokesperson, and empowered them to confront the Pharaoh and organize the people to leave Egypt. As the story progressed, God began to be involved in every detailed aspect of organizing, while also giving the vision of the promised land. This plot reveals that God's deliverance was not a random, incidental reaction to the pain of His people, but a comprehensive and deliberate plan to organize them into a new people. Just as a skillful community organizer, God tapped into people's discontentment, suffering, and desires, and invited them to be His partner to build a new society. One should also notice that the process of liberation included the rise of a new awareness (conscientization), in which their folk religion exercised a formative role.

> The Moses group [freed slaves], in rejecting both the physical and psychic bondage of the Egyptian socio-political and economic system, had also abandoned the religious ideology that legitimated and reinforced that system. In replacing the Egyptian gods, whose son the Pharaoh claimed to be, they chose, or claimed to have been chosen by, Yahweh, the god of the oppressed, a god who stands by the poor and frees those enslaved. The religious cult they began to develop would also serve as a binding and legitimating force for the new people now being created in the hill country of Canaan.[7]

Despite God's promise, the liberation of the Hebrews did not happen immediately because of Pharaoh's hardened heart. Pharaoh not only rejected Moses' offer (Exod 5) but also intensified his mistreatment of the Hebrews, which led to God's judgment of the Pharaoh through the ten plagues.

Judgment

In the Exodus story, Pharaoh symbolizes the epitome of an unjust social system where power (political, economic, and cultural) was concentrated in the hands of a few: its political economy was aimed at endless acquisition at the expense of human lives and families; the strangers (migrants) were mistreated; families broke down under the pressure of economic exploitation; ethnicity became the basis of social exclusion; infants were the victims of a genocidal government policy. The Pharaoh symbolized the force of anti-life, anti-community, and anti-creation, because his policies were the utter opposite of God's design for humanity (Gen 1–2) to multiply and be fruitful. He was an anti-God figure because the Pharaoh, posing as a deity, used religion to justify systematic exploitation as part of "natural" order.

Hence, God's judgment and triumph over the Pharaoh in Exodus had a profound moral meaning. Michael Walzer's comment is apt on this point:

> The Exodus is not a lucky escape from misfortune. Rather the misfortune has a moral character, and the escape has a world-historical meaning. Egypt is not just left behind; it is restricted; it is judged and condemned. The crucial terms of that judgment are *oppression* and *corruption*.[8]

Plagues

The plagues were the vehicle of God's punishment of the Pharaoh. They were God's public demonstration and judgment against injustice. Terence Fretheim claims that we should see the plagues in terms of the symbiotic relationship between creation order and moral order in biblical thinking: "The divine power over all forms of Pharaonic power is demonstrated through the moral order for the purpose of re-creating justice and righteousness in the world order."[9]

This means that God's judgment is not arbitrary, a simple bias in favor of Israel over Egypt. God's judgment is based on justice, embedded in God's moral order. God acts as both the creator and the universal judge. God does not violate the limit that He Himself set through the order.[10]

> The theological understanding for the plagues is an understanding of the moral order, created by God for the sake of justice and well-being

in the world. Pharaoh's moral order is bankrupt, severely disrupting this divine intent, and hence he becomes the object of the judgment inherent in God's order.[11]

In other words, the plagues are the results of accumulated injustices. The story of the plagues demonstrates that there is an intrinsic causal relationship between God's judgment and human moral life; God's punishment grows out of human malice.[12] The effects of human deeds are revealed in due time.

The plagues had several effects on Egyptians and Hebrews:

(1) Through the plagues, God disrupted the system of injustice and the entire social order that the Pharaoh symbolically represented. God's plagues demonstrated who is the true Lord and who is truly in charge in history. The statement "You [Egyptians] shall know that I am the Lord" is repeated throughout the entire plague narrative (Exod 6:7, 7:5, 7:17, 8:22, 10:2, 14:4, 14:18).

(2) The plagues altered the Hebrews' perception of power and power relations as they saw that the imperial power of Egypt counted as nothing under God's judgment. The Hebrews gained a new awareness that their God, YHWH, is not just an ethnic God, but the true Lord and King of all the earth. Consequently, the demonstration of God's power in the ten plagues restored the moral agency of the Hebrews. It is not difficult to imagine that despite oppression, leaving the land where they had lived for four hundred years was a difficult decision. The Hebrews could have negotiated new terms of relationship and power with the Egyptians. The plagues assisted in the development of a new social consciousness. While watching God's power in the plagues, the Hebrew slaves were persuaded to leave Egypt willingly and to participate in God's vision of a new society. Their decision reveals their changed mindset (conscientization) resulting from God's judgment.

Divine-Human Collaboration in Liberation

Liberation was possible thanks to God's sovereign power. However, contradicting a conventional interpretation, the literary composition and structure of the chapters show that liberation was not solely God's work (as a lone ranger), but the collaboration of God and courageous human agents. The opening narrative of the book, as aforementioned, implies that the Hebrews took some initiative in their resistance. God responded to their cry, visited his people, saw their suffering, and decided to intervene.

Even in performing the plagues, "God is explicitly active in only six plagues (1, 4, 5, 7, 8, 10). Aaron/Moses are involved in three of them in a dual role (1, 7, 8) and alone in plagues 2, 3, 6, and 9 (see 7:1!)."[13] Sometimes the text even attributes a passive role to God: "God acted according to the word of Moses" (Exod 8:13). These examples show that "[b]oth God and human beings are agents. Moses and Aaron would not be effective without God's power working in and through them, and God is dependent on Moses and Aaron, working in the world through that which is not divine. Both God and Israel recognize this dual agency (Exod 3:8-10; 14:31)."[14]

An Alternative Society

In the Exodus narrative, whereas Egypt symbolized "the house of slavery," the promised land symbolized a new alternative society. The promised land and Egypt stand in complete contrast. Michael Walzer notes, "Canaan is a promised land because Egypt is a house of bondage."[15] In the scheme of God's organizing, judgment (liberation) and alternative (reconstruction) are inseparable. God's goal was not to establish another nation alongside other nations, but to create a new peoplehood that would act as a catalyst for the transformation of the world.

For the Israelites, the promised land signifies not only a liberated society but also a newly organized society based on justice and love, fulfilling God's intention for humanity.[16] The vision of the promised land was a necessary moral response to Israel's experience under Pharaoh's system, and the Sinai Covenant and God's law offered a roadmap for building such a society.

With the Exodus and the Sinai Covenant, a new notion of community was born, an alternative to the surrounding city-states and Egypt. Through covenant, Israel was organized by God as a society of freed slaves who sought an alternative society compared to the pyramidal social stratification of Egypt.

> Thus a new notion of community was born with the exodus. In compromising or denying it, as Israel repeatedly would, Israel would compromise or deny its own essential being as a people called by God, a community of freed slaves within which the pyramid of social stratification consigning certain classes to lives of ease and others to relentless suffering and deprivation was to be banned forever.[17]

Under the covenantal vision, Israelites endeavored to build an anti-Pharaonic society reflecting God's moral character of compassion, justice, and peace (solidarity with the poor). This endeavor was reflected in the political economy of Israel.

> Yahweh intends that Israel be a nation of sisters and brothers in which there will be no more poor (cf. Deut. 15:4). This in itself makes clear that, according to the Bible, the poor of Egypt are to become, through the Exodus, a kind of divinely-willed contrast-society . . . In fact, the new society that Yahweh creates out of the poor Hebrews through the Exodus is not only in contrast to the Egyptian society they have left behind, but beyond that it is in contrast to all other existing societies in their world [it is thus a task directed not just at Israel's good but to the good of all humanity].[18]

The Israelites relied on covenant in constructing an alternative society. The covenant had a leveling effect on social inequality and privilege; it checked the tendency to stratify people along the lines of power, privilege, and status; it reversed hierarchies and inequality while nurturing a solidaric, reciprocal, and public spirit. Exercising a new moral imagination inspired by the covenant, the Israelites invented a new model of society that overcame the painful past of oppression and exploitation. The result was transformation from a hierarchal state model to a covenant model—"a decentralized, egalitarian, tribal mode of life."[19]

Constituting a People

The first phase of God's organizing work, liberation, climaxed at the crossing of the Red Sea and the drowning of Pharaoh's army; the second phase began with the formation of the people at Sinai. The Bible's insight is that liberation alone does not guarantee a new community. Rather, a new community needs to be carefully designed and structured, and its members need to be trained and disciplined in their new civic responsibilities. Without this constructive phase, the achieved liberation is politically fragile and socially unstable, often resulting in chaos or another form of tyranny.

The Sinai Covenant played a critical role in this transition from liberation to a new society, serving as the organizing framework of a new people. The Sinai Covenant transformed *goy* into *am*, an ordinary nation into a people with a distinctive vocation and identity: a priestly kingdom acting as a light to the nations. Community organizing began with God's deliverance, but its concrete form, structure, and collective identity emerged through covenant.

The Hebrew word *edah* captures this constitutive power of covenant in organizing the Israelites as one people. *Edah* was what emerged as the result of the covenant. It describes the "congregational assembly, in the republican sense of a governing body [with a decision making power] that meets at regular intervals (*moadim*)."[20] Consisting of all men, women, and children, it was equivalent to a modern sense of civic duty, and thus, "from Sinai onward, constitutional decisions were taken by the entire *Edah*, men, women, and children, assembled together to give their consent."[21]

The idea of *edah* displays that ancient Israel had a popular, republican form of polity based on the covenant. Each member, regardless of gender, age, or class, participated in the common life as an equal and responsible citizen, although important decisions were made through the tribal leaders who represented the *edah* (e.g., Exod 18).

Freedom: Its Bilateral Nature

Covenant is symbolized and concretized in a genuine moral community based on the free consent of people, which was emphasized in the bilateral nature of the Sinai Covenant (Exod 19:5–8).[22] Although covenant was initiated by God, the making of the covenant was ultimately the free choice and decision of Israel. The Israelites were not forced to agree to the covenant.

In Exodus 24:3-8, the Israelites gave their pledges to God a second time in response to Moses' delivery of the Book of the Covenant. This stresses the significance of the people's free decision for and participation in their covenant relationship with God. Every member of the community believed that he/she was individually covenanted with God, and thus, no activity was exempt from the obligations specified by the covenant. In other words, covenant itself is the proof that humans are not God's robots. The bilateral covenant, with its requirement of human free consent, was the sign that former slaves were treated as God's partners and equal among themselves, with the freedom to decide their own destiny. A new collective identity arose as they entered into a covenantal relationship with God.

By the standard of Moses' time, the Sinai Covenant was inclusive and democratic; women, children, servants, strangers, rich, and poor had equal citizenship (membership)—equal rights and responsibilities in the covenant. In Israel there was one law binding both citizens and aliens (Lev 24:22). The requisite of consent in the covenant-cutting ceremony indicated a political body that developed as the result of a common will and the decision of the people, rather than on a sheer biological basis.

Justice

For the Hebrews, covenanting was a process to form a just community. This was a strong demand in response to God's deliverance in Egypt. Israelites were required to live by a high standard of righteousness and justice in every domain of life, including special care for the weak and the poor, and humane treatment of animals.

There are two biblical principles of justice that play an important role in God's organizing: *tsedakah* (Hebrew: צדקה) and *mishpat* (Hebrew: מִשְׁפָּ), translated, respectively, as "righteousness" and "justice" or "judgment." While *mishpat* is concerned with the basic rights (sanctity) of each person, *tsedakah* has to do with moral requirements intrinsic to specific social relationships.

To be righteous means to live according to the moral standards and expectations intrinsic to a specific relationship, or "correspond correctly to the values of the relationship, such as parents, spouse, friends, business partner, judge, politician."[23] Hence, *tsedakah* is a relationally bound notion because it pertains to the very nature of a specific social relationship.

Mishpat has to do with governance—the judgment or execution of an ordinance of God or a king in organizing and ordering a society. It is closely tied with the modern idea of human rights—thus universalizable moral requirements of how to treat others. *Mishpat* is stipulated in the specific codes of the behaviors that are required to protect the rights of each person,[24] in particular, the weak and the needy.[25] This requirement of justice for the weak and the needy was specified in terms of the responsibility of a king to protect the rights of the poor and the weak, and of the judge to settle legal disputes in fairness. The violation of these laws was believed to bring God's judgment against the nation (Jer 22:3; Ezek 22:7, 29; Mal 3:5; cf. Ps 94:6), because mistreatment was regarded as a breach of their covenant with God. This principle of justice also gave a theological basis for people to challenge abusive rulers.

These two different ideas of justice show that covenant organizing was highly sophisticated in its consciousness of the reality of power (financial, political, clerical, military) and the complexity of human life.

The law was designed to prevent its abuse and misuse, to protect the weak, and to be relationally sensible by attending to the moral nature of social relationships.

The Sinai Covenant

The Sinai Covenant broadly refers to the event of God's entering into a relationship with the Israelites, as portrayed in Exodus 19. The Sinai Covenant includes two parts of stipulations: the Ten Commandments as its constitution, and the Book of the Covenant (or the Covenant Code, Exod 20–23) as its detailed statutes.

Ten Commandments (Exod 20:1-17)

The Ten Commandments, as the summary of the moral law and the constitution of Israel, offer the encompassing framework of life for the Israelites. Constituting the relationship itself, the Ten Commandments describes the fundamentals of the spiritual and moral relationship between God and Israel. God, humans, and the biotic world are intimately connected—God is the life source of both human and biotic worlds under his covenant. The Ten Commandments has two parts, the two tablets, revealing Israel's understanding of what constitutes a true moral community. The first tablet has to do with worship of God, while the second has to do with the ethical life of the people of God. The structure of the Ten Commandments shows not only the unity and order between worship and ethics in the covenantal life of Israel; the Ten Commandments also teaches piety toward God and justice toward other human beings.[26] Both piety and justice are indispensable for the building of a community.

If the Ten Commandments served as the constitution of Israel as a unified political body, the Book of the Covenant concretized the religious and moral demands of the Ten Commandments in the form of civil, criminal, and cultic laws, statutes, and ordinances. The Book of the Covenant supplements the Ten Commandments, delineating how to lead a life in great detail—what the way of life under God's covenant should be like. It offers numerous stipulations that guide and regulate sacrificial rituals (Exod 24:3-8), covenantal meals (Exod 24:9-11), the erection of the tabernacle (Exod 25–27; 35–40), and the consecration of Aaron and his sons as priests (Exod 28–29).

In Israel's life, the Sinai Covenant indicated an encompassing organizing framework regulating and guiding every aspect of Israel's life:

worship, family, economics, politics, and international relationships. Israelites were required to exercise covenantal faithfulness in every domain of their lives—in eating (selecting proper animals that were properly slaughtered), in treating strangers, in relating to the land and to neighbors, and in time (Sabbath). It helped to organize and guide Israel's relationship with God and other nations and its own internal life.

The Law

The law specified the moral obligations required of God's partners, specifying what God's justice/righteousness are. Predicated on a covenant relationship, the law was not heteronomous, but instructional and informative. However, because of the intimate relational nature of the covenant, the law is more filial than judicial. The law did not exhaust or substitute the covenant, because in the covenant, the law was never intended to be an end in and of itself, and never to exist separate from the relationships with God and other people. Therefore, obedience to the law was driven not by fear of reprisal but by a free willingness to reciprocate God's love and faithfulness. In this respect, from a biblical viewpoint, the law was paradoxically the sign of human freedom rather than subjugation:

> [T]he law points up the fact that God has chosen not to do everything in this world by himself. . . . the law insists that there are important human initiatives and responsibilities to be undertaken. Human beings are given important tasks in furthering the cause of justice and good order in Israel and the larger creation.[27]

The law (as covenantal stipulations) played an important role in the organizing of people and their community by offering principled consistency and reliable behavior to the members of a community. Its specific guidelines and directives offered the structure and order necessary for personal and social life. That is, it specified concretely what mutual expectations of righteousness and justice were, and what responsibilities looked like in relationship. Keeping the covenantal promises enhanced mutual trust and strengthened solidarity among covenant members. The Ten Commandments and the Covenantal Code, as covenantal stipulations, served as a plumb line not only for covenantal participants' own moral actions, but for other nations' behavior as well,[28] according to the principles of justice. Violations were believed to invite divine judgment.

Unity in Diversity: Tribal Confederacy

The Sinai Covenant built a new community on a federal arrangement (a separation of powers) while seeking to build a collaborative system based on justice. Ancient Israel was covenantally organized around a loose union of twelve tribes. This union, perhaps the first true federal system in history, was bound together by a common constitution and law but maintained by relatively rudimentary national institutions grafted onto more fully articulated tribal ones.

By intention, the confederate tribal system did not have a centralized government with a king at the top. It aimed at a federal political entity—the unity of Israel in the diversity of twelve tribes. They were unified as the one people of God, sharing a common historical memory, collective identity, and the Torah, but living as the twelve tribes. While the constitution was comprehensive in its scope, the role of government was limited and local in nature.[29]

> Thus the local arena becomes the most important arena of governance and primarily self-government. Local elders, constituting a local council (*shaarei ha-ir*), handle day-to-day matters, primarily of adjudication, subordinate to the general assembly of the local citizenry (*ha-ir*).[30]

Confederacy was designed to protect smaller units of a society, resonating with the principle of subsidiarity, in which powers were divided among federal authorities, such as judges and civil servants, and local ones, such as tribal and familial leaders.

> The classic biblical commonwealth was a fully articulated federation of tribes instituted and reaffirmed by covenant to function under a common constitution and laws. Any and all constitutional changes in the Israelite polity were introduced through covenanting and even after the introduction of the monarchy, the federal element was maintained until most of the tribal structures were destroyed by external forces. The biblical vision of the restored commonwealth in the messianic era envisages the reconstitution of the tribal federation. Certain of the American Puritans and many Americans of the Revolutionary era among others, were inspired by the Biblical polity to seek federal arrangements for their polities.[31]

Covenant had the effect of organizing the twelve tribes to avoid the danger of both tyranny and separatism. Joshua distributed the land according to tribes, each of which elected its own officers (Josh 1:13) and had its own economic basis.

Separation of Power

As described above, the Exodus and the Sinai Covenant show acute concern about the issues of power and justice, embodied in the separation of powers and authorities. In the polity of ancient Israel, we see the primordial form of the separation of powers.

Within God's covenantal relationship with Israel (*edah*), the idea of three *ketarim* (literally, "crowns") captures the structural division of power and authority. *Keter malkhut* (the crown of governance) describes the authority of civil governance that represents people at both the local and the central levels; *keter kehunan* (the crown of priesthood) describes worship, rituals, and sacerdotal matters; *keter torah* (the crown of Torah) is responsible for the interpretation and teaching of the Torah in order to teach and judge over people.[32] This responsibility started with Moses, was shared with the seventy elders, and later was taken up by the prophets and rabbis. In their use of power, leaders were required to follow the principles of justice and the law.

Even after Israel moved to monarchy, this covenantal passion for justice and the principle of the separation of power did not cease, but continued in the tripartite offices of priest, prophet, and king. The prophets checked kings and the corruptive influence of priests over kings while hearkening people to return to living faithfully before God. The priestly class was protected by God's covenant with Aaron and his sons, giving priests divine authority.

Political Economy

Using covenant as their roadmap and constitution, the Israelites were called to build a society based on justice and compassion. The covenanted people were called to reciprocate God's compassion and love through their commitment to freedom, equality, and care for the poor and the oppressed.

In particular, using covenantal organizing, Israelites built a political system that was anti-hierarchal, decentralized, egalitarian, and confederal, which was in sharp contrast to the hierarchal and centralized structure of Egypt. There was no king and no centralized power. God was their king, and under God's reign, each person was equal and held accountable to others. Regardless of their social status and economic standing, every Israelite was an equal member of God's covenant, and covenant legally protected their equal status in God. This was legally and religiously symbolized by the participation of women in the covenanting rite at Mount Sinai.

The confederacy of the twelve tribes served as a system of horizontal collaboration and checks and balances so that none could be inordinately wealthy and powerful enough to oppress and exploit others. In light of their past suffering in Egypt, there was a deep constant warning against the danger of inordinate greed and power. This concern is expressed through the emphasis on their equal status before God and society's responsibility toward the weak and the poor.

Economic System

A similar idea is found in the Israelites' view of the land and redistribution of resources. Their political economy emphasized sharing and public service in place of acquisition and domination. They were critical of greed and possessiveness of wealth. The land was integral as it belonged to God; it was distributed among the tribes, and then among the clans and families within each tribe. Each family had an inalienable right to an inheritance, which was their permanent possession; even a king was not to meddle with the inheritance (1 Kgs 21:3). Such strict prohibition was part of covenantal ethics: the economic rights of each family were crucial for the commonwealth of individuals and society, the basis of their social freedom.

Under a covenantal moral vision, the Israelites built an economic system that protected the subsistence of every family and clan. It was based on the belief that the land was not private property but God's property, and humanity used it only as God's stewards (tenants). Specifically, "The covenant required that each extended family have access to the basic resources for survival, particularly through the spirituality and practice of the Sabbath Day, the Sabbath Year, and the Jubilee."[33]

Extended families (*bet-abot*) formed the base, living in close proximity and reaching 50–100 people of various generations and relations. Access to the land was the primary basis for subsistence, identity, and self-determination. These extended families were gathered into associations or clans (*mispajah*) for mutual support and protection at the level of villages or neighborhoods, insuring the survival of each family against military intrusion, providing wells and terraces and communal lands for grazing, offering loans without interest, organizing work teams, and celebrating festivals. These associations together formed tribes for mutual defense and aid at yet another level as regional alliances to protect their independence and meeting internal crises, and they in turn formed the Israelite intertribal confederation or alliance.[34]

As a result, Israelites did not have the typical burdens that other ordinary people had in the city-states of the ancient Near East. They were not exploited for tributes or into forced labor imposed by city-state rulers. They were also able to overcome the threats of droughts, insects, disease, and bandits through mutual support, care, and collaboration built upon the tribal covenant.

> By means of this alliance, Israel achieved political self-government, economic development, military defense, and a cultural identity that gave prominence to their religion as the ideological base of the system and the source of its legitimacy and efficacy. Israel's egalitarian tribalism [covenantal social system] functioned as an alternative to the centralized and hierarchal state.[35]

Through their historical experiences, the Israelites were keenly aware that economic subsistence—providing the resources to meet basic needs of food, clothes, shelter, etc.—was critical for maintaining basic human dignity and integrity as free people. They learned that there is no genuine freedom without economic freedom. The decrees of the Sabbath Year and Jubilee (every seventh year and every fiftieth year, respectively) constituted the heart of covenant economics. The decrees were designed to avoid the concentration of power, thus reenacting the message of the Exodus. Hence it is correct to say: "Jubilee is exodus spelled out in terms of social salvation."[36] These decrees were intended to protect people's basic economic rights by institutionalizing periodic corrections of economic inequality (through forgiveness of debts and release from slavery) and offering equal opportunities for all. The ultimate goal was to restore a just community.

For the prophets, the practice of covenantal economy was a major criterion to test Israel's covenantal fidelity toward God. Worship and ritualistic sacrifice could not replace the requirements of covenantal political economy because exploitation and oppression are inimical to God. This means that worship and sacrifice cannot be compartmentalized or divorced from the economy of a society.

The Organizing Power of Worship

The worship of the Israelites, like their ethics, was a covenantal practice. Worship indicates the occasion of a communicative interaction between God and Israel in which both parties were fully present, challenged, reaffirmed, and redefined.[37] Its structure and liturgical plot were covenantally informed. The Israelites' experience of slavery and God's deliverance were permanently commemorated in a communal ritual: the Passover.

Worship was specifically designed to remind, strengthen, and renew the Israelites' covenantal relationship with God.[38] Worship was the occasion to communicate with God and others; it had the effect of reorganizing a community. Worship carries in it the memory of God's liberation and deliverance, and the hopeful expectation of and commitment to a just society. Through ritual, the covenanted people are repeatedly called by God not to forget God's liberation, but to renew their own commitment to God and God's justice. In Israel, rituals served as the occasions of covenantal renewal.[39]

Of their rituals, the observance of the Passover through the sacrifice of the Pascal lamb is one central to Israel's life. The Passover offers a public occasion for God's redemptive story to be redramatized and reenacted.

> [I]n and through the celebration of the Passover God works salvation initially, and ever anew, in the lives of the participants, (re)constituting them as the redeemed exodus community . . . "As such, it is a sacramental vehicle for making the exodus redemption real and effective for both present and subsequent generations." Thus "When Israel reacts the Passover, it is not a fiction, as if nothing really happens in the ritual, or all that happens is a recollection of the happenedness of an original event. . . . It is an entering into the reality of that event in such a way to be reconstituted as the people of God thereby."[40]

The experience of deliverance (memory) is shared and passed down in the community in the form of a narrative and rituals.[41] When they lose this memory and its meanings, then the covenant itself loses its moral anchor, and the loss of identity (resulting in confusion, corruption, or decay) is inevitable.

The Passover is deliberately designed to pass the memory of the Exodus event to subsequent generations. Children hear the story of the Exodus from their parents, eat the bitter herb, and remember the suffering of their ancestors under slavery. Through the ceremony the Exodus is relived—not as some antiquated event but a living reality for today. Through a shared story and a meal, children learn the values of their community and freely participate in God's covenant as God's people.

Organizing Power of the Sabbath

As part of their covenantal stipulations, the Sabbath practice plays an important temporal and social role in organizing Israel's life and community. Israel's understanding of the Sabbath is tied with two major narratives: creation and Exodus.

The Sabbath practice addresses God's entire economy (*oikonomia*), encompassing both the human and biotic worlds. In a symbolic way, the Sabbath repeats God's creation event. The Sabbath is the occasion of God's cosmic reorganizing. Humans cease economic activities and focus on the renewal of their lives in relationship with God and others.

On the Sabbath, God empowers each member to find its natural rhythm and pace, attuning to the flow, loops, and circulation of creation itself. The Sabbath restores and refreshes the agency and power of each creature. Every creature, especially the weak and the marginalized, reclaims its own space and boundary. As God originally organized the space to secure the place where creatures can flourish, the Sabbath is the time that God reorganizes time and space by resetting boundaries and putting a creative space between all competing/contesting parties (humans and land, farmers and domestic animals, masters and maids/servants). Through the Sabbath the creation is reordered, reoriented, and renewed, foretasting God's shalom.

As much as it stemmed from the creation story, the Sabbath was also associated with the Exodus story. Indeed, the Sabbath connected creation and Exodus. The Sabbath reminded Israelites of God's deliverance in the Exodus event and beseeched them to live up to their covenantal obligations—to practice an alternative economic system to the Pharaoh's slavery system. "[Sabbath] is rather an icon for a socio-economic political arrangement of social power in a distinctive way that is critical of and an alternative to other social arrangements that are authorized by other gods."[42] Through its exploitative system and greed, Egypt (and Pharaoh) indicated the utter violation of the moral vision of the Sabbath. The Sabbath was the antidote to the predatory Pharaonic system of Egypt. Alexia Salvatierra and Peter Heltzel note, "When sabbath is kept, oppression and exploitation can be ended, and there will be universal well-being throughout the whole community of creation."[43]

A regular, periodic rest on the Sabbath alleviates the stress and burden of each member of society. However, it is more than the stoppage of work and activity. The Sabbath and Jubilee statutes show an inherent affinity between God's organizing work and socioeconomic justice of all creatures. The Sabbath is a community-affirming and community-celebrating practice. In connection to creation and Exodus, the Sabbath offers the reminder that genuine rest comes from a just and righteous moral order, where everything is in right relationship with others through a harmonious attuning of life to God.

The Sabbath has a profound economic message for us today. By setting a boundary against human economic activities, it warns against the danger of human overproduction, overwork, and over-ambition, and it protects the rights of vulnerable humans, animals, and the land from exploitation.

Wilderness: A Divine School

It is quite an audacious task to transform former slaves into model citizens of the world (as a priestly kingdom), and God's organizing work takes a different form after the crossing of the Red Sea. God's organizing of the Hebrews occurred in two phases: pre-Exodus and post-Exodus. While the first organizing was to empower and motivate the Israelites to leave Egypt, where they had lived for four hundred years, the second phase of God's organizing happened in the wilderness. The sign of the unconditional love of God and the ten plagues in Egypt boosted the courage of the people to sever their ties with Egypt and follow Moses' lead. The organizing in the wilderness was to equip and train them to be capable of entering the promised land. However, thanks to the Sinai Covenant, the people of Israel did not wander in darkness, but embarked upon their journey toward a new community with a clear moral vision and concrete guidance.

The wilderness served as a divine school providing the opportunity for collective reflection, identity formation, and the shaping of a new community tradition. The separation from Egypt—in a liminal space, belonging nowhere—offered an opportunity to undo the moral and psychological effects of slavery, that is, to desocialize (deorganize) the Israelites from Egypt and to resocialize (reorganize) them as the free people of God. Power has a strange mystique to lure the oppressed to envy, admire, and imitate their oppressors, even while simultaneously hating them. The slaves inevitably internalized the social worldview, cultural habits, and negative self-images and stereotypes instilled by their oppressors ("lazy, stupid, unworthy, cursed").

For freed Hebrew slaves, such a reformation occurred through a carefully conceived and crafted curriculum of worship, community life, and ethics under the Sinai Covenant. The Israelites were systematically trained in organizing every aspect of their lives: worship, family (clan/tribe), economy, and politics. Covenantally informed communal practices in worship and ethics shaped them with a new distinctive spiritual and moral identity and vision, and enhanced their moral capability and agency. Their shared experiences of life together in the wilderness, in a long journey under God, gave rise to a common tradition and collective memory.

The motif of wilderness reappears in Christian spirituality in close association with pilgrimage and spiritual discipline (e.g., the Desert Fathers). The journey through the wilderness implies that a sudden radical transition is not plausible for the formation and organizing of a new community. Learned habits are obstinate, the resilient formation of peoplehood takes time and effort, and even the pain from a deep learning curve is inevitable. Furthermore, this phase of internal transformation is uneven, as people respond differently in faith. Thus, the liminal space is indispensable.

Intergenerational Education

Later biblical writers share the conviction that the Sinai Covenant binds all generations of Israel, that all Jews, including the unborn, were present at Sinai. Hence, every generation needs to be reminded of their covenantal relationship with God and others. Educating a new generation is necessary to help them understand what Israel is, what it means to live under God's covenant, and what their rights and obligations toward God and others are. Without education, covenant cannot be maintained. The study of Torah was the heart of their education. Thus, covenantal renewal had a pedagogical purpose in passing down the covenantal tradition from one generation to the next. The prime example was Moses' covenantal renewal in Deuteronomy.

Called *Divrei HaBrit*, the Words of the Covenant (Deut 29:8),[44] Deuteronomy presents an excellent example of the renewal of the covenant with a new generation in a new historical context. Moses' renewal speech, on the plains of Moab prior to crossing the Jordan River, was delivered to the entire assembly of Israel (the *edah*) who were born in the wilderness. While the Exodus was intended for the people in the wilderness,

Deuteronomy was meant for the people settling in their land—designed for a settled people with their own "permanent territorial divisions with a fixed central shrine" (Temple) and the institution of the kingship.[45]

Legacy

The Exodus-Sinai story was permanently etched in the mind of Israel and exercised enduring influence on later generations. As the ancient Hebrews reflected upon and remembered the Exodus, "ideas and expressions in the original situation [event] give rise to [core] symbol, and become a motif"[46] and embodied practices of a community in the form of shared history, memory, and expectations.

One form of expression was the prophetic tradition in Israel, which was another historical expression of covenantal ethos.[47] Importantly, the prophets, while interpreting major historical events in terms of moral cause and effect, typically relied on the Sinai Covenant as the moral basis for their criticism of idolatry and social injustice. A covenantal pattern of judgment and restoration appeared in their proclamations and denunciations.

The prophets were advocates of justice, defenders of the weak, the vulnerable, and the oppressed victims of injustice. Their list of violations also included idolatry, sexual promiscuity, and violence. They warned the people that neither the Temple and its rituals nor a biological lineage could protect Israel from God's judgment unless they practiced covenant fidelity to God and God's law. The prophets threw stinging indictments toward the people of Israel for their breach of covenant with God.[48] They beseeched them to return to the Lord, following the ways of justice and righteousness stipulated by the Sinai Covenant.

The prophets played an important role in passing on the Exodus-Sinai story to future generations. A large portion of prophetic literature in the OT tells how the covenantal tradition is central to the biblical understanding of God and humanity.

Conclusion

The covenant pattern of God's organizing and judgment-restoration (the motifs of liberation, justice, and a dream for a new society) played a normative role throughout the OT, and later the NT. Hence,

> [The Exodus-Sinai story] is a much bigger concept than merely the liberation of the Hebrews from the oppressive iron furnace of the Egyptians.

It is about God's crafting a people for himself by bringing them to the very abode of his presence at Mount Sinai. Yet there is more. Just as there was an anticipated goal at the beginning of creation in the Garden of Eden, so also there is an anticipated goal for Israel. The deliverance from Egypt did not stop at Sinai, where God meets with his people. This deliverance was intended to include the Promised Land.[49]

The Exodus-Sinai event is an inspiring story of how a vulnerable people, when organized and guided by God, can build an alternative community and teach a new way of organizing the world.

The Exodus-Sinai event shows that a distinctive aspect of God's organizing in history is God's bottom-up method. God identifies Himself with the oppressed. God embraced the "rabble of slaves" as God's partner. In contrast to other gods, what characterizes the God of Israel is His passion for justice and willingness to maintain solidarity with the poor and the marginalized (Ps 82:3-4). The Exodus story portrays God as the deity who is in conflict with other gods and the oppressive power of the empire sponsored by those gods.[50] God sides with the oppressed in diametric opposition to the gods of Egypt, who protected and perpetuated a hierarchal social caste with the Pharaoh at the top and the Hebrew slaves at the bottom.

This pattern of God's bottom-up solidarity echoes throughout the Bible. In history, God uses the downtrodden and the marginalized to organize a society into a new form—more egalitarian, in a deeper union. This is by God's wisdom, according to Paul, in order to shame the wise and the strong (1 Cor 1:27-29).

> Yahweh is a God who forcefully, decisively, and willingly enters into solidarity with a group of helpless people. That solidarity is for the benefit of people who cannot act for themselves. That solidarity is an act of risk for Yahweh, for it puts Yahweh in conflict with other gods and with the awesome power of the empire. It is this act of enduring, risky solidarity that most decisively characterizes the God of the Bible. . . . risky solidarity [is] what we mean by covenant.[51]

The Exodus-Sinai narrative describes in dramatic detail how passionately (and intelligently) God is committed to organizing a new community. It reveals that God is not a remote, impersonal God, but a covenantal God who liberates the oppressed and partners with them to build a just new society. He is an active God who is involved in history in order to organize humanity and creation toward His vision of shalom community.

God uses covenant as a primary means of organizing His people. Worshipping the God of the Exodus is always to revive and refresh the memory of His liberation, rekindle the people's commitment to justice and compassion, and draw them to participate in God's organizing work already taking place in history.

> [I]n essence there was already revealed in this event both the nature of the God Yahweh, and the nature of the community of faith that Yahweh's nature implied . . . In the deliverance from Egyptian slavery, Israel encountered a God whose nature and whose corresponding plan for reality stood in diametric opposition to the gods of the Pharaoh.[52]

The Exodus story presents covenant as a central biblical method of organizing God's people and their society. Interpreted in the context of the organizing intention of the Exodus, covenant is a revolutionary idea that prioritizes freedom, equality, peace, and solidarity over oppression, privilege, and exclusion in human relationships. It indicates a world-shattering way to organize a community—from oppression to justice and peace.

The story of God's organizing continues to be remembered today whenever the Exodus story is told and celebrated. The story of the Exodus evokes a passion for justice—resistance against unjust, unequal social structures—and the longing for a just, righteous community. An important message of the book of Exodus is that God hates injustice, and God's people are called to resist oligarchic, tyrannical rule (empire), whether it occurs in their own community or in broader society.

Ancient Israel was not a democratic society based on popular sovereignty in a modern Western form. But seminal democratic ideas were already present in the Sinai Covenant. The separation of powers, the rule of law, and the periodic correction of economic inequalities were direct products of the Sinai Covenant. These ideas have made a huge impact on the politics of the West.[53] The vision and norms embedded in the Exodus and the Sinai Covenant can inform and guide how people actually govern themselves, how they distribute resources, and how they enact justice.

3

Jesus

The Kingdom Organizer

"[T]he sole meaning of the entire activity of Jesus is the gathering of God's eschatological people."[1]

Jesus is the central figure of Christianity. For Christians, Jesus is the Lord, the savior, and the messiah who came to save humanity from sin and death, and fulfilled his mission on the cross. His salvific work transcends time and space. In a rampant milieu of individualistic understandings of Christian salvation, Jesus' earthly ministry, let alone his Jewish heritage, often loses its soteriological significance. His earthly ministry is regarded as supplying proofs of his supernatural power or superhuman morality and virtues. Far worse, Jesus' Jewishness is treated as irrelevant, either because he has fulfilled all the requirements of the law, or because he is the universal Son of God who transcends any particular ethnic origin. Undoubtedly, the Christian misunderstanding of the law, Marcionism, the Protestant tendency toward antinomianism, and anti-Semitism have resulted, to a considerable degree, from the decoupling of Jesus' life and ministry from his Jewish heritage, specifically the Exodus-Sinai tradition.[2]

This chapter studies Jesus' earthly ministry, in particular, community organizing, from a covenantal perspective.[3] I claim that standing in the Exodus-Sinai tradition, the center of Jesus' ministry was the organizing of God's new people (both Jews and Gentiles) through the renewal of the Sinai Covenant. A covenantal interpretation of Jesus' ministry and ethics is plausible because Jesus was a quintessential Jew who lived in Palestine, speaking Aramaic; his upbringing was deeply rooted in the Jewish religious tradition informed by a covenantal worldview. Jesus was well versed in the Mosaic laws, the Psalms, and the Prophets (especially Isaiah). For Jews in Jesus' time as well, the covenant was a prevalent thought-pattern forming their religious worldview and practices,[4] and Jesus was not an exception. Jesus was a real Jew, rooted in the historical nation of Israel. Just as the Exodus-Sinai story delineates the biblical model of God's redemption, so does the redemptive work of Jesus. Hence, his preaching, ministry, moral teachings, and death are incomprehensible apart from the Jewish understanding of covenant. The significance of the idea of covenant only increases if we recognize how Jesus himself is remembered to have invoked the covenant in his explanation of his death in the Last Supper (Matt 26:28 and par.). Indeed, Jesus presented his death as the culminating shape of his life/organizing, joining discipleship and soteriology.

Historical Contexts: Roman Imperialism and the Jesus Movement

In studying Jesus' organizing work, we need to briefly survey the political and economic situation of Palestine under Roman imperial rule during Jesus' time, because his ministry was partly a religious response to this situation. In ruling its vast conquered territory under its imperial domination, Rome employed indirect and direct methods of control—directly through an appointed governor over the region, and indirectly through the patronage system, that is, by installing client kings as proxies for their imperial rule.

In understanding Jesus' historical time and social context, the indirect rule of Rome deserves our brief attention because in Palestine, Rome ruled indirectly through the Herodian family and the high priests in Jerusalem. Operating under the patronage of a Roman aristocrat or emperor, client kings were typically natives who pledged their loyalty to and collaborated with the Roman Empire in order to maintain control and gain self-preservation or protection from other hostile factions. Client kings were responsible for levying taxes, securing *Pax Romana*, suppressing revolts, financially sponsoring imperial games, constructing buildings, maintaining military bases, and encouraging emperor worship in return for Roman protection of the client king's rule and control over a certain territory. This pyramid of patronage naturally indicated multiple layers of rulers and domination, adding to the demands of taxation and other economic social burdens on the people at the bottom.[5] For example, people in Galilee were forced to pay all sorts of taxes to every level of the pyramid—Rome, Herod, and the Temple—and their tributes, tithes, offerings, and dues went to the construction of temples, cities, buildings, and roads.[6]

Only through brutal oppression and systematic economic extraction from the occupied was the Roman Empire able to defend its expansive borders, maintain its armies, and fund its massive construction projects for Roman rulers and their client kings in imperial metropolitan centers. Hence, tax burdens for farmers reached more than half of their harvests.

Absentee landlords living in Jerusalem took advantage of the situation to steal farmers' lands; they charged high interest rates and forced farmers to mortgage their land to pay their taxes. Debt collectors also extorted the people; they added to the taxes their own fees and unfair fraudulent charges for profit. When people couldn't pay, their lands were expropriated and commercialized.[7] Losing their inherited ancestral land, farmers became tenants of the rich Herodian family, royal officials, and high priestly aristocrats.[8] Many were displaced from their ancestral villages and became day laborers or tenants of the rich and the ruling elites. Village economies were drained by tributes, taxes, construction projects, and imperial expeditions. People were forced to borrow from others. When they become insolvent, many sold their children as slaves, losing their familial, cultural, and religious resources of mutual aid and care.

To maximize its tax revenues and subjugate the people, Rome resorted to brutal violence and terror, crushing even the slightest sign of resistance against its rule. For example, Galilee was a terrorized area; in addition to the brutal experience of the initial conquest, Rome enslaved thirty thousand people in 53–52 BC around the town of Magdala. At the time of Jesus' birth, Varus' army burned down the town of Sepphoris (only several miles away from Nazareth), and massacred and enslaved its inhabitants in response to a local rebellion.[9]

People were physically and psychologically traumatized by forced labor and constant intimidation. Under excruciating hardship, families and village communities were disintegrating. It is not farfetched to regard multiple incidents of demon possession, masochistic behaviors (e.g., Mark 5:1-20), irregular menstruation cycles (e.g., Mark 5:2-35), physical and mental illness, and other self-destructive behaviors as psychosomatic reactions to unbearable suffering under prolonged oppression.

Thus, one can imagine that the power-question was existentially acute for Jesus and the local people. Palestine faced a major crisis as economic difficulties undermined the very fabric of society. As will be discussed later, the prayer that Jesus taught to his disciples (the Lord's Prayer) addressed the desperate economic hardship of the people.[10] Far from being a mere ritualistic phrase, the petition for daily bread and debt forgiveness had a concrete social meaning that reflected the desperately impoverished economic condition of the people.[11]

Cultural Context: Jewish Worldview

Living under Rome's harsh and brutal rule, Jesus' contemporaries generally regarded their communities as living in conditions of manifold decay and foreign oppression proscribed by the covenant, and therefore hoped for the fulfillment of covenantal promises of liberation. They earnestly longed for the full restoration of Israel. There was a high eschatological anticipation that Israel's God would soon intervene, liberate God's people, and become their king again.[12]

Such a collective longing, and interpretation of their historical situations, was deeply influenced by the covenantal tradition and its thought patterns. In particular, Jews interpreted historical events and religious experiences in reference to the Exodus narrative,[13] which served as the metanarrative of various prophetic movements and revolts against Rome. Metaphors and performative actions associated with the Exodus story were prominent among the Jewish people's imagination, religious behaviors, and literature (including the Gospels).

The central confession of the Exodus event is of God as the liberator King who liberates His people from oppression (embodied by the Pharaoh). But following the pattern of the Exodus, the return from the exile also means God's reconstitution of God's people, which happens through the renewal of the covenant. God calls His people to enter a (re)new(ed) covenantal relationship with him.[14] The coming of God's kingdom means the gathering of God's people; God's reign cannot be separated from the gathering of people. "The rule of God presupposes a people of God, in whom it can become established and from whom it can shine forth."[15] God's reign is actualized in a community through His people. In this sense, the return from exile is a new Exodus, and God's rule is a new covenant that entails the establishment of a new community (a new people of God) with new creeds and new moral standards.

During Jesus' time, Jews were geographically scattered and socially and economically fragmented, which, in their moral worldview, signified the curses that the covenant prescribed. In this context, the new covenant was understood to mean the healing of this scattered condition—the bodily gathering of people with geographic, social, and economic bonds within a newly restored covenantal community.

Jesus' Ministry of
Community Organizing

The above discussion of the historical and cultural contexts of Jesus' time is necessary for understanding the background of Jesus' kingdom ministry—its goal, intention, and choice of message and method. In his daily life as a carpenter before his public ministry began, Jesus must have closely witnessed the debilitating effects of Roman imperialism (e.g., the massacre at Sepphoris) and Herod—the collective trauma of people under exploitation. There is little doubt that his religious and moral consciousness was profoundly shaped by the brutal social and economic situations of the poor Jewish people.[16]

It is evident that Jesus' teachings and parables addressed the social, economic, and political hardship of the people: poverty, hunger, debt, anxiety/fear, despair, powerlessness, mutual hostility, envy, shrinking opportunities, distrust, violence, disputes over property, and other conflicts—the symptoms of disintegrating families and villages. No doubt, given the political and social conditions of Galilee's subjugation under Rome, power and poverty were the two most acute social questions. Many of Jesus' parables and teachings were related to the use of power (including violence) and economic issues reflecting the deep concerns of his audience/followers (e.g., Luke 12:29-31).

Jesus started his ministry of community organizing in his native region of Galilee with the poor and other socially marginalized as his primary audience. Tremendously traumatized by Roman violence, Galilee during his time was under the jurisdiction of Herod's son Antipas. Jesus' community organizing was informed and guided by the biblical tradition of covenant. Covenant is manifested in the various aspects of Jesus' ministry: gathering disciples, healing people, and preaching of the kingdom, judgment, deliverance, and restoration.

Judgment and Restoration

Jesus started his ministry with the announcement that "the Kingdom of God is near," a central message throughout his ministry. We need to briefly analyze this message. As we discussed in chapter 2, kingship is a political notion, and it is associated with God's organizing work, which is expressed through judgment against evil and striving toward a new just society. In Jewish thinking, judgment, deliverance, and reconstruction are typical exercises of God's kingship. Hence, in the long-standing history of Israel, Jesus' proclamation of the kingdom of God simultaneously indicated judgment against oppressors and the restoration of Israel. Richard Horsley affirms this point: "The Gospel has two complementary aspects, the renewal of Israel and the condemnation of the rulers."[17] God's judgment indicates the beginning of God's deliverance from the power of sin, evil, and death (the ending of the old order) and the advancement of a new one.

Judgment

Jesus was critical of the abuse of the wealthy (against the poor), the powerful (against the meek), and the privileged; the Sermon on the Mount is not always peaceful, but at times confrontational and judgmental against the rich, the proud, and the powerful. For example, Jesus preaches the promises of blessing and the kingdom to the poor, the hungry, the meek, and those who mourn (society's victims). This amounted to an indirect critique of the political and social system that produced these victims. For Jesus, God is on the side of the meek, not the ruler. Jesus was especially critical of the perversion of God's intent for the law and the distortion of the divine purpose in dominant Jewish religious practices and ethical life. Jesus' cleansing of the Temple and denunciation of it as "a bandits' den" was emblematic of his condemnation of the Temple system. His crucifixion was the response of the powerful to Jesus' public agitation and challenge. Jesus' ministry was a serious threat to the ruling class of his time, as it undermined the very theological and moral foundation of their rule.[18]

It is true that Jesus was far more direct in his confrontation with Jewish religious leaders than with Roman imperial power. But even if not publicly confrontational against Rome, Jesus' organizing work was still politically subversive. For example, his message of sole loyalty to God indirectly criticized and rejected the supremacy of Rome and the power of Caesar. Jesus' anti-imperialism was never more explicit than in his favorite self-designation as "Son of Man" (an allusion to the promised eschatological figure in Daniel 7 who exercises the judgment against empires). Clashes of reigns were inevitable in the life of Jesus, as he embodied a qualitatively different reign of power than the worldly one. His crucifixion by Rome demonstrates that Rome and Jesus were incompatible.

The titles given to Jesus in the NT—the Son of God, Lord, Savior, and bringer of peace—originally belonged to Caesar Augustus. By assigning these titles to Jesus, Matthew subversively challenges the dominant religious-political ideology and presents an alternative kingdom (way of life) to Rome, with the effect of undermining Roman agendas and claims. This is not so different in Luke. Despite his apologetic tone/gesture in the opening, one sees a similar subversion in Luke. The message of a newborn king in Luke was given to shepherds—the outsiders of their time.

Similarly, the values that Jesus preached and practiced were the opposite of those of the Roman Empire. His sermons, parables, and symbolic actions showed ethical criticism of Roman rule. His welcoming and embracing of every person as equal brother and sister was a critique of rigid social stratification on the basis of various social categories.

God's judgment was also manifested in Jesus' exorcism. Exorcism in the context of the Kingdom of God was political as well as religious. Exorcism implied the defeat of Satan—a mysterious dark source of evil and demonic power that feeds on and fuels the destruction of human lives. The defeat of Satan meant God's eschatological judgment of the powers, principalities, and spirits of the world, including the imperial power of Rome and its political economy.

Exorcism was an integral part of God's liberation of his people—a sign that God was directly intervening in their midst, in a manner parallel to the ten plagues in Egypt. The key feature of exorcism is that it sets people free from being possessed by oppressive evil forces, including imperial military power (Luke 8:26-39). Imperial power is demonic, as it belongs to Satan—the ruler of the world. Rome was simply one of its manifestations.

However, God's judgment did not only target rulers and the elite, but also called for the repentance of the people—their departure from the old habits and prevailing patterns of their society (cf. Rom 12:1-2) and their adoption of new sets of values. This too is an aspect of God's internal moral organizing of people. N. T. Wright explains that Jesus' call for repentance was "a political call, summoning Israel as a nation to abandon one set of agendas and embrace another."[19] Repentance entails living out a new moral and social possibility. Jesus invoked judgments against unrepentant towns where he had worked in the same manner as the prophets (Amos 6:4-7; Mic 2:1; Zeph 2:5). Jesus pronounced eschatological threats against the Galilean towns that were not responsive to his mighty deeds and wonders by predicting God's judgment upon them because they refused to repent (Matt 11:21-23; Luke 10:13-15). In other words, since they refused his call to pursue the covenant justice of God's kingdom, their inherited patterns of injustice would culminate in destruction, as prescribed by the covenant.

Restoration

It is a distinctive pattern of God's reign that when God delivers God's people, God also organizes them by renewing His covenant. This was the case with Jesus. Together with deliverance, the restoration of the people of Israel was a central theme of Jesus' ministry. Restoration aims at the reconstitution of people under God's rule (the formation of a new peoplehood), which typically entails the realignment of worldview, identity, community life, social relationships, and praxis.

Specifically, restoration means reentering into a covenant relationship with God, so that God becomes their God, and they become God's people. Inspired by Isaiah's eschatological vision, Jesus introduced God from a fresh perspective: "Abba" (Daddy) as well as the creator ("the maker of heaven and earth"). The God of Jesus was not a holy, transcendental, remote God, but a powerful yet intimate God. Together these two images portrayed God as the reliable provider of daily necessities.

Morally, restoration indicates the renewal of justice in the community, the reestablishment of justice in social relationships. The biblical idea of covenant is not purely religious but evidently social (in fact, there was no separation of religion and politics). In a pattern similar to the Exodus-Sinai story, a new community was built upon God's covenant, intending to be an alternative to the hierarchal, exploitative social economic system.

Through the message of God's kingdom, Jesus offered a counter-social vision and value system against the dominant ideology and practices of the Temple and Rome that perpetuated the concentration of wealth and power, and justified exploitation and violence. Jesus' approach was neither violent nor nationalistic, but militant in its spirit and subversive to the dominant pattern of society in his time. He attempted to build a contrasting community with a different vision, ethic, and lifestyle than contemporary Greco-Roman society.

Jesus identified his mission with this task of covenantal organizing, and it was the heart of his kingdom message. Jesus' Nazareth Manifesto (Luke 4:18-19), a crucial descriptor of his mission, concisely captures the key motifs of covenantal organizing: judgment and restoration.

> "The Spirit of the Lord is upon me,
>> because he has anointed me
>> to bring good news to the poor.
> He has sent me to proclaim release to the captives
>> and recovery of sight to the blind,
>> to let the oppressed go free,
>> to proclaim the year of the Lord's favor."

As one can see, while the words "release" and "let the oppressed go free" have do to with the motif of judgment, "recovery of sight to the blind" and "to proclaim the year of the Lord's favor" pertain to the theme of restoration. The idea of bringing good news and the year of the Lord's favor (Jubilee) serve as an inclusio, framing the content of judgment and restoration. This manifesto is important because, borrowing from Isaiah 61, Jesus recapitulates the Exodus-Sinai story in emphasizing God's commissioning a deep passion for justice and care for the marginalized through the message of Jubilee. In short, the Manifesto presents Jesus' vision of covenantal community in undeniable continuity with the Sinai Covenant.

The Eschatological Nature of Organizing

For Jesus and his followers, God's judgment and restoration are eschatological in nature, the fulfillment of Israel's ultimate covenantal hopes. His incarnation and ministry are not a mere repetition of the past, but rather the beginning of a new creation. They extend God's reign from the restoration of Israel to the ingathering of all nations, even encompassing the restoration of creation. Jesus' collaboration with the Spirit is another indication of the extraordinary, eschatological nature of God's organizing.

However, the full eschatological meaning of his ministry can be comprehended only in reference to the past history of Israel. He is the final fulfillment of the past promise, but the fulfillment does not mean the nullification of the past. One cannot understand what is fulfilled without what was promised before.[20] In Jesus, God fulfilled the promises of the past by using the same paradigm of Exodus-Sinai (this is at least what Matthew tries to achieve), and this fulfillment is ultimately to bless all nations. Following the pattern of the OT, the task of the Church as a newly covenanted people is to bring God's blessings to all nations, fulfilling God's call to Abraham. The newly organized community has a mission. It is the priestly kingdom, salt and light to the other peoples.

Jesus' gathering of Israel (the lost sheep of Israel) was neither exclusive nor final, but rather instrumental in inviting other nations and peoples to God's reign. Thanks to its theological nature and eschatological horizon, Jesus' organizing work was more communal and universal than nationalistic. While rooted in the local, Jesus set off an inclusive community, organizing it under God's reign through a network of strong local communities. From a sociological perspective, the organization of local villages and communities was strategic because it had the effect of creating and consolidating a firm communal basis that sustained people against various oppositions and suppressions.

Covenantal Renewal

The above observations lead us to claim that Jesus' kingdom ministry took the form of covenantal renewal, which we discussed in chapter 1. Jesus' ministry directly addressed the disintegration of the village communities of Israel under the pressure of poverty, debt, and violence by reorganizing and renewing village communities according to the Exodus narrative and covenant. Jesus creatively adapted the Exodus tradition in his own social context by reinterpreting and reapplying the Torah.

Jesus' moral emphasis was theologically informed by Israel's covenant tradition, but it also addressed the harsh social realities of his people under Roman rule. His renewal of the Mosaic covenant was inseparable from the regeneration of the people and reconstitution of their families and communities.[21] Jesus reinterpreted the covenantal values and standards of the Torah in his social context to help people resist the vicious circle (and death trap) of domination, subjugation, and violence, and to build an alternative form of life in sharp contrast to Rome: one marked by forgiveness, serving, sharing, and nonviolence.

Covenantal renewal is, for example, found in Jesus' reinterpretation of the Torah in the Sermon on the Mount, which not only revives but also intensifies the covenant tradition of Israel; in particular, the six antitheses (two triadic sets) in the Sermon on the Mount (Matt 5:21-48) that begin with "You have heard that it was said . . . But I say to you that" redefine Mosaic laws in a new and far more radical and intensive form.[22] With its focus on the transformation of the desires of the human heart, Jesus' ethic goes beyond the Decalogue. Jesus calls for the uprooting of sin in all its forms in order to maintain an intimate and loving relationship with God.

Although the covenant is not explicitly mentioned in the Sermon on the Mount, Jesus is teaching the covenant in the Sermon on the Mount by presenting all of its instruction as the fulfillment of "the law and the prophets," which is in fact a way of naming the covenant in the Bible. Biblical scholars have noticed a close affinity between the story of the Mosaic Covenant (Exod 20; Deut 5) and the Sermon on the Mount (Matt 5–7), and agree that the Sermon on the Mount is reminiscent of the Sinai Covenant. Here are a few examples:

- The opening two verses of Matthew 5 ("[Jesus] went up the mountain; and after he sat down, his disciples came to him. Then he began to speak, and taught them") are reminiscent of Moses' ascension of Mt. Sinai and his reception of the law from God to give to the Israelites. As Moses did, Jesus teaches on the topics of murder, adultery, divorce, almsgiving, oaths, revenge, and forgiveness. This means that Matthew is introducing Jesus as a new Moses!
- Matthew 4:23–5:2 tells that Jesus' ministry of healing and deliverance preceded the Sermon, just as the Exodus event preceded the Decalogue. That is, God's initiating act of love and grace takes place before the giving of the law and the Sermon.
- Each beatitude is structured in a promise-fulfillment pattern, linked by motivational device "for" (*hoti* in Greek), which is typical for covenantal documents in the OT.
- The core values that Jesus emphasizes in the Sermon on the Mount, such as loyalty to God, trust, love, and justice, are essentially covenantal in nature.[23]

These are only a few examples. There are several other passages in the Sermon on the Mount that connect Jesus to Moses and the Sinai Covenant. Just as the Sinai Covenant (the Ten Commandments) served as the constitution for organizing the Israelites as a new, independent people, so did Jesus' Sermon on the Mount act as the charter of his new community.

If Jesus' ministry was the renewal of the Exodus-Sinai tradition in an eschatological context, then how was Jesus' ministry related to community organizing? How did covenant assist his organizing work?

Strategies of Community Organizing

Gathering

Jesus' ministry revealed the covenantal pattern not only in its message but also in its organizing practices. His restoration work begins the calling and gathering of his people (Israel in the OT) as a sign and vehicle of God's salvation. Gerhard Lohfink says that "the sole meaning of the entire activity of Jesus is the gathering of God's eschatological people."[24] Jesus labored to rebuild the house of Israel and to restore and reconstitute the lost sheep under the good shepherd, Jesus himself (John 10). This idea of "the lost sheep" has historical background in Ezekiel and other OT passages. The lost sheep are in a miserable situation because they are deprived of protection and guidance; they are extremely vulnerable to predators. Jesus' ministry was to bring them back to the fold of God's protection and to reconstitute (reorganize) them as a new people.

Jesus called and installed the twelve disciples (Mark 3:14-16). Jesus' calling of the twelve symbolized the restoration of Israel as the original twelve tribes. Jesus was not simply calling individuals separately to invite them to heaven or individual blessings of self-fulfillment; rather, Jesus called the twelve as a symbol of Israel, that is, the entire people as his followers and community. The symbolic meaning of this act should not be underestimated. Jesus publicly, not secretly, called and named them as his companions and sent them out to preach the Kingdom of God, to heal the sick, to raise the dead, and to expel demons. This public demonstration (installation of his twelve disciples) is Jesus' performative action to announce the regathering of Israel under God's reign from exile. The reference to the twelve disciples (symbolic of the twelve tribes) preaching the Kingdom of God and casting out demons pronounced the inauguration of the eschaton, raising eschatological expectations among people. It fulfilled the prophecy of Ezekiel (37; 39:23-29; 40-48) that at the end time, the twelve tribes, all scattered or lost, would be restored and brought back to the land. The reconstitution of the twelve signified the return of Israel from the exile and their gathering as God's elected people—all by the sovereign power of YHWH, who is the maker of heaven and earth, and whose reign has already been inaugurated.

Empowering People

Jesus' community organizing included several moral, psychological strategies to empower people, such as visiting local villages, preaching, teaching, exorcism, healing, and table fellowship. Using these methods, Jesus helped people find a new source of power (faith, trust), and regain a sense of dignity and their subjectivity (agency) by reaffirming God as their king. Typical symptoms of unorganized people under unbearable oppression are a sense of powerlessness, internal fights and conflicts (disunity) over limited resources, violence against weaker members because of eroding traditional communal ties and family bonds, and callousness toward others. Oppressors deliberately employ this divide and conquer strategy against the oppressed to maximize their control and profits. A vicious circle of despair and violence (against others and oneself) then yields self-destruction.

(1) Through exorcism and healing, Jesus helped the people discover a new source of agency and hope. Exorcism has a double political meaning; it is the defeat of unjust forces as well as the restoration of people's agency (*imago Dei*) and freedom. Psychologically, exorcism addresses the question of the agency of victims (the possessed) in its core. Liberated victims are no longer possessed (owned by alien forces) but restored to be free and responsible children of God. A demon-possessed man in Decapolis and a Syrian-Phoenician woman's daughter are only a couple of examples.

(2) Jesus' message of kingdom sets people free from the distorted ideologies and myths that legitimized their oppression and alienation, such as the false belief that their misery (poverty, debt) was the result of their sins. Jesus opened his Sermon on the Mount by pointedly addressing the people's debilitating belief that their poverty, hunger, and general misery were God's curses for their own sins. Horsley notes:

> By transforming the blessings and curses that had worked to make the people feel hopeless, proclaiming blessings on the poor and hungry but woes against the wealthy, Jesus declares God's new action in the present and future to deliver the people from their oppression.[25]

(3) Jesus' message of God's forgiveness and grace helped people to shed their self-indictment, shame, and guilt, injecting a new sense of hope and energy. It made his audience conscious of their intrinsic worth as children of one Father (Matt 6:26; 18:10-24). It also had the effect of building trusted relationships among his followers.

(4) Jesus strategically focused on renewing marriage, family, and village life, strengthening their bonds of unity on the basis of God's justice. While gathering the lost sheep of his people, Jesus also called people to repent from unjust or corrupt patterns of marriage, family, and village life for the sake of God's kingdom. The sort of unity that Jesus built was not an uncritical uniformity, but prophetic and moral in nature in its conformity to the covenantal pattern of God's reign.

In particular, Jesus reached out to those who were marginalized and alienated in Jewish society and invited them back into his renewed community. Social exclusion or ostracism is the typical means of social control—punishing those who do not comply with dominant social norms and rules. Challenging this practice, Jesus welcomed people who were previously displaced and disenfranchised in Israel, even those who were traditionally not regarded as members of the Jewish community (e.g., a Samaritan woman, a Syrian-Phoenician woman, a Roman centurion). In the eyes of religious leaders, Jesus' welcome of sinners and outcasts was regarded as blasphemous and disruptive of conventional social norms, blurring the boundary between the sacred and the profane, the clean and the unclean. In the eyes of zealots, Jesus' acceptance of tax collectors, such as Matthew and Zacchaeus, was unpatriotic. However, for those who participated in table fellowship with Jesus, the spiritual and psychological effects were unparalleled. They felt welcomed, restored to a community, and forgiven by God, which manifested in a renewed life under God's reign.

Jesus' community organizing was intentional, strategic, and sophisticated by today's standards:

(1) Jesus went into the midst of the people. His itinerant preaching and pastoral circuits were part of his community organizing. Rather than confining himself to a sacred place with historical import, Jesus regularly visited local people in their local, family contexts—synagogues and private houses, the countryside, and public places. According to Sean Freyne, it is likely that Jesus would have covered all regions of the northern part of the inherited land of Israel, inspired by his ideas and hope of Jewish restoration eschatology. Expressions such as "throughout all Galilee," "the surrounding territory of Galilee," and "through cities and towns" in the Bible display the broad scope of Jesus' itinerant ministry.[26] Jesus met people where they were rather than forcing them to come to a permanent religious place such as the Temple. His peripatetic

ministry was replicated in his sending of the disciples, two by two, to different towns and villages to build a communal network.

These regions that Jesus regularly visited were ecologically, politically, and culturally diverse.[27]

> These different sub-regions had given rise to different modes of human interaction with, and opinions about the natural world. How might his experience of and reflections on these regional variations have coloured his actual sense of his ministry and mission in the light of the received tradition?[28]

Jesus might have reacted to these different village subcultures and environments with different attitudes, sensibilities, and strategies.

(2) In his community organizing, Jesus tapped into a longer local religious tradition, namely the Exodus-Covenantal tradition, which was still alive in the villages of Judea and Galilee, serving as their common religious and moral framework. Consequently, his message of the kingdom, which was an adaptation of the Exodus-Sinai story, deeply resonated with the people, as we see in their stunning response to his ministry.

(3) Jesus utilized the established Jewish and social community structure.

> When Jesus repeatedly goes into a/their "synagogue," he is not going into a religious building, but into a local village assembly (1:21; 3:1; 6:1). . . . these assemblies met once or twice a week. So Jesus was deliberately visiting a given village on days that the people would be assembled for community discussion, business, and prayers. In that context he carried out his teaching and healing and exorcism. He was pointedly dealing with whole communities, not just individuals, in the context of their meeting for self-governance. He was not dealing only with what we moderns call "religious" matters, but with the more general political-economic concerns of the village communities as well . . .[29]

This practice was very strategic, given that socially the primary location of Jesus' ministry was the villages and towns in Galilee. Jesus attempted to strengthen the primary institutions of family and village life. As we saw, the Sinai Covenant (especially the fifth and sixth commandments) emphasizes the importance of the family unit and protects its financial viability and mutual trust among Israelites.

(4) In particular, well-publicized to both his friends and opponents through his routine practices, Jesus' table fellowship with sinners was an

effective tool of community organizing.[30] Jesus' reputation as the "friend of sinners" reveals how frequent and active his table fellowship was. It typically has a stronger bonding effect than other relationship-building techniques. In biblical times, the very fact that people typically ate and talked for two or three hours over a meal indicates how central table fellowship was to community life as a strong tool of social bonding and networking that generated the social capital of trust, friendship, and belonging.

Common eating is a widely accepted social practice that delineates and reinforces social boundary, status, and membership. Even today, who one eats with is telling of one's social status. Sharing a meal symbolizes acceptance, intimacy, and friendship, while its refusal means disapproval and rejection. A common meal signifies the de facto boundary and membership of a community.

Inclusion or exclusion in a common meal had a communal disciplinary function—to approve or disapprove certain behaviors and to maintain social status. During Jesus' time, the Pharisees used table fellowship as a primary tool of social control to protect the holiness and purity of the Jewish community. Their table fellowship was the community of separation.[31]

In the ancient Middle East, the practice had a covenantal connotation; covenanting includes sharing of meals accompanying an exchange of pledges. Sharing a meal implies that a covenantal relationship exists among the participants. In the Gospels, "covenant" is at its most explicit around the meal table (Matt 26:28 and par.; cf. 1 Cor 11:25).

Jesus' table fellowship with sinners, outcasts, and prostitutes had the effect of building a community through mutual acceptance, personal acquaintance, and trust, which had a therapeutic and restorative effect. Marcus Borg notes:

> Clearly, given that sharing a meal symbolized acceptance in that culture, eating with a Spirit person [such as Jesus] with a powerful numinous presence could mediate a profound sense of acceptance and be an instrumental part of the therapeutic process whereby the internalized alienation of the outcasts was overcome and they would once again be able to see themselves as part of the people of God.[32]

Jesus' table fellowship was the symbolic re-inclusion of the outcasts into the covenant, who were previously outside the covenant. The inclusion was Jesus' organizing outreach toward people who had forfeited their status and membership within a community.

When Jesus shared a meal with outcasts, he was mindful of the table fellowship of the Pharisees. By eating with the sinners and the outcasts, Jesus was performing a strategic, subversive action against an exclusionary social paradigm built upon holiness, purity, and ethnicity. John Dominic Crossan writes:

> What Jesus was doing is located exactly on the borderline between the covert and the overt arts of resistance. It was not, of course, as open as the acts of protesters, prophets, bandits, or messiahs. But it was more open than playing dumb, imagining revenge, or simply recalling Mosaic or Davidic ideals. His eating and healing were, in theory and practice, the precise borderline between private and public, covert and overt, secret and open resistance. But it was no less surely resistance for all of that. A further question: Did Jesus have any type of organized social program for others to adopt and follow? We know already that he had a magnificent vision of the Kingdom of God here on earth and that by his own actions he already practiced what he preached.[33]

Jesus' table fellowship aimed at the deorganizing of the Pharisees' exclusionary community in order to reconstitute a new community; it had the effect of shattering rigid social boundaries and hierarchal structures and building a new inclusive, reciprocal, egalitarian community.[34] Table fellowship sent a public message that the outcasts and sinners were equally the children of God, and Jesus came to restore them to God's community. Crossan notes:

> Open commensality is the symbol and embodiment of radical egalitarianism, of an absolute equality of people that denies the validity of any discrimination between them and negates the necessity of any hierarchy among them.[35]

Nonviolent Resistance

In his community organizing, Jesus taught his followers the strategies of resistance. His teaching in Matthew 5:39b-41 is superbly original in its moral imagination and potential political impact: turning the other cheek, giving the undergarment, going the second mile. Walter Wink is a biblical scholar who identified these as three practices of nonviolent resistance with a profound political meaning. According to him, Jesus' teaching his disciples to "turn the other cheek" was not a sign of subservience but rather a clever and firm way to protest the insult of the oppressor. To turn the other (left) cheek is to indicate that one is willing to be struck again with the back of the left hand of an assaulter. This was impossible in the Middle East culture, because to strike anyone with the left hand was forbidden; its use was only for unclean things. Similarly, getting naked in court (by giving the undergarment), and insisting on going the second mile are equally unsettling to the oppressor, like turning the other cheek.

What was Jesus' intention in teaching these practices? Jesus wanted people to recognize their own power and stand on their own moral ground. That is to say, with these acts of nonviolent resistance, Jesus was teaching people how to use their meager power to protect their basic humanity and resist intimidation and subjugation. By taking these creative, unexpected actions, the oppressed send a clear message to the oppressor: ". . . 'I deny you the power to humiliate me. I am a human being just like you. Your status does not alter that fact. You cannot demean me.'"[36] Such subtle protest would take the oppressor with complete surprise and set them off balance; the oppressors might feel ashamed and see the oppressed in a new light.

Jesus was deeply aware of the abysmal imbalance of military power between the Roman Empire and the Jewish people (hence the futility of military resistance). In a situation of overwhelming power imbalance, Jesus' solution was neither utopian nor escapist but politically clever and realistic. Despite hardship, Jesus wanted to encourage people to seize initiative, rather than being kept in passivity and cowering subjugation, and to "assert their dignity in a situation that cannot for the time be changed."[37]

At the same time, the nonviolent resistance of Jesus was based on the moral conviction that God is still the sovereign Lord and everything is under God's power, and every person is equal in God. It was first a spiritual practice as a confessional act of faith before it was political. It was a sign of courage that one does not fear the oppressors. Jesus was reminding these humiliated people of their God-given dignity and spiritual-moral power that they still possessed. I guess that such a bold spirit and assertion of dignity was palpable in the world-defying faith of early Christians, and their newly discovered moral agency and sense of dignity in Jesus served as moral resources to build their new community together.

Unfortunately, until Mahatma Gandhi's first application of Jesus' teaching to a political change, Jesus' teaching on the three practices was, on the whole, dismissed as impractical and self-destructive. However, from the perspective of community organizing, these tactics are the gem of Christian grassroots organizing and political engagements. Wink comments:

> No one, not only in the first century but in all of human history, ever advocated defiance of oppressors by turning the cheek, stripping one-self naked in court, or jeopardizing a solider by carrying his pack a second mile. For three centuries, the early church observed Jesus' command to nonviolence. But nowhere in the early church, to say nothing of the early fathers, do we find statements similar to these in their humor and originality. These sayings are, in fact, so radical, so unprecedented, and so threatening, that it has taken all these centuries just to begin to grasp their implications.[38]

These actions of nonviolent resistance are realistic (in accounting for the reality of power imbalance), creative (in moral imagination and political savviness), and morally consistent (in rejecting the use of violence).

In fact, the political assumptions behind the strategies of Jesus are strikingly similar to those of Saul Alinsky's community organizing, especially his "12 rules for radicals," which emphasize the agency and initiative of the oppressed through creative identification and mobilization of their power and resources in order to break the cycle of humiliation and restore their dignity. Alinsky's method, as we discuss later, focuses on unsettling the oppressor's sense of security and predictability by shaming them and debunking their moral hypocrisy through the use of innovative tactics. It is to deprive the oppressor of the initiative and sense of superiority by refusing to play into their planned domination scheme.

(5) Jesus trained his disciples into kingdom organizers. Jesus built a small core group around his twelve disciples and empowered and educated them toward his vision by sharing his life and strategy with them. Through his mutual fellowship with his disciples, Jesus built trust and friendship that reoriented their mindset and gradually transformed their worldview and psychological habits. Even after his resurrection, Jesus spent forty days with his disciples and acquaintances to deepen his relationships with them and reinforce his message of the kingdom in light of his victory, rather than engaging in a new, post-resurrection political or social project. His decision has strategic value in nurturing and training a kingdom of community organizers.

Summary

Jesus' organizing practice offers a wonderful model for understanding local covenantal organizing with a global vision. Using the strategies and methods above, Jesus reinstituted people into a new (extended, or surrogate) family of God. He organized them into a new cohesive entity (by means of apostles) through the complete sharing of life, food, journey, and ministry for three years. His approach brought internal unity, recalibrating their commitment and instilling a new sense of mission. Thanks to these strategies, Jesus' organizing was powerful enough to build a strong popular movement within a short period of time. Jesus brought together small villages into his broad kingdom movement and its vision through his network of disciples and friends. Many living under Roman rule joined Jesus' community. The quick spread of the movement of Jesus indicates that his message resonated deeply with people, as we find in the comments that "he speaks with authority, unlike the Pharisees and scribes" (Matt 7:29). Indeed, the Gospels report people displaying wonder and amazement about Jesus' preaching and ministry.

Jesus' covenantal renewal incurred clashes with the Jewish rulers and religious authorities of his time, who rejected Jesus' teachings of the law, identity, and mission of the Jewish people as expressions of Israel's covenant with God. Conflicts with the Pharisees, the temple system, and Roman power were inevitable. Wright explains the implication of Jesus' approach:

> [I]t was *because* Jesus' agenda was "theological" from first to last that it was "social" . . . It was because this way of life was what it was while reflecting the theology it did, that Jesus' whole movement was thoroughly, and dangerously, "political."[39]

To preach that God is the king carried radically subversive meanings and revolutionary ramifications, inviting the suspicions of (and clashes with) the ruling powers, ultimately leading to Jesus' death.

Equipped by Jesus' vision of the kingdom, his followers, after Jesus' resurrection, were nonviolent but militant enough to be willing to endure suffering brought by Rome due to their confession of Jesus as the Lord (as opposed to the Caesar) and their distinctive ethics and lifestyle.

The New Way of Life

Jesus' covenant renewal entailed the revision of conventional norms and the conventional praxis of the people in order to spiritually and morally form and shape them into a new collective moral entity. Through the renewal of covenant, Jesus organized people into a new, egalitarian, reciprocal community with a distinctive spiritual vision, identity, and ethics.

The renewal of covenant entailed the renewal of membership (contra marginalization), worship (contra idolatry), and ethics (contra sexual promiscuity and violence/oppression) through recommitment to God and God's sovereign will. For Jesus and his followers, the eschatological vision and belief in the advent of the messiah expanded the meaning of a community (God's family), its membership, and its ethics.

The new covenant needs a new community structure, just as Jesus preached that new wine needs new wineskins. Alongside new membership, Jesus changed religious rituals and identity markers that separated the people of God from outsiders; these were a major part of his covenantal renewal. The redefinition of membership, rituals, and ethics was an inevitable process of redrawing the boundaries of a new community. If God's eschatological reign was new wine, then new wineskins were necessary because the old wineskin of the Mosaic Covenant could not handle its power. A new community—with new ethics, rituals, and practices—emerged around a new covenant.

Membership

Organizing a new community is inseparable from the question of its membership.[40] Jesus' renewal of covenant inevitably, and controversially, touched on this subject, as we see in his disputes with the Pharisees. Jesus redefined the membership requirements of his new covenantal community in accordance to God's reign. Traditional identity markers such as dietary laws, cultic laws, purity laws, and practices (such as cleaning, Sabbath, and fasting) were reinterpreted in light of the covenantal renewal.

Rather than these external criteria, Jesus emphasized internal values—allegiance to the living God and an eschatological nationhood. For Jesus and his followers, their religious identity rested on God's grace and His new covenant. The ground was substantially leveled before God. Everybody was in need of God's grace and mercy. The true condition of belonging to God's community was one's genuine and willing openness to God's grace. No personal merit, social status, religious lineage, or family heritage could replace or compete with God's grace.

Ethics

In the covenantal framework, God's reign always calls for new human moral responses to reciprocate God's deliverance, responses which include the renewal of ethics.[41] Just as the Torah was the constitution of the order and life of Israel, Jesus' teaching, such as the Sermon on the Mount, constituted a covenant charter on the model of the Torah.[42] Setting higher moral standards and practices, it gave instructions on how to live as God's new covenant people.

One sees a covenantal pattern in Jesus' community. Those who joined the new community were required to demonstrate a new lifestyle fitting to the covenant. His ethics aimed at building God's new people. Violence, lying, and coveting were condemned because they eroded trust and bonding among the community members. Their community life practices were to reflect God's character—God's generosity and righteousness. Jesus identified the triad of justice, mercy, and faith as the "weightier matters" of the Torah, and taught the love of God and the love of the neighbor as the two greatest commandments of the law that constituted the center of the covenant relationship.[43] The practices of this new ethic gave Jesus' followers the spiritual and moral high ground over occupiers, no matter how great the military power of Rome.

One distinctive aspect of Jesus' ethics was nonviolence (Matt 5:43-48). Reliant on God's reign, his followers recanted retaliation and violent means of resistance, and were willing to suffer if called upon. They were to be free from violence internally and externally. Instead they were committed to active, nonviolent forms of resistance.

Political Economy

Jesus practiced a counter-imperial political economy among his followers. The ethos of Jesus' community was communal and egalitarian. This new community was based on serving and sharing in *koinonia*, not domination, exploitation, and violence. Since absolute power, rule, and honor belong to God alone, all other forms of power, honor, and prestige were relativized. In contrast to the rigid structure of domination under Rome, Jesus instructed the renunciation of domination and the practice of serving and caring for others, as evident in Jesus' criticism of the Gentiles' lifestyle (Matt 20:25-28).

In the manner of the Sinai Covenant that did not allow a king for Israel, Jesus taught his disciples that their community should have no "father" or "teacher" other than God. In place of competition and envy toward others, he taught love and solidarity. His performative action of washing his disciples' feet demonstrated how power should be used in God's family. He declared that the least will be the greatest and the greatest will be the least.

The communal nature of his community is found in Jesus' expansion of the meaning of family to transcend a biological group and include all in God's family. For example, Jesus declared, "Whoever does the will of my Father in heaven is my brother and sister and mother" (Matt 12:50).

Jesus encouraged voluntary sharing, mutual aid, and deep compassion in the manner of God's love (*hesed*). Instead of obsessive possession or exploitation, generous sharing of material goods to meet human needs was a major characteristic of Jesus' community. It was based on the belief that the redistribution of resources meets the demands of God's covenant, and is indispensable in building a free egalitarian community.

In memory of the covenantal economics of Moses, Jesus requested his disciples to practice the Jubilee principle in their social relationships. One of those examples was the forgiveness of debt, which was seen as an enslaving power: "Forgive our debts as we forgive our debtors" (Matt 6:12).

This practice of pooling resources together and forgiving debts helped to protect people from further disintegration, despair, and desperation. By practicing Jubilee economics (Acts 2:44-45), Jesus' community provided a safety net for every member; they experienced God's generosity, mutual love, and affection among themselves, which in turn provided succor and energy to continue their lives under oppression while dismantling that oppression. The effect of Jesus' covenantal organizing is found in Acts 4:34, which was reminiscent of the sabbatical year in ancient Israel (Deut 15:4).

Conclusion

Standing within the Exodus-Sinai tradition, Jesus' movement was a covenant renewal movement emerging throughout the villages of Palestine, resisting the forces of exploitation and disintegration, and building a new alternative community.

Like the Exodus story of the Hebrews, Jesus' ministry displays the inseparable connection between covenant and community building. While God's organizing in the Exodus was national in its scope, Jesus' organizing was local in nature while guided by a grand eschatological vision. Eschatological in nature, Jesus' organizing work started in Palestine but was not confined to it. Indeed, its horizon and scope reached the entire world (the Great Commission in Matt 28:16-20). In a final analysis, his exorcism, miracles, preaching and teaching, and table fellowship contributed to the empowerment of his people and the building of a new covenant community of trust, mutual aid, and hope.

Jesus' answer to an excruciating social situation was neither withdrawal from society nor violent resistance, but the organizing of a new community of sharing, care, and generosity in God. Under the scaffold of the covenant, Jesus' organizing was communal but not exclusive, political but not nationalistic, religious but not parochial. Instead of advocating a violent political revolution against Rome, Jesus unleashed a social revolution that had wide and profound political implications: "Anyone announcing the kingdom of YHWH was engaging in serious political action."[44] Likewise, "[a] social revolution becomes political when it reaches a critical threshold of acceptance; this in fact did happen to the Roman Empire as the Christian church overcame it from below."[45]

Jesus' ethics of love, forgiveness, sharing, and justice had the effect of building kinship and cooperation among his followers. A sense of acceptance, belonging, and unity had the effect of healing.[46] A new life in a community staunched the further deterioration of society, revitalized family and village life, and enhanced both individual and collective resilience and solidarity against the disintegrating power of their rulers. It empowered the moral agency of his followers as individuals and as a group by removing their sense of marginalization, alienation, and exclusion. Jesus' covenantal organizing contributed to the long-term sustainability and solidarity of his community against exploitative forces. As time went by, his movement increasingly represented a serious challenge to existing social structures.

> [I]t is in circumstances of relative powerlessness vis-à-vis the Roman imperial order that Jesus called for the renewed commitment to covenantal economic and political values and behavior in their communities. But it was precisely in those circumstances of poverty and powerlessness that Jesus and his followers found it essential to struggle to practice those values and principles of justice, cooperation, and solidarity. The imperial order was still in place. But Jesus was calling people to take control of and rebuild their own community life in the confidence that the imperial order stood under God's judgment.[47]

Such an approach, as we will see later in Alinsky's community organizing, had the effect of empowering people by enhancing their sense of mutual trust, self-esteem, and internal unity. Through the organizing work of Jesus, people were freed from isolation, competition, despair, guilt, and hopelessness; instead, they built an alternative community where they were able to find dignity, support, and hope. By modern standards, some might say that Jesus' organizing was relatively stronger in the aspect of community development than direct political advocacy, but his community was not withdrawn in isolated self-sufficiency like that of the Essenes. His advocacy was both religiously active and politically subversive. Although Jesus did not apply the accumulated power to directly challenge Roman imperial rule (which was embodied in local political and economic habits and structures, particularly as these were networked across localities), Jesus' focus on intermediate, local manifestations of Roman power should be regarded as an equally potent way of resisting Roman imperial rule as a direct challenge.

Jesus' local organizing offers a wonderful example for understanding covenantal organizing. Jesus' model has wide applicability for people living in excruciatingly oppressive situations. It is not outright confrontational against oppressive regimes, especially a society or nation that is undemocratic and does not protect freedoms such as association, speech, and conscience. Furthermore, it shows that a community can take a political disposition that is neither otherworldly nor rash and reckless (e.g., centering on military action). While building up the internal strength of a community in a nonviolent way, it waits for the fitting time to mobilize its accumulated power and resources for structural change. Jesus' community gradually but steadily undermined the very moral foundation of the imperial reign. Empires rule and control with the fear of death and the threat of dispossession. For those who do not fear death and belong to a healthy community, imperial rule loses its teeth. This is a quieter, more sustainable revolution (cf. Matt 12:15-21).

One sees a similarly strong motif of organizing in the letters of Paul and other NT epistles with different tones and emphases. For example, Paul's ideas of the church and the Eucharist are rich with this motif. This motif has been expressed in many different forms in Christian history, one of which was the Puritan movement, in which we find a powerful, systematic, actional expression of covenantal organizing.

4

Puritans

Covenantal Politics and Democracy

"One of the great common patterns that guided men in the period
when American democracy was formed, that was present in their
understanding and in their action, and was used in psychology,
sociology and metaphysics as in ethics, politics and religion, was the
pattern of the covenant or of federal theology."[1]

In popular imagination, Puritans are envisioned as overly serious, intolerant, ascetic, and somewhat depressed people who did not know how
to enjoy life (the Thanksgiving holiday notwithstanding). Some of these
cultural caricatures might be true, but the Puritan contribution to American democracy and their influence on culture and social institutions
should not be underestimated. Hence, any renewal of democracy today
requires us to critically and seriously engage with our complex heritage
from the Puritans. This chapter studies the covenantal organizing of the
Puritans: how and why they adopted covenant as their central religious
symbol and used it in newly organizing society in early modernity; what
impact it has left on US democracy and politics; and what its implications are today.

Puritan contributions to American democracy (constitutionalism,
rule of law, limited government, separation of powers) and capitalism have
been well documented by other scholars. Hence, my focus in this chapter
is on the role and function of covenant as an organizing principle for
churches, social institutions, and civil society. My objective is to show
how the stream of covenant thinking that originated in the Bible was
connected to the organizing of a democratic society in the US, and how

the Puritans explicitly expanded the democratic thrusts and motifs of covenant (such as voluntary participation and communicative deliberation) found in the Bible in order to develop a coherent, theologically informed political theory of democracy and civil society. This observation is important because Puritan social-political experimentation with covenant bridges the biblical idea of covenant with Saul Alinsky's community organizing.

Reformation and Covenant

The primary intention of Protestantism, which arose, as its nomenclature suggests, to protest the abuse and corruption of the Roman Catholic Church (e.g., indulgences, Simonism, papal abuse of authority), was theological; its scope was initially limited to the internal reform of the Roman Catholic Church. However, it had the impact of transforming the entire European society, precipitating the rise of modern society. Marking the end of the Roman Catholic Church as the sole determiner of truth and morality, the Reformation unleashed strong aspirations for freedom for the rest of society, as well as religious communities. With the erosion of Roman Catholic control, European society experienced radical turmoil in every aspect of its social life. The question of order (how to organize a society) became acute and urgent as traditional social structures and institutions were severely challenged: people asked where true moral authority comes from, and how to harmonize their rediscovered human drive for freedom with the necessary requisites of social stability and order.

Protestant Reformers, including Lutherans, Anabaptists, Anglicans, and Reformed, took several different approaches in addressing these questions. Among them, Reformed theologians such as Zwingli, Bullinger, and Calvin rediscovered the biblical idea of covenant as the constitutive organizing principle of religious and social organizations.[2] These early Reformed theologians identified covenant as a consistent method that God relies upon in dealing with humanity, and conceived the whole of human history as covenantal history—from the covenant of works to the covenant of grace.[3] In covenant they found a theological notion that effectively mediates the divine and the human, church and state, eternal and historical without collapsing one into the other. For them, covenant offered an encompassing, ready-at-hand notion that accounted for the question of political order in theological terms and vice versa. Their approach was in contrast to Lutheranism, Anglicanism, and radical reformation wings that disclosed a certain thread of theological reservation or indifference toward the idea of transforming civil government. The Reformed Protestants embraced the reorganizing of civil government as an integral aspect of the Christian witness, and vital for the moral sanctification of a society. Daniel Elazar writes:

> The federalist politics of the Reformation was an answer to two older theories of Christianity and the political world. One, dominant among Roman Catholics and to a great extent among Lutherans as well, held that princes possessed absolute and unlimited civil power, and the other, the pietistic theory of the first Christians revived by the Anabaptists, that denied that civil government filled any significant role for Christians. The federalists sought the Christian commonwealth, recognizing the importance of civil government for maintaining the fabric of human society against human vices, especially greed, overweening ambition, and lawlessness.[4]

Puritans

Theologically, the Puritans further developed the idea of covenant and applied it more extensively as an organizing principle of society. The Puritan movement arose in the late sixteenth and seventeenth centuries to thoroughly reform the Church of England toward the side of Protestantism. As second-generation Calvinists, they embraced Calvin's basic theological outlook such as concern for social order and sanctification. But their understanding of covenant was more influenced by the Swiss Reformed theologies of Zwingli and Bullinger than Calvin's.[5] They understood covenant in a more reciprocal and conditional way compared to the unilateral and unconditional terms of Calvin, thus allowing human free will and responsibility to play a more significant role in bargaining with God. This bilateral emphasis had the effect of mitigating the fatalist tendency inherent in Calvin's idea of predestination, and countering the authoritarian (aristocratic) nature of Calvinism in the sixteenth century.[6]

The Rediscovery of Covenant

In developing their theory of organizing, Puritans drew upon the thoughts of a variety of Calvinist thinkers in Europe (e.g., Theodore Beza, Johannes Althusius, and others) and applied them to their own political and religious contexts, in critical conversation with Roman law, republicanism, medieval natural law, and conciliar tradition. Their search for the free exercise of faith and practical necessity of order compelled them to find in covenant a coherent organizing principle of life, in contrast to the traditional model. It met their religious vision of a new divine society while addressing the reality of sinful human nature, and the inevitable diversity of opinions and views found in social life. Covenant indicates a free, cooperative human endeavor to build a moral community under the guidance of God.[7] Covenant values free consent in organizing a society rather than coercion or biological affinity.

For Puritans, a good social order was not something naturally given once and for all, but something that was to be achieved through the willful struggle and decision of human agents.[8] They believed that genuine order was based on freedom, and only achieved when a human being freely obeyed God; even the Word of God was effected only when its listeners responded in free obedience. Inspired by grace, perfect order resides in humanity's free consent to God; coercive order falls short of perfect order. For Puritans, covenant provided a theological ground for an order based upon free human consent, which served as social glue. The subordination of individuals to the state was justified only by their voluntary consent. The idea that free consent provides a legitimate basis for order was revolutionary for democratic thinking.

> Consent becomes the instrument for establishing authority in the community and for expressing the sovereignty of God. God transmits his sovereignty to the people through the broader covenant, and they in turn convey his sovereignty to the rulers on the basis of the specific covenant creating the civil community. The people's consent is the instrument for linking God with those holding temporal authority, whose authority then is viewed as sanctioned by God. Because this temporal authority comes through the people, however, the rulers are beholden to God through the people and thus are immediately responsible to them. This, the original basis of popular sovereignty, had been independently developed by both Protestant and Catholic thinkers during the sixteenth and seventeenth centuries.[9]

With "consensus" as the basis of social order, covenant harmonizes the demands of freedom and order. In a covenantal relationship, freedom is not anarchic; order does not suffocate individual freedom and creativity.[10] By utilizing covenant, Puritans in both Old and New England were able not only to espouse individual freedom (freedom of conscience, speech, association) over hierarchal structures, but also to defend the value and importance of the common good and legitimate authority over individual freedom.[11] Under this covenantal social vision, their goal was not merely to protect individual freedom, but also to build a holy commonwealth.

Judgment and Restoration

As we saw in chapters 2 and 3 (the Exodus movement and the Jesus movement), the overarching covenantal pattern of judgment and restoration is also found in the Puritan movement. Deeply inspired by the Exodus story, Puritans, in various ways, attempted to reactualize it in their own political contexts. Confronting the entrenched political and religious status quo and its hierarchal social structure that refused any meaningful reform, Puritans organized themselves into a political group. In Europe (where Catholicism, Lutheranism, or Anglicanism was the established state religion), the covenant served as a theological instrument of ecclesial reformation and political revolt. One sees such examples in Oliver Cromwell's English Revolution and the Dutch Revolt against Spanish rule in 1565.

The overarching covenantal pattern of judgment and restoration, resistance and alternative vision, is also found in the Puritan movement that took covenant as its central religious symbol. Puritans used the idea of covenant as their method of resisting traditional order, both religious and political, and building a new church and political society.

Exodus

In their fight against the traditional political and religious authorities, Puritans gained inspiration from the Exodus-Sinai tradition.[12] Exodus imagery (such as "Egypt," "Jerusalem," "wilderness") and rhetoric reverberated through Puritan political and religious speeches and writings. Puritans interpreted their collective life—its origin, journey, and destiny—as paralleling the biblical narrative of Israel.[13] Avihu Zakai notes, "For English Puritans in general, the exodus theme of Israel's flight out of Egyptian bondage indeed became the mirror of the whole history of human redemption and salvation."[14]

For instance, the centrality of the Exodus in Puritan collective imagination is evident in the picture located in the title page of the Geneva Bible of 1560. Often called the "Puritan Bible," it portrays a scene of the Israelites on the shore of the Red Sea, their backs to the Egyptian army and their faces toward the promised land. As the ancient Israelites, the Puritans wanted to actualize God's reign (through the medium of God's law) in every realm of life, the religious as well as the political.

Interpreted through a Christian apocalyptic vision, Puritans believed, initially, that the English nation had a providential role as God's chosen people in history to achieve God's purposes. Following the covenantal pattern of blessing and curse (punishment), however, they also believed that God's election and blessings were dependent on the purity and dedication of the Church of England. If the latter refused to obey God, then imminent judgment was in store for England and its people; God would desert England and choose another people for His purposes.[15] In particular, they tied divine election of the English people to the progress of the reformation in the Church of England.

However, the failure of reformation under King Charles I of England led the Puritans to take a bold decision: migration to New England.[16] With a change in sentiment and context, their interpretation of history and God's providence also shifted; they now compared Old England to Egypt and New England to Canaan, a sacred place in which God's providence in history would unfold. Seeking psychological assurance and moral guidance from the Bible, they imagined themselves a New Israel, called to reenact the Exodus event in a new historical time. Migration to New England was compared to Israel in the wilderness.

New England Puritans

Feeling betrayed by the delay of reformation in England and Charles I's anti-Puritan policy, the first band of separatist Puritans ("Pilgrims") fled from Yorkshire to Holland in 1608 and then to Plymouth, Massachusetts, in 1620 on the *Mayflower*. They wanted to practice their faith according to their conscience and build a community grounded in biblical principles. The core members of the Pilgrims' immigrant group were separatists, members of a Puritan sect that had split from the Church of England, the only legal church in England at that time. Others in the group, however, had remained a part of the Church of England, so not all of the Pilgrims shared the same religious beliefs: "The religious dissenters who were prominent in the first waves of migration came to America to establish their own communities where they could practice their religion free from outside interference."[17]

Signed on November 11, 1620, by the adult male passengers, the Mayflower Compact served as a legal instrument that bound the Pilgrims together when they arrived in New England.

> In the name of God, Amen. We whose names are underwritten, the loyal subjects of our dread Sovereign Lord King James, by the Grace of God of Great Britain, France, and Ireland King, Defender of the Faith, etc. Having undertaken for the Glory of God and advancement of the Christian Faith and Honour of our King and Country, a Voyage to plant the First Colony in the Northern Parts of Virginia, do by these presents solemnly and mutually in the presence of God and one of another, Covenant and Combine ourselves together in a Civil Body Politic, for our better ordering and preservation and furtherance of the ends aforesaid; and by virtue hereof to enact, constitute and frame such just and equal Laws, Ordinances, Acts, Constitutions and Offices from time to time, as shall be thought most meet and convenient for the general good of the Colony, unto which we promise all due submission and obedience. In witness whereof we have hereunder subscribed our names at Cape Cod, the 11th of November, in the year of the reign of our Sovereign Lord King James, of England, France and Ireland the eighteenth, and of Scotland the fifty-fourth. Anno Domini 1620.[18]

The Mayflower Compact is rich with a thick covenantal vision and motifs that were shared among the Puritans. While framed in a monarchic system, the Compact emphasizes the reciprocity and commitment among its members under God's sovereignty, the motifs being equal laws and the common good. The Compact relies on covenant as a principle of organizing a new society ("Covenant and Combine ourselves together in a Civil Body Politic, for our better ordering and preservation and furtherance of the ends aforesaid").

This covenant made a huge impact on later generations and the founding of the United States of America.[19] In 1802, John Quincy Adams described the agreement as "the only instance in human history of that positive, original, social compact,"[20] and it is popularly believed to have influenced the Declaration of Independence and the US Constitution.

Ten years later, another group of people, led by John Winthrop, arrived in New England and founded the Massachusetts Bay Colony. Winthrop's famous speech onboard the flagship *Arbella* also offers a precious window into the mindset of the Puritans—how he and other Puritans used covenant as an organizing principle in forming a new community. The Exodus and the promised land imagery, together with the pattern of liberation and restoration, were prominent in his speech. He identified the passengers as people leaving the old England (Egypt) to journey toward God's promised land. Winthrop reminded them of their obligations under their covenant with God. If they remained faithful to God, they would be blessed; if not, they would be punished.[21]

With the speech, Winthrop's goal was to prepare people for the unknown future as they were about to enter into wilderness, that is, to impart a new moral purpose and identity. What is notable is that Winthrop used the Exodus story to lay out the vision for a godly commonwealth and encouraged his fellow Puritans to commit to the common task; he relied on covenant to achieve his goal of forming a new people. He emphasized equality among the members—"noe man is made more honourable than another or more wealthy &c., out of any particular and singular respect to himselfe, but for the glory of his creator and the common good of the creature, man."[22] He stressed mutual obligation and unity based on covenant between the rich and the poor. The speech intended to draw covenantal pledges from fellow Puritans. With the famous biblical metaphor, "City on the Hill," which appears in his speech, he was dreaming of building a model society in New England in direct contrast to the ways of Old England. Winthrop, relying on covenant, attempted to turn uncertainty, displacement, and risk (coming from migration) into an opportunity of cultural self-invention and a new collective identity.

Free Church Congregationalism

Opting out of the established church and building an independent congregation (free church) was an attempt to protect the purity of the gospel and the conscience of the believer from abusive power and corrupting influences on their faith. Against a traditional Episcopalian parish model, the Puritans adopted a congregational model of the church—the independent assembly of the faithful with free and equal status before God, loosely connected people in a confederate relationship. Covenant served as the theological basis of congregational organizing. The church was not a natural community, but an intentional association, built upon the basis of free, equal participation and voluntary consent and commitment of the members.

Covenant theology provided a theological justification for congregationalism; for Puritans, the church, in the tradition of the Hebrew idea of *edah* (assembly),[23] meant a covenantal body organized through the exchange of mutual oaths to God and others with Christ as the head, not the pope or a king. It was the belief of the Free Church Puritans (called "Separatists") that the church should be independent from any external intervention or control by any political authority, and that an independent congregation was best to protect the freedom of conscience and purity of the church. The free church meant people had freedom to organize themselves into a congregation and to worship free from government control, and the right to "to determine its own conditions of communion and to discipline its members" according to their own conscience and the teachings of Scripture.[24] The state had no right to appoint church officers or interfere with its internal administration.[25] This claim of the church's right over the state was rooted in the conviction that God is the ultimate authority of the church, and thus people are in direct communication with God without the mediation of a political or papal authority. That is, the covenant between God and God's people is prior to any political and religious authority, and is thus inviolable.[26]

Within the broader Puritan movement, free church advocates expanded the prophetic and democratic streams within Puritanism while mitigating the authoritarian streak of the early Calvinists. In particular, it should be noted that the Anabaptists, Mennonites, Baptists, and Quakers made an important contribution to democracy and human rights especially through their advocacy for religious freedom: "It was their advocacy of religious liberty and independence of churches from the state that became the First Amendment to the US Constitution."[27]

Unlike their mainstream Calvinist counterpart, who emphasized "order" and used the "covenant" to oppress African Americans and Native Americans, the free church advocates were more thorough in their commitment to religious freedom and more consistent in standing for the free church principle. The Baptists and the Quakers relied on peaceful means, such as education, public discourse, and moral persuasion, rather than coercion. They were committed to the equality of all humanity and rejected any special favor or privilege of Europeans over Native Americans. They did not impose their form and practice of Christianity upon others. In his article, "Is There a Common American Culture?," Robert Bellah claims that a "founding" political thinker in the United States was Roger Williams rather than John Winthrop, given Williams' firm commitment to religious freedom and individual rights.[28]

The Free Church tradition expanded beyond specific religious boundaries and created a distinct arena for human freedom and community organization. Under the influence of Puritanism and its covenant theology practiced in Old and New England, various forms of congregationalism with diverse theological expressions bloomed: Presbyterians, Baptists, Congregationalists, Methodists, and others. This insight spilled over to other forms of social institutions, including political and familial. Stackhouse says:

> The basic, primordial freedom of the church to order its own life is taken as the basis for the organization of political, economic, educational, familial, and other aspects of life. Political authority does not grant "concessions"; it does not have the authority to allow or disallow these groups to be formed, or to give or to withdraw permission— quite the contrary.[29]

The covenant served as an organizing principle for the formation of churches and modern civic organizations. By providing a new organizational model or exemplar for a society as an alternative to the traditional one, it also played an instrumental role in the emergence of modern types of institutions; covenantally organized free churches served as a model of organization for other institutions. Stackhouse attributes the origin of modern voluntary, intermediary institutions and community organization to the Free Church movement:

> [T]he Free Church Tradition, although now expanded beyond specific Christian confession, created a distinct arena for community organization, a social space for participation and membership in voluntary associations, that is prior to and inviolable by public authority.[30]

Practiced through the free church on a regular basis, covenant inspired people with organizational imagination. Covenantal practices in the free churches helped create the necessary organizational habits, civic virtues, and behaviors necessary for proper functioning of various civic organizations. Inspired by the free church, individuals were free to organize various associations under God's law. Many modern associations—the university, corporation, guild, and political party—attained "theological legitimacy based on the analogy of a free church."[31] The fast spread of a covenantal mode of organizing was possible because it deeply resonated with human yearning for freedom, creativity, justice, and productivity. Because of this historical influence, modern institutions took on a quasi-covenantal quality. To the Puritans, the covenant served as a comprehensive and coherent worldview of God, self, and society and its institutions.

> [T]he covenant gave them [the New Englanders] a rudder by which they could conduct their daily lives, a means by which they could articulate their individual, ecclesiastical, and societal purposes in a "mission statement"—much like contemporary companies and organizations develop mission statements to remind employees of the larger goals that should transcend the daily routine.[32]

The practice of covenant in a congregational model has the effect of delimiting political power, cultivating and spreading a democratic ethos throughout the entire society. The right to freely organize the church was the prototype of modern human rights. Stackhouse observes,

> The churches prepared the way, demanding a guaranteed autonomy from exterior control. The autonomy was, at first, to ensure the freedom of worship and the congregation's right to govern its own affairs. But as the implications of the message and the polity were translated into habit and public behavior, the pattern inevitably spilled over into the reform of professional, political, economical, and familial institutions.[33]

Participation in those groups signified the beginning of democratic politics in its truly modern sense. Churches taught people their birthright to oppose abusive powers.

> Dissenting pastors focused on encouraging the ordinary people to understand their own natural rights and have confidence in their own judgment rather than passively deferring to the upper classes. They used the basic human rights to strengthen people's confidence in speaking out against injustice, in discussing issues, and in voting. They advocated for "the consent of the governed" and "human dignity."[34]

As time went by, the experience in free churches naturally led to a prophetic posture toward the established economic system and political status quo. Free churches and their members spoke out for civil rights, fair taxation, care for the poor and working class, democratic elections, and civic responsibilities.[35]

Political Covenant

In their fight against established religious orders and political powers, the Puritans developed a radical political theory (of democracy) centered on covenant. Covenant offered a theological basis for "radical political ideology"[36] (natural rights and popular democracy) and a new organizing of the church in contrast to monarchy, aristocracy, and the Anglican Church. Puritan theology produced a new kind of politics, which was "purposive, programmatic, and progressive in the sense that it continually approaches or seeks to approach its goal."[37]

Modern democratic ideas of popular sovereignty, governance by the people, developed out of Puritan covenantalism. Puritans understood the political community (the government) in covenantal terms. Following the governance model of the free church, they believed that government is constituted by a covenant between rulers and people under God. They embedded the authority of princes (kings) in the divine-human covenant, with the resulting effect of relativizing the power of rulers (as it is derived from God's authority and power) and holding them accountable to God's justice and the people with whom they entered into a covenantal relationship. Kings were obligated to protect the freedom and rights of the people consistent with God's law because the rights of people were antecedent to the kings' authority. The goal of politics was to advance the commonwealth of the people, not the ambition and greed of kings. This was possible under a righteous political order created by a covenant.

The political covenant between a king and the people is subject to the covenantal relationship between God and God's people. The latter covenant circumscribes a king's authority over his people. In other words, a king cannot override the moral status or standing that people acquire in their relationship with God. God is the guarantor of their rights. Through their covenant with God, God's people obtain the right and authority to enter a covenant with a king. Hence a king is bound to God and to his people. Thus, a king's law cannot supersede God's law, and the people have the right to hold the king accountable to the law.

This covenantal theory of political power provided a theological basis for revolt, resistance, and even regicide and revolution in some cases.[38] Covenant gives "a moral right (and not merely a religious duty) to resist any ruler who fails in his corresponding obligation to pursue the welfare of the people in all his public acts."[39] According to Theodore Beza, covenant gave Christians the right (and natural rights) to organize resistance against tyranny, although this right was confined to the lower magistrates in the beginning, and only later expanded to include ordinary people.

Formation of a New People and a New Society

As mentioned above, for New England Puritans, covenant served as the key organizing principle of their new society. Away from their homeland in a new place ("wilderness"), they needed to come together and organize afresh their political, social, and religious lives. The settlers treated the new territories as "a political tabula rasa, the state of nature" that needed to be filled in newly designed institutions, constitutions, and ways of common life.[40] Puritans were free from the customs and obligations of the old world to newly dream and conceive a new society and implement theory (religious faith) into social-political practices that were impossible in the old world.

The combination of this environmental necessity and their religious fervor led Puritans to engage in a unique and radical experimentation of organizing a society through covenant. In organizing a new society and new institutions in a new place, covenant, along with colonial charters, offered the colonists an organizational scheme by which to constitute their own institutions to practice self-government. Learning from the churches, "[t]he civil authority adapted the well-known practice of church covenanting to legitimize itself."[41] The narratives surrounding their covenantal documents (records on the covenanting of the church) were patterned after the OT story of the Israelites (assembly at Mount Sinai or Ezra's covenantal renewal), which was marked by the dedication of an entire day for solemn worship and rituals.[42]

These founding covenantal documents were highly religious in nature, including those designed for civil purposes,[43] and followed the pattern of the Sinai Covenant. Donald Lutz directly attributes these founding documents' original inspiration and imagination to the Bible (the Sinai Covenant, in particular), which was ubiquitous in the colonies. Lutz notes,

> In almost every significant detail the church covenants written in early colonial America resemble Jewish covenants, with one important exception—they do not establish a specific form of government. When colonists found themselves in the position of having to create a government, therein to flesh out a government granted in the charter, they tended to add this element to the church covenant form and thereby completely recover the foundation elements in Jewish covenants. They did not do so consciously, perhaps, but the radical Protestant return to biblical sources for ordering their lives led to their becoming, to a far greater extent than they realized, precisely what they saw themselves as metaphorically—a modern version of the Jewish people.[44]

Political covenants, while derived "from the use of covenants for the foundation of religious communities," rather quickly evolved into the compact form. The use of compact for political organizations was a critical step toward developing a more inclusive form of democracy (thus moving away from theocracy) and the idea of popular sovereignty.[45]

Designing a society in a covenantal pattern, Puritans relied on a sophisticated theology of covenant, with the covenant of works and the covenant of grace. The two covenants explain the connection and difference between religion and (its influence on) civil and political covenants. The covenant of works that describes God's covenantal relationship with Adam was "not only salvific but institutional, binding all people everywhere to the stipulations that God had ordained" in nature (the natural law).[46] Adam, the federal head of humanity, had a relation with God in which all humans participated. It was not a special, privileged relation for the elected few but a natural, inclusive relationship for the entirety of humanity.

Puritans did not understand the covenant of works and the covenant of grace to be necessarily antithetical; rather, the two covenants were the different dispensational aspects of the one and the same divine providence (cf. Westminster Confession of 1647). For them, God was the creator of the universe, and thus the source of order and morality, as well as the redeemer. God's power and rule reached every corner of the universe and every realm of human life beyond the Church. This made possible the creative embrace of the religious and political spheres, the covenant and the compact, without confusing, mixing, or separating the two.

Unity in Diversity: Civil Society

Covenant offers the scaffold of our social life that helps to unify and harmonize diverse social institutions in light of God's rule. It envisions a form of interdependent, organic, differentiated society with God as the center and ground of human existence. For Puritans, covenant offered a necessary and fruitful social imagination that conceptualized the complex relationships of church, state, and other social organizations in a coherent way—affirming the autonomy of each in mutual coordination, with checks and balances. It was natural that a modern form of civil society grew out of such a religious and moral ecology.

A close connection between covenant and civil society is found in the federal structure of civil society in which social institutions are "partly interdependent and partly autonomous," as Stackhouse explains, "each of which may be formed by covenantal traditions."[47] This confederate polity is the outworking of the unity-in-diversity principle of covenant.

In addition, the Protestant idea of vocation empowered the autonomy and mission of each institution in seeking the commonwealth. Each institution was not just the place where individual Christians lived out their vocations. Rather, it was believed that various social institutions were called by God to "fulfill certain functions of and for humanity . . . to define, obey, and enhance the specific values and purpose that are proper to it."[48] It was the duty of the church to work together with society as a whole in order to see that these vocations were met and the purposes of God fulfilled.

The Separation of Powers

Standing in a Calvinist tradition, Puritans had a deep awareness of human fallibility and corruption, including the destructiveness of unchecked power and authority.[49] They believed that every human power had a tendency to exalt and absolutize itself, tempted by the desires of domination, greed, and indulgence. Hence its control and restraint required a just and adequate form of social arrangement, as well as constant inner renewal and moral transformation by God's grace.

In a covenantally informed civil society, government and social organizations maintain their relative autonomies, and power/authority is distributed throughout society among multiple spheres. For example, neither political power nor ecclesial power may exercise direct control over the other.

The Rule of Law

In their search for a wise political design that would prevent the abuse and misuse of the power, Puritans relied on natural law in addition to the consent of people, and natural law served as a cornerstone of their jurisprudence and the rule of law. Puritans inherited the natural law tradition from the Catholic scholasticism of the Middle Ages.[50] Natural law, the knowledge of which God has endowed humanity at creation, offers a minimal moral foundation for all humans despite their religious and cultural differences. When God created the first human being, God enabled him to discern the laws of nature and morality by the light of reason. Moral laws provided a secure basis of social morality and order. Based on this idea, Puritans believed that all authorities are morally accountable to God.

However, unlike Catholics, Puritans theologically understood the idea of natural law in the framework of covenant, namely the covenant of works. Natural law was the order instituted by God for the rule of the universe, and hence universal in nature. Civil law was to be based on natural law, which was itself based on divine law (such as the Ten Commandments). Puritans, while believing that an organization should be formed on the basis of the agreement of the people, also insisted that such an agreement should not be arbitrary (based on people's own invention), but rather should cohere with God's justice and righteousness (the knowledge of which natural law provided, and which the Bible articulates further).

The modern idea of the rule of law developed out of concern over the abuse of power. Bestowed with authority independent from any specific political authority, it restricts the arbitrary use of authority by subjecting it to defined, well-established law. The rule of law would exercise institutionalized restraints and check against the abuse of power in order to maintain the effective implementation of justice. A lawful rule was necessary to secure the predictability of governance, the protection of basic rights, and the correcting or removing of abusive rulers when necessary. The rule of law had roughly two moral grounds: 1) the natural law that provided its moral substance; 2) and the consensus or democratic will of people (through legislation of their representatives) that provided its legitimacy.

The natural law and the rule of law are closely associated. For Puritans, who believed that both the state and public life must be governed by a public standard instead of the whims or personality of a monarch, both the natural law and the rule of law offered such a standard and public procedure for governance, which helped to prevent the abuse and misuse of power and to justly guide a common life.

Empowering People

Exemplified by the Sinai Covenant and Jesus' New Covenant, the biblical idea of covenant is designed to empower people. This equally applied to the Puritans. The covenant with God granted people a new identity, along with the rights and authority to live with a sense of dignity. As we saw in the Reformed idea of popular sovereignty, people acquired political agency through their covenantal relationship with God. In a covenantal framework, all worldly powers and authorities were relativized because they were secondary to God's antecedent covenantal relationship with God's people. Within this covenant community, members were empowered to defend and stand up for one another during trials and tribulations.

Likewise, the idea of natural rights (freedom of speech, association, conscience) and the rule of law empowered the Puritans to legally protect themselves by delimiting the king's power. Also, their participation in the free church and civic organizations helped them to develop leadership skills and democratic power.

Additionally, an emphasis on voluntary participation and the consent of the people in community life and its decision-making processes empowered the voice of the people. There was no better evidence of that which affirms the freedom and self-determination of people than having an independent social space for worship and ecclesiastical self-governance free from the interference of the state.

Covenant had the power to transform people from passive objects into free, active subjects. In the Reformation era, covenant was instrumental in setting people free from medieval passivity and loyalty; it trained and equipped them with new disciplines and public virtues.[51] Any form of tyranny was rejected, along with individual selfishness and unruliness. Members were disciplined on the basis of covenant, especially through the guidance of God's law. People were no longer passive subjects, but active agents who participated in the decision-making processes of the church and other organizations. They actively participated in politics and civic life, as they believed they were called as God's instruments for justice and the common good. Walzer says:

> [I]t was the Calvinists who first switched the emphasis of political thought from the prince to the saint (or the band of saints) and then constructed a theoretical justification for independent political action. What Calvinists said of the saint, other men would later say of the citizen: the same sense of civic virtue, of discipline and duty, lies behind the two names. Saint and citizen together suggest a new integration of private men (or rather, of chosen groups of private men, of proven holiness and virtue) into the political order, an integration based upon a novel view of politics as a kind of conscientious and continuous labor.[52]

The attempt to empower each Christian was also expressed in the Puritan passion for education. Puritans recognized that literacy and civic education were indispensable for living responsibly as God's saints in the world. To be God's covenant partner required the moral ability to spiritually and ethically discern what was happening—what is right and wrong, good and bad—and to collaborate with others for solutions.

Free consent had to be informed and rational rather than uneducated or impulsive. Out of this awareness, the Puritans set up various educational institutions and literacy programs across New England. Through these institutions, they trained and equipped people to live as responsible citizens in building God's commonwealth. The following quote offers a snapshot of the percolating democratic passion and energy of the people for civic participation and organizing, motivated by their covenantal faith.

> People in some 550 towns in New England had engaged in civil self-governance, and many had acquired experience in the direction of church bodies in that region and elsewhere in the nation-to-be. The perceived element of gift differed in the two settings, ecclesiastical and civil. Religious people recognized God as the giver of gifts, including the gift of their common life as a people and their duties as citizens. Others would not use biblical language, but the element of gift was there in civil discourse. They began with the given of their life together as citizens, which they respected by engaging in public deliberations, complying with the law, and serving variously their neighbors and the public good. Either way, whether as members of civil or ecclesiastical bodies, people were used to the rough carpentry of legislating, the business of executing and enforcing laws, and the solemn task of judging disputes among themselves. Together these functions constituted the public life of a people, and these activities constituted what John Adams and others at the time called their "public happiness," a phrase that sounds odd to modern ears.[53]

Similarly, the idea of vocation helped people to develop and exercise their moral agency. Following Luther and Calvin, the Puritans taught that each Christian has a vocation to serve God and contribute to the common good. The idea of vocation helped respect the individuality of each person in connection with the common good.

Impact

Covenant served as a comprehensive social vision and moral worldview for Puritans, touching almost every aspect of their life from worship and vocation to religious life, civic life, and political participation. In creative interface with Enlightenment humanism, it made a profound contribution to the development of modern theories of democracy, social contract, human rights, and civil society. Elazar observes,

> The road to modern democracy began with the Protestant Reformation in the sixteenth century, particularly among those exponents of Reformed Protestantism . . . who developed a theology and politics that set the Western world back on the road to popular self-government, emphasizing liberty and equality.[54]

Preceding about one generation (or one century), Puritanism influenced the rise of social contractarians, such as Thomas Hobbes, John Locke, and Jean-Jacques Rousseau, who understood society as a self-consciously organized body on the basis of rational agreement among free individuals. Government represents the common will of a society to procure the general interest (Rousseau); to prevent anarchy, disorder, and lawlessness (Hobbes); or to protect natural rights such as liberty, life, and property (Locke).[55] Again, Elazar notes:

> Thus they [Puritan settlers] were the first people at the eve of the modern epoch or after its beginning to develop constitutions of government of their own, based on civil principles or, in many cases, on the half-civil, half-religious covenants they had established for themselves as their initial means of self-organization.[56]

Puritan covenant theology and its democratic principles and organizing ethos left a lasting impact on the establishment of the new nation, as we see in the Declaration of Independence and US Constitution. The American Constitution was deeply influenced by the covenantal documents of the early settlers. As Elazar notes, "American constitutionalism fits exactly into the covenantal mold and indeed represents the successful adaptation of that mold to modernity."[57] He explains:

> [T]here were no extant models for the framers of the US Constitution except New England. Furthermore, representatives from New England, especially Connecticut and Massachusetts, were influential in the Constitutional Convention. The principal compromise of the Convention, the Connecticut Compromise, was initiated by those delegates accustomed to the New England legislative system in which one house provided for representation of towns.

The Constitution had the effect of transforming "the disparate colonists into an organized people" with a shared moral vision, a new identity, and common interests.[58] The Declaration of Independence is also covenantal in nature. In a manner analogous to the Ten Commandments, it "sets forth the fundamental principles that define the character of the

American people, their basic purposes, and the nature of good government for such a people."[59] For example, its opening statement reflects the core values and principles of the covenant: equality, inalienable rights, and consent of the people.[60] The Declaration of Independence has historically served as a sort of founding covenant of the United States. Although it does not have a legally binding force, it espouses the vision, higher values, and principles that guide and inform the US Constitution and "serves as the standard against which particular constitutions are to be judged."[61]

Conclusion

This chapter demonstrated how covenant served as the organizing vision and principle of the Puritans. For the Reformers and the Puritans, covenant offered a theologically informed practical method of organizing a society that was undergoing massive ideological and structural changes in the wake of the Reformation.

Inspired by a covenantal vision, New England Puritans practiced a seminal, burgeoning form of democracy among themselves—a form of Puritan democracy. The political system of early New England was far from a mature or perfect form of democracy by today's standards, but it was revolutionary in its own time, even more democratic than their counterparts across the Atlantic Ocean.

However, one should not miss the major flaw (and inconsistency) in the Puritan practice of covenant. Driven by an overly ambitious desire for transformation and sanctification, one must acknowledge that they sometimes used covenant to suppress theologically divergent views and practiced racial exclusion and domination, especially toward Native Americans, African Americans, and other people of color. While protecting their own rights of freedom of speech, association, and conscience, they did not equally and consistently apply and enforce those rights for others. This hypocritical tendency was especially strong when their political and economic interests were at stake (e.g., slave trade, territorial expansion, etc.), such as during the period of colonial expansion to the West and the spread of mercantile capitalism when the slave trade was a lucrative international business. Puritans, many of whom were involved in commerce, did not turn away from the economic opportunity it brought. One also sees a similar abuse of covenant in American imperialism in the past and present under the ideologies of Manifest Destiny and, more recently, American exceptionalism.

But this is not an intrinsic flaw of covenant. There is redeeming potential in covenant theology thanks to its intrinsic liberative and universalistic dispositions. Covenantal vision and ideas permeated Puritan culture and offered "the firm but flexible framework of political change" in the United States.[62] In particular, due to its inherent liberative and democratic impetus, throughout US history the covenant tradition has contributed to generating many transformative social movements.

> In the nineteenth and twentieth centuries, this same pluralistic, covenantal model became the basis of mass movements for abolition of slavery, reform of women's status, prohibition of alcohol abuse, control of child labor, defense of consumer rights, and dozens of other movements.[63]

While seeking full-fledged membership into the nation, these movements typically appealed to the foundational documents of the nation (the Declaration of Independence, the US Constitution, and the Bill of Rights). Guided by the ideas of human dignity and natural law, they utilized both public discourse (communication) and grassroots politics in critiquing various injustices based on race, sex, gender, class, disability, etc. These movements appealed to covenantal ethos and principles in mobilizing the public for their moral causes. This affirms the efficacy of the idea of covenant.

The stream of covenant has run deeply through the history of US society in both religious and secular realms. Through multiple avenues, especially various Protestant denominations, Puritanism has influenced the civil and political ethos of the United States. Its thought patterns, political insights, and civic mindsets have been passed down to the twentieth century, forming a distinctive American worldview and political practices.[64] One strong piece of evidence of the profound influence of covenantalism on US society is what Robert Bellah calls American civil religion, in which God and certain covenant values serve as transcendental principles of self-criticism and the source of collective identity (a chosen people with a special mission).[65] Hence, it is not an exaggeration to say that without covenantalism, US democracy would be quite different from what it is today.[66]

In the twentieth century, covenantal organizing had two major manifestations in the United States, one secular and one religious: Saul Alinsky's community organizing and Martin Luther King Jr.'s Civil Rights Movement, the topics of the next two chapters. Both addressed the entrenched social evils of their times: poverty in the wake of the Great Depression and segregation under Jim Crow. While their political agendas, ideologies, and paths were quite different, they creatively utilized the tradition of covenantal organizing at the core of US society in their own social settings.

Between them, King, relying on the Bible and the American democratic tradition (inherited from Puritans) attempted more fully to actualize this universal covenantal ideal by correcting the wrongs of the Puritans—dismantling racism, classism, and militarism—and renewing American society into the vision of the beloved community—an alternative society of love, justice, and peace.

5

Martin Luther King Jr.

Organizing for the Beloved Community

"When evil men plot, good men must plan. When evil men burn and bomb, good men must build and bind."[1]

Martin Luther King Jr. is one of the most influential spiritual and moral leaders of the twentieth century. King is best known by the public as an activist, a preacher, a prophet, and a leader of the Civil Rights Movement. However, not many people know that he was also a skilled community organizer with a deep understanding of power as well as the shrewd strategies and tactics necessary to achieve his goals. The Civil Rights Movement is often understood as a dramatic mediagenic event, driven by King's charismatic leadership and soaring rhetoric, which generated marches and demonstrations. But this perception is mistaken. The Civil Rights Movement could not have achieved such success without numerous hours of extensive, rigorous, tedious grassroots organizing work. Although King's leadership played an important role in energizing people, the Civil Rights Movement was not a movement led by a single individual.

This chapter studies the formative role of the idea of covenant in King's community organizing in the Civil Rights Movement, focusing on how key theological themes, motifs, and practices of King's community organizing were associated with covenant. Covenant provided a broad theological-ethical framework for his organizing and movement.[2] One sees in King a wonderful synthesis of three strands of covenant traditions: Exodus, Jesus, and US democracy (the American Puritan tradition).[3] King combined a moral vision of a just society found in the

Exodus story with the moral ideals of freedom and democracy articulated in the founding documents of the United States (the Declaration of Independence, the Constitution, the Bill of Rights, and later, the Emancipation Proclamation), while using nonviolence, inspired by Jesus, as the primary means of political action. In this chapter I ask: How did covenant inform and guide King's organizing and movement, especially in addressing the evils of racism, classism, and militarism?

Community Organizing and the Black Churches

African American churches have a history of community organizing even older than Saul Alinsky. African American churches have always carried within themselves the indigenous knowledge, wisdom, and experience of community organizing. From the beginning of their history, African American churches organized themselves not only as a religious body but also as a political and social advocacy group fighting against racism. Living under the constant threat and intimidation of whites, African Americans could not do otherwise. No matter how meager their resources were, they tried to mobilize to fight racism. Their building of independent black churches and denominations, schools and colleges, were attempts to keep and nurture their own power sources and social bases.[4] The mission statement of the AME Church, the oldest African American denomination, unambiguously declares that throughout its history, African American churches have served as bases of black community organizing and vehicles of the liberation movement. Consequently, African Americans naturally consider their churches as organizing bases for social change; this tradition made a huge contribution to the success of the Civil Rights Movement. Many African Americans learned their associational habits through the churches, especially Protestant churches whose polity was congregational, and thus covenantal in nature.

Organizing work was not, however, confined to churches. Even before the Civil Rights Movement, many civic organizations, inspired by Christian faith, were fighting against segregation. For example, around the turn of the twentieth century, a number of African American women were involved in the work of community empowerment and social justice by organizing black women's clubs, charitable societies and ladies' auxiliaries, daycare centers, orphanages, nursing homes, and anti-lynching campaigns.[5] The Southern Christian Leadership Conference (SCLC) served as an auxiliary extension of the Black Church,[6] while African American pastors were founding members, supporters, and field organizers of the movement.

Exodus

The Exodus-Sinai narrative has played an important role in the organizing work of African American churches. Many, along with King, consistently embraced it as their collective narrative in their resistance to racism by offering with it a moral framework to interpret their political situation. Like the Jews before them, African Americans found their most appropriate spiritual symbols and moral vocabularies in the Exodus-Sinai story.[7] As for the significance of the symbolism of the Exodus story for social activism, William Watley observes,

> The towering figure of Moses as leader, Egypt as the condition of oppression, Pharaoh as oppressor, the Red Sea as an obstacle to freedom, the wilderness as the transition period between slavery and freedom, and the Promised Land as freedom are all paradigms for those who were themselves engaged in a similar struggle. The Exodus drama was tailor-made for those like King who believed that God was not just involved in the historical; God was actually directing the events of history.[8]

Unlike many white evangelicals, African American clergy refused to allegorize the Exodus story as one of individual salvation from the power of sin to gain entrance to heaven. The Exodus story conveyed God's unfailing care and intervention on behalf of the oppressed. It enjoyed paradigmatic religious symbolism and moral status and inspired various religiously motivated black political movements.[9] The imagery and symbols of the Exodus narrative are strongly present throughout Negro spirituals, gospel songs, poems, and sermons.

Their love of the Exodus story meant that African American churches naturally embraced the covenant pattern embedded in the Exodus narrative. As a linchpin between the Exodus (judgment) and the promised land (restoration), covenant, though not always explicitly acknowledged or elaborated upon by African American churches, is also integral to black religious and political thinking, evidenced by many metaphoric references and hints in their spiritual life. Through the formative role of the Exodus narrative on their spiritual life, the overarching covenantal pattern of "judgment" and "restoration" and the vision of a new moral community were naturally accepted in African American churches, including by King. For them the God of the Exodus is one who liberates oppressed people from the yoke of injustice and invites them to build a new, just society. The black church tradition's emphasis on the parenthood of God and kinship of humanity summates this biblical vision of covenant in an explicitly non-racist term.[10]

At the same time, noticing the covenantal moral underpinning and the idea of natural rights in the Declaration of Independence and the Constitution, African Americans used these moral ideals and norms for their liberation. From early on, they held onto these founding documents to morally and politically hold whites accountable to their own standards.

Jesus

Similarly, African Americans interpreted the gospel stories as God's solidaric and liberating story for humanity in Jesus. They interpreted Jesus in continuity with the divine redemptive story of the Exodus and the moral judgment of the prophets in the OT. Their Christology was not abstract and philosophical, but spiritual, personal, and practical in nature. In Jesus' suffering they saw their own suffering, such as lynching. They were able to see in Jesus God's inseparable solidarity with the poor and the oppressed.[11] They saw in Jesus the incarnation of none other than the God of the Exodus and the prophets. For African Americans, the cross of Jesus was God's "message of justice in the midst of powerlessness, suffering, and death."[12] Their special affection for the cross of Jesus was not out of masochism or self-denial alone, but identification with Jesus' suffering and promise of his victory. While identifying with Jesus' suffering, they also saw the assurance of hope and redemption in Jesus' resurrection—God's vindication of the victims: "The enslaved African sang because they saw the results of the cross—triumph over the principalities and powers of death, triumph over evil in the world."[13] For them, there was no separation or incongruence between the resurrected Jesus, the crucified Jesus, and the Galilean (socially marginalized) Jesus.

Organizing and Covenant in King

King lived in a longstanding organizing tradition of protest and resistance in African American churches, which he tapped into and relied on. As a black Baptist pastor, organizing was very natural to King, who learned from his ancestors' prophetic faith and organizing skills and elaborated upon and expanded them to a new, deeper level. This included his critique of the tripartite evils of racism, classism, and militarism, as they are inextricably linked with one another.

King believed in the potency of organized people; only organized and unified masses could generate power and achieve necessary social justice. He said, "When one Negro person stands up, he is run out of town. But when a thousand stand up together the situation is drastically altered."[14] King knew that meaningful social change happens neither by chance nor by a mere progression of history (time), nor by the mercy of whites, but by the collective actions of African Americans themselves, because oppressors never voluntarily share their power. Hence, they needed to organize themselves and stand up for their cause. He reminded people that even new legislation in Congress could not guarantee its implementation; laws of the nation only designate rights, but do not enforce them.[15]

Out of this awareness, King understood African American churches as a collective moral agent of God for social transformation. He declared that the churches "have always been our refuge, our source of hope and our source of action."[16] Through his father's ministry and that of others, he witnessed the positive role of African American churches in the lives of African Americans. From the first year of his pastorate, King called on people to participate in civic organizations, such as the NAACP, and to make individual contributions. King himself served as a member of the executive committee of the local branch of the NAACP.

Covenant played a formative role in shaping his organizing. As a third-generation African American Baptist pastor, King experienced the profound influence of the Bible on his religious life, particularly through the narratives of the Exodus and Jesus. Thus, King naturally adopted a covenantal vision and value system pervasive in the Bible, interpreted through his unique African/African American spiritual heritage and experiences and the US democratic tradition. King's extensive reliance upon the Exodus, Jesus, and the American democratic tradition for his community organizing exhibits his affinity with the covenantal framework.

Exodus

The Exodus narrative plot (storyline of liberation-wilderness-promised land) appears repeatedly in his sermons, speeches, and writings; in fact, it forms his basic moral worldview. In the Civil Rights Movement, King used the Exodus story as the paradigm of resistance as well as a collective call for the redemption of the US. He theologically interpreted the Civil Rights Movement as a metaphorical parallel to the Exodus story,[17] comparing black segregation to bondage in Egypt, genuine integration to the promised land, and the Supreme Court decision against segregation (*Brown vs. Board of Education*) as the parting of the Red Sea!

> God has a great plan for this world. His purpose is to achieve a world where all men will live together as brothers, and where every man recognizes the dignity and worth of all human personality. He is seeking at every moment of His existence to lift men from the bondage of some evil Egypt, carrying them through the wilderness of discipline, and finally to the promised land of personal and social integration.[18]

Familiar to both whites and blacks, the Exodus story offered a paradigmatic symbol for King and his followers by offering a political vision that helped mobilize the spiritual and moral energies of the people. Hence, one may say that his Civil Rights Movement was the application of the Exodus-Sinai paradigm to American situations (racial, economic, and international relationships).

Jesus

In the same footsteps as his ancestors, King deeply identified his own ministry with the prophetic ministry, crucifixion, and resurrection of Jesus. King frequently cited Jesus' Nazareth manifesto in his sermons, a favorite of many African American preachers. King's interpretation of the incarnation (nativity story), earthly ministry, death, and resurrection of Jesus was not much different from that of his ancestors. That is, King saw the Christ event in the framework of God's judgment against injustice (liberation) and reconstruction of a new society.

King presented Jesus as a moral exemplar of nonviolent ethics, a covenantal person par excellence, the perfect and creative incarnation of divine love, justice, and power. King saw in Jesus a brave soul who creatively used his power to love while refusing to conform to the unjust and immoral pattern of the world—a transformed nonconformist who condemned all destructive forces against human well-being, including violence, greed, jealousy, hatred, and oppression. Following Jesus means to be creatively maladjusted to dominant cultural practices, any exploitative ethos, and systems of injustice.

The US Democratic Tradition

King also imbibed covenant streams and insights through his study of the social philosophy of the founding fathers of the United States, modern Western philosophy, and white liberal theology (Henry David Thoreau,

Personalism, and the white liberal theology of Walter Rauschenbusch that embraced or engaged with the Bible and the American democratic tradition).

In his speeches, King constantly referred to the foundational documents of the nation, treating them as its covenantal charters. King considered the United States to be the first government in the world based on the theory of natural rights and the justification of revolution. He saw no incongruence between the creeds of the Declaration of Independence and the core values of Judeo-Christianity.

Democracy

King was committed to democratic values and norms such as freedom, equality, and justice. Unlike some communitarian Christians today (e.g., Stanley Hauerwas), King was keenly aware of the importance of human rights, democratic principles, and democratic government for the wellbeing of humanity. His first speech at the Holt Street Baptist Church is revealing, as it extensively mentions democracy, the Constitution, and human rights. As he did on many other occasions, King began his speech with a quote from the Declaration of Independence. King accepted democracy as the best form of government because it respects human rights, including the right of citizens to resist injustice. However, he had a more expansive understanding of human rights and democracy than liberal Enlightenment philosophers. He called on the government to ensure the protection and actualization of human dignity to the fullest extent; economic rights must be guaranteed by the Constitution, not only civil and political rights.

Covenantal Renewal

Through his movement, King attempted to renew and revise the US covenant to be more faithful to the spirit of the nation's sacred documents. King inherited and creatively adapted the deep covenantal tradition of American Protestantism that goes back to the Puritans. While the Puritans used covenant to lay the foundation for democracy, constitution, and civil society in the United States, King attempted to deepen and expand the American covenant by correcting its distorted practices and incompleteness. That is to say, King attempted to correct the racial distortion (unfaithfulness) of the covenant that began with the inception of the republic, and to liberate it into the sort of new, more inclusive covenant community of God as the Declaration points toward. He challenged whites to accept and embrace the full humanity and kinship of people of color and to apply the promise of freedom, equality, and justice to everyone in a manner consistent with the founding documents. He claimed that the passage of the Civil Rights and Voting Rights Acts were indispensable (as an integral requisite) toward keeping the integrity and credibility of the covenant and in renewing the covenant for the nation.

As the audacious motto of his movement, "To Redeem the Soul of America," indicated, King's movement was for the renewal of the American covenant. He was deeply aware that the nation needed spiritual and moral transformation in addition to judicial changes. To be persuasive, King appealed to the Bible and the Declaration as the shared foundations of the nation's vision and moral principles. While many of the moral principles he advocated—such as freedom, equality, justice, and unity—were consistent with those of the American democratic tradition embedded in the foundational documents, King also added new values. The most important of these include love, solidarity, nonviolence, forgiveness, and self-sacrifice.

> More than a test of law was at stake in King's civil protests, however; King asked Americans to judge themselves and their institutions according to values and commitments that transcended and informed constitutional choice. From the perspective of African-Americans, the injustices of ordinary law and the imperfections of the federal Constitution impelled not only constitutional tests, but also a movement to rededicate American constitutionalism to natural right, equality, and justice. Only by returning to the precepts articulated in the Declaration of Independence could Americans elevate their founding principles above constitutional compromises. For King, the political principles of equality and liberty articulated in the Declaration referred to religious insights concerning the inherent worth of God's creation.[19]

However, King did not stop with fidelity to the founding documents. He labored to expand and deepen the documents toward a more authentic moral reality and union. His advocacy for an economic bill of rights and his organizing of the poor people's campaign were examples of this attempt at expansion. Through his speeches and political campaigns, King appealed to poor whites to join the campaign for the renewal of the American covenant. Furthermore, through his vision of the great world house (his vision for the beloved community), King envisioned the covenant at a global level, as his support for the United Nations, human rights, and global peace movements indicates.

Covenant Motifs

In his community organizing, King framed his speeches and political practices in deep covenantal theological terms. Here are some concrete examples of how covenantal motifs and themes appear in King's theology and ethics:

God

King's view of God is also consistent with the covenantal understanding of God presented in chapter 2. For King, God is personal, moral, and relational, not an impersonal principle or a monistic ideal. God wants to enter into and maintain fellowship with humanity. God is responsive to human beings and deeply engaged in human affairs; God evokes and answers human prayers,[20] as the Psalms vividly describe. King portrays God as an organizing God—the arch builder of the beloved community. The following statement concisely expresses King's theological view of God's intention and determination on community building:

> The cross is the eternal expression of the length to which God will go in order to restore broken community. The resurrection is a symbol of God's triumph over all the forces that seek to block community. The Holy Spirit is the continuing community creating reality that moves through history.[21]

God condemns systems of evil and injustice, and God labors to build the beloved community in history. As with the Exodus, Jesus, and Puritan movements, this judgment-restoration presupposes God's reign and power; King firmly believed in God's sovereign power and its benign and just nature. He declared that "God is able" and "The arc of history bends toward justice." For King, God's sovereignty is the unrelenting source of encouragement and hope for humanity because no evil can stand against God. God is the bulwark of hope against the entrenched structures of evil. Grounded in the biblical idea of covenant, King called God the eternal companion in the human struggle for justice.

Judgment and Restoration

Like Jesus and the Puritans, the vector of King's ministry moved from resistance of social injustices to the formation of a new, just society. In a manner parallel to the pattern of the Exodus story (Egypt → Wilderness → Promised Land) that King and his predecessors heavily relied on,

King's broad organizing pattern flowed from resistance against tripartite evils (racism, classism, militarism) → struggles (especially reflected in the metaphor of "marching," which resonates with Israel's journey in the wilderness) → the beloved community.[22] This covenantal pattern of judgment and restoration is found in many of his speeches and sermons. For example, his famous speech "I Have A Dream" begins with his stinging criticism of white American hypocrisy in failing to fulfill the covenant and its promises, and it concludes with his vision of a new community of freedom, equality, and solidarity. Appealing to the long tradition of American constitutional democracy and moral idealism, the speech calls for a new, more faithful covenant relationship among members of society.

Judgment

King's organizing work and movement began with the fight against racism. Racism is based on the false belief that one race is congenitally inferior to others and does not deserve equal treatment or reciprocal interaction. From King's perspective, segregation was anti-humanity and anti-community; it violated the transcendental worth and equality of all humanity and the kind of inclusive community intended by God.

Despite his prioritization of fighting racism in his public campaigns, King never lost sight of classism and militarism. He was cognizant of the dehumanizing forces of poverty, unemployment, and poor education. His march on Washington was a march for freedom and employment as his movement expanded to economic rights by demanding equal housing, healthcare, and employment. Civil rights and voting rights are empty without economic rights, as economic power is as important as political power. King had a heightened awareness of the urgency of economic justice. From King's perspective, poverty was also a violation of basic human dignity, particularly as it manifested through squalid environments, dilapidated living conditions, and permanent unemployment. An empty stomach was as tormenting as lynching and racist violence, as both types of assault corroded human dignity. Between late 1967 and early 1968, King began planning the Poor People's Campaign through a coalition of diverse racial and social groups such as labor unions, poor whites, and academic communities.

On the international front, King was aware of the danger the United States posed to international peace and justice. In US foreign policies, King saw the same racial supremacy that he encountered in white segregation in the South, as attested to by the extraordinarily high death rate of African Americans and poor whites in the Vietnam War. King saw the wastefulness of the Vietnam War, for it suctioned precious resources away from domestic necessities, such as urban revitalization, education, healthcare, and housing, in order to fund a needless war. United States arrogance toward small nations, such as Vietnam or the Dominican Republic, was nothing but another form of racism.

King believed that the tripartite injustices of racism, classism, and militarism were destroying Western civilization. These evils are inter-linked; one cannot be solved without solutions for the others. To address the triadic, interrelated evils of racism, classism, and militarism, King called for the revolutionary change of society through the redistribu-tion of power and the transformation of the nation's values. To achieve this goal, King also invited all conscientious citizens to be united, orga-nized, and mobilized for the task, using mass civil disobedience as a pri-mary method of resistance, which was more radical than conventional methods of nonviolence such as sit-ins, demonstrations, and marches. On the global front, King called for an international coalition among third-world countries to resist US militarism, declaring that the freedom and wellbeing of African Americans were dependent upon that of other oppressed peoples of the world.

Restoration

King's vision of the beloved community served as a concrete goal of com-munity organizing that consistently inspired and propelled his move-ment. Going beyond dismantling segregation or securing black freedom alone, King's community organizing work in the Civil Rights Move-ment ultimately aimed at building the beloved community. The mission statement of the SCLC reads, "The ultimate aim of SCLC is to foster and create the 'beloved community' in America where brotherhood is a reality."

As a rephrasing of the Christian idea of the Kingdom of God, the beloved community refers to an inclusive, mutually cooperative, and interracial society characterized by freedom, justice, and love among its members.[23] It indicates a fully integrated society where no one is unfairly discriminated against and the particularity of each person is celebrated while everyone cooperates with everyone else for the enhancement of the common good in God. Interpersonal and inter-group mutuality and cooperation characterize the beloved community.

In a biblical sense, one may say that the beloved community is a covenantal community. The beloved community cannot be legislated. It requires the voluntary participation and cooperation of all members. The beloved community is not naturally given but something that all humanity accomplishes by working together. It is the community where both the demands of love and justice are simultaneously met, where members respect and care for each other, and one's powers are used to serve others and the common good.

Empowering People

Any organizing includes the empowerment of people, which can be accomplished in several ways. From the start of the bus boycott, King labored to empower people. As Jesus did with his disciples from Galilee, King attempted to undo the brainwashing and indoctrination of racial inferiority and fatalism internalized among African Americans through the centuries-long exercise of racism. He utilized his oratorical skills, intelligence, and moral convictions to convince people to shed fatalism and inferiority and to stand up for their dignity. He persuaded African Americans that they were not wrong to protest for their constitutional rights. For example, King morally framed the Montgomery Bus Boycott as a rightful African American struggle for democracy, for rights protected by the Constitution. He declared, "If we were dropped in the dungeon of a totalitarian regime we couldn't do this. But the great glory of American democracy is the right to protest for right."[24]

To empower people, King called African Americans chosen people, evoking another covenant motif of the Bible. Like some black leaders preceding him, he even suggested that the uniqueness of their suffering made them the chosen people with a special purpose.[25]

Desires for change (justice) were immediately provoked by unjust situations that people experienced in their communities, but they were equally powerfully guided by the moral mission of building a new society. By appealing to his Christian faith and US democratic tradition, King was effective in sublimating people's anger at injustice (their immediate motive for participation in campaigns) into a noble dream and aspiration to build a new, just society (the enduring and empowering motive for staying in the campaigns, enabling some to dedicate their lives beyond their self-interest).

Unity in Diversity

King's communal cosmology, which undergirds his vision of the beloved community, describes the intrinsic unity and interdependence of all lives.

> [A]ll life is interrelated. We are caught in an inescapable network of mutuality, tied into a single garment of destiny. Whatever affects one directly affects all indirectly. We are made to live together because of the interrelated structure of reality.[26]

However, this unity is different from uniformity as it is based on mutuality and reciprocity among people, mediated by the principles of justice. Unity is found in the vision of the beloved community that actualizes the interconnectedness and interdependence of humanity and the foundational universal norms that bind all people.[27]

As much as all lives are interdependent, they are also diverse. Only love (forgiveness, reconciliation), justice (respect of the rights of each), and dialogue can achieve the goal of unity. King believed that diversity is God's creational plan, an expression of the richness of God.[28]

> Because God brought things into being in order that his goodness might be represented by his creatures. And because his goodness could not be represented by one creature alone, He produced many and diverse creatures.[29]

King came to believe that unity among diverse persons and groups is possible without the imposition of uniformity. Hence, for King, integration does not mean uncritical, unilateral assimilation into white culture, ideology, and systems, but the beautiful harmony of diversity. It describes the moral state in which each community affirms its distinctive culture while acknowledging and seeking unity with others through love and justice. In addition, King contends that the issue of integration must be approached not in sentimental terms but in political and moral terms, in concrete reference to the alteration of existing power relations. For him, integration without the sharing of power and justice is meaningless. This relationship of unity and diversity serves as a philosophical basis for his coalition building, as we will discuss shortly.

Love, Justice, and Power

As mentioned in chapter 1, covenant is the creative composite (or dialectic ensemble) of love, justice, and power. King's ideas of love, justice, and power display this covenantal understanding. Borrowed from Paul Tillich's theology, the triad provided King an ethical manual in community organizing. For King, organizing refers to an intentional method that accumulates power among the oppressed to correct injustices on a road to build the beloved community.

Power

King affirmed the indispensable nature of power for human existence and emphasized that power itself was not evil. Human existence is impossible without the exercise of some form of power. Yet King recognized that the exercise of power in history has always been precarious. Power can be both destructive and constructive. There is no moral guarantee that every exercise of power in history will be consistent with moral requirements.

Power has many different manifestations in society: political, economic, military, and cultural. A dominant group controls and uses various kinds of powers (physical, military, technological, economic, cultural-symbolic) to maintain the status quo. King and his colleagues endeavored to mobilize a variety of resources to enhance the power of African Americans. Some of their objectives were the election of black political leaders, leveraging buying power for employment, progressive politics, and economics, and a collective voting bloc that could be seriously reckoned with in national elections. King paid special attention to developing the political and economic power of African Americans out of his belief that in modern society, the transformative edge (the leverage of power) lies primarily with political and economic power.[30]

King rejected a common perception that the oppressed were entirely deprived of power. In addition to conventional sources of power, King tapped into different sources of power to confront segregationists. Inspired by Gandhi, he believed that the oppressed possess a formidable form of power in their hands, a power he called soul force, or truth force. Also, faith in God's justice, a hope for vindication, is a form of power (spiritual and moral capital, so to speak). Soul force is the power of the human spirit in relation to God and the purpose and meaning of life. Often, this power is as strong as other powers because it could enable people to confront injustices even at the risk of one's own safety and life. King's idea was partly inspired by the amazing spiritual resources of African Americans, which enabled them to survive the terror and oppression of slavery, lynching, and segregation without forfeiting their souls.

King felt that the challenge was how to use power (either by the haves or the have-nots) as a moral force for a just cause. If the use of power is disconnected from a right moral purpose, power becomes violent and demonic. For King, the goal of power should be justice (as the immediate objective) and love (as the ultimate goal). That is, power should be both a liberating power that dismantles injustices and a joining power that creates community.

Love

Agape is not sheer self-sacrifice (or paternalistic philanthropy), but relational in nature; it also presupposes self-love. For King, love is the power that overcomes indifference, alienation, and hostility to create a true community. He said,

> Agape is love seeking to preserve and create community. It is insistence on community even when one seeks to break it. Agape is a willingness to go any length to restore community . . . It is a willingness to forgive, not seven times, but seventy times to restore community.[31]

Love does not deny power, but rather presupposes power to establish a just, harmonious relationship.[32] A careful analysis shows that King's idea of love is covenantal in nature in affirming both self-love and other-love in the context of the mutuality and solidarity of humanity in God. Although love is the ultimate goal, the achievement of love begins with meeting the requirements of justice.

Justice

Justice is based on enlightened self-interest—awareness of the rights of self and others. Delineated in universal norms, such as human rights, freedom, equality, and fairness, justice offers specific moral guidance for the use of power in achieving love. One may say that justice is the structure or channel through which power reaches toward love. Without the guidance of justice, power becomes immoral and abusive, and love becomes sentimental and romantic. Justice helps to discern a right means in achieving love. It specifies what the minimal demand of love is in concrete human relationships.

Justice mediates love and power in history by offering the form and structure of mutuality between persons and groups. The triadic relationship of love, power, and justice is brilliantly summed up in King's statement: "Power at its best is love implementing the demands of justice, and justice at its best is power correcting everything that stands against love."[33]

This statement emphasizes a delicate and dialectic balance between love, justice, and power in a concise way, indeed, in a way astoundingly similar to the covenantal view of love, justice, and power that we examined earlier.

The Rule of Law

Like the Puritans, King believed in natural law and the natural rights articulated in the founding documents of the nation.[34] He declared that the moral laws of the universe are just as binding as its physical laws.[35] They are indispensable in organizing a just society. Humans have a moral obligation to collaborate with God in order to create a just social system that reflects God's moral laws and to build a social condition that fulfills God's intention for humanity.

King's moral justification of civil disobedience was grounded in the idea of natural law. He claimed that a person has the moral obligation to stand against unjust laws through civil disobedience. King's idea of civil disobedience was congruent with Puritan political theology, which holds that it is morally valid to challenge an unjust ruler or law. The purpose of the law is to establish and maintain justice; when laws are unjust, they become dangerous impediments to the well-being of a society, and it is the citizen's responsibility to take action to correct the unjust situation. Specifically, in his justification of civil disobedience, King relied on Augustine and Thomas Aquinas.

> I would agree with Saint Augustine that 'An unjust law is no law at all' . . . How does one determine when a law is just or unjust? A just law is a man-made code that squares with the moral law or the law of God. An unjust law is a code that is out of harmony with the moral law. To put it in the terms of Saint Thomas Aquinas, an unjust law is a human law that is not rooted in eternal and natural law.[36]

For King, the criterion was human dignity: any law that respects and enhances human dignity is just, while any law that undermines human dignity is unjust. All the statutes of racial segregation were unjust because they degraded human dignity.

The concrete demands of the natural law are discernible through the critical use of reason and conscience: "[M]oral experience reveals the reality of an objective moral order, just as sensory experience reveals an objective physical order, and this universe of order can be understood as the activity of a generative supreme mind."[37]

Despite his use of civil disobedience, however, King's objective was not to deny the legal system itself, but to correct unjust laws within it. It was King's belief that civil disobedience should be used only as a last resort. While it is the moral responsibility of citizens to resist unjust laws, King felt that it was also important to accept the penalty for doing so. This willingness to accept the penalty for breaking an unjust law is what makes civil disobedience a moral act and not merely an act of lawbreaking.[38]

Means of Organizing

In his organizing work, King used several means: moral persuasion, education, nonviolence, agitation, confrontation, conflict, and coalition.

Moral Persuasion

King's oratorical skill is globally known. With his intelligence, logic, rhetorical skill, and personal charm, King engaged in civic discourse in various social settings, such as churches, university lecture rooms, and the public square, in order to persuade his foes and mobilize people. King's moral persuasion was framed by his criticism of the tripartite injustices (racism, classism, militarism) as well as his invitation to the shared vision of the beloved community.

A covenantal pattern (motif) appears in his rhetoric as well. As the Hebraic prophets used the Sinai Covenant as the basis of their moral criticism, King used the Bible and the foundational documents of the nation (the Declaration of Independence, the Bill of Rights, the Constitution, and the Emancipation Proclamation) as his moral reference point.

In persuading whites, King exploited the gap between the promise of the documents and the nation's actual practices, with the effect of shaming whites for their moral hypocrisy. Like African American leaders before him, King condemned slavery and segregation as not only inconsistent with the moral creeds of the founding documents but also as constituting grave breaches of the covenant.

> When the architects of our republic wrote the magnificent words of the Constitution and the Declaration of Independence, they were signing a promissory note to which every American was to fall heir. This note was a promise that all men, yes, black men as well as white men, would be guaranteed the unalienable rights of life, liberty and the pursuit of happiness.[39]

King's moral persuasion inspired people to collectively work for change. King attempted not only to correct current unjust practices in light of the national covenant, but also to transform political life in a way more consistent with the covenantal vision of the Bible and the Declaration of Independence. As Jesus did, King appealed not only to the text but also the spirit of the Constitution and the principles of other authoritative documents. King appealed to whites to join the beloved community by newly covenanting with blacks and other people of color by accepting their full humanity in order to form kinship bonds.

Education

Under King's leadership, the goal of the Civil Rights Movement was more than dismantling the segregation system, but changing people and society through a revolutionary transformation of values, which touched every aspect of life. To achieve this objective of transformation and to organize people into a more effective and enduring life, King felt the necessity of educating ordinary people on their social conditions and issues: "The only truly responsible consensus will emerge when grassroots people know the issues, articulate their demands, and become a part of the democratic process."[40] Similar to Paulo Freire's pedagogy, King's approach integrated theory and praxis, mind and heart, head and hands. He said:

> Education without social action is a one-sided value because it has no true power potential. Social action without education is a weak expression of pure energy. Deeds uninformed by educated thought can take false directions. When we go into action and confront our adversaries, we must be as armed with knowledge as they. Our policies should have the strength of deep analysis beneath them to be able to challenge the clever sophistries of our opponents.[41]

King used James Lawson's workshop on nonviolence as a training ground where participants in nonviolent resistance, including future leaders (outside Montgomery), learned the philosophy, vision, and method of nonviolence.

Nonviolence

King was adamantly insistent on nonviolence as the primary means of his movement. Nonviolence is not passive, inactive resignation; it is the exercise of the organized power of the oppressed to correct social injustices. King reminded his followers that one could be strong without using violence. He contended that only those truly strong and courageous could choose to be nonviolent, because nonviolence puts a higher and more stringent moral demand on its practitioners. It requires real courage and strength of spirit to resist the evil within (such as hatred and vindictiveness) and without (mob activities and police brutalities). True strength lies in one's ability to control violent emotions and desires, and to overcome enmity with friendship. King believed that nonviolent resistance is the only realistic alternative to the violent reactions, resignation, withdrawal, and cynicism that pervade the lives of the marginalized.

Nonviolence integrates the communal and the political as well as the normative and the strategic aspects of community organizing.[42] Nonviolence is communal as it seeks community building, but it also fosters political change as it employs countering forces and negotiations to achieve justice (including via pressure to bring the opponents to the negotiation table). For King, although the immediate goal of nonviolence was to achieve justice, the ultimate goal was always the building of the beloved community.

Although he was deeply aware of the depth of suffering and injustice in his community, King rejected violent means. He rejected the utilitarian idea that the end justifies the means. A moral means must be consistent with the moral end it pursues; violence cannot be a moral means to achieve the beloved community. In addition to political change, nonviolence aims to win the friendship and understanding of the other, not to retaliate against them.[43] Furthermore, he recognized that violence abets violence; it engenders hatred and ruins the character of all who use it.

This ideal of nonviolence was deeply rooted in the Christian belief in the sanctity of all human beings (justice) and the intrinsic interdependence of humanity (love). Also, it represented Jesus' way; for King, Jesus was the primary example of the relational exercise of power—communal power—to build community. In particular, for Christians, nonviolence should be a way to live out the love ethic of Jesus. King promoted the study and practice of nonviolence as a way of life for humanity. He noticed the character-building effect of nonviolence: those who fight for a single issue (e.g., racial segregation) through a nonviolent means find themselves fighting for other issues of injustice as well, because they build new habits in the process of their struggle.

Agitation, Confrontation, Conflict

King was neither a naïve idealist nor a Machiavellian realist. He was a pragmatic idealist.[44] Despite his idealistic vision and lofty moral rhetoric,

King was astute in his power analysis; in his organizing, he was savvy in his choice of targets. He believed that a grassroots campaign required shrewd political tactics and clever strategies in addition to moral persuasion. For example, in his movement against segregation, King decided to focus on a single and distinctive aspect of segregation, such as a segregated lunch counter or bus, believing that this would be strategically more effective than a general attack on segregation. This strategic approach is found in his bus boycott; it was successful because he targeted the bus company whose major clients were African Americans. The boycott severely hurt the bus company's economic interests and forced it to come to the negotiation table.

Similarly, King did not hesitate in employing clever tactics to achieve his goals. In the Birmingham Campaign and the Selma March, he deliberately focused the media's attention on living incarnations of evil in people like Bull Connor of Birmingham and Jim Clark of Selma. In his Birmingham campaign, over the opposition of some critics, King controversially recruited African American children to march against the abusive power of Bull Connor.[45] His strategy was to use Connor's brutality to turn public opinion to his side.

More than anybody else, he understood the power of television. In the mid-1950s, sixty-five percent of US households had television sets. King knew that visuals would make a difference in getting people's attention—he recognized the power of public opinion in a democratic society. He said that whenever the white segregationists "reached for clubs, dogs, and guns, they found the world was watching, and then the power of nonviolent protest became manifest."[46]

King was not afraid of intentionally creating conflict by using tactics of agitation such as sit-ins, boycotts, demonstrations, marches, and civil disobedience. King believed that in order to achieve social change, creating a crisis and tension was necessary to get the attention of oppressors and bring them to the negotiation table. He claimed that not a single civil right of African Americans in the United States was attained without their dogged struggles, public pressure, and protest.[47] King did not always see conflict (induced by nonviolent means) and crisis negatively, but saw them as necessary in order to collectively confront deeper problems and bring about overdue changes such as desegregation.[48]

Coalition

In his movement, King worked closely with people of different religious, racial, and ideological backgrounds and built coalitions with them: evangelicals, atheists, blacks, whites, liberal Protestants, Catholics, Jews, and people of other nationalities. King called them "partners in power."[49] These coalitions served practical and moral objectives for his movement. Practically, they helped accumulate the power of his movement by expanding its political base and power resources.

> In a multiracial society no group can make it alone . . . To succeed in a pluralistic society, and an often hostile one at that, the Negro obviously needs organized strength, but that strength will only be effective when it is consolidated through constructive alliances with the majority group.[50]

Morally, coalition building was a concrete way to practice and actualize the vision of the beloved community. King believed that coalition offered the process and opportunity to build mutual understanding and reconciliation among different groups. In light of his communal vision, King was critical of the separatist ideology of the Black Power movement. King declared that in isolation from other racial groups there cannot be "salvation" for African Americans,[51] because the destiny of African Americans is tied up with that of other racial groups and humanity itself. Indeed, in his later years, King also sought to engage in international coalition building based on the common cause and concerns among people of color in America, Africa, and Asia, who were struggling to overcome racism and the legacy of colonialism.[52]

Summary

For King, covenant served as a latent framework of organizing as it held whites accountable to their promises by connecting vision (the beloved community), values, and practice (nonviolence) and by bringing different groups into coalitions for a common cause. He offered a deeper, broader, and higher moral basis for community organizing while aiming at both internal (identity, character, and self-esteem) and external changes (laws and policies). King's example exhibits how covenantally informed community organizing could be effective and inspiring.

King understood community organizing as a way of life for the oppressed rather than one-time political activism. In his last years, he was concerned about the enduring, long-term development of power within African American communities. Although he spent most of his public life in the movement, he believed that the movement was not sustainable without the ongoing work of grassroots organizing. Likewise, even legislative successes, won by the blood and sweat of many, could be easily reversed without the vigilant unified work of grassroots organizing.[53] Similarly, government social welfare was never sufficient by itself, nor could it be a solution. When ordinary people have accumulated unified strength, then legislation or the launch of a new program becomes virtually a matter of a simple administrative procedure. What really matters is people's power to make things happen rather than the program.[54] Government programs could never replace the self-organizing effort and power of people. When they do, they cultivate dependence.[55] When considering organizing as a daily practice of the oppressed, King was thinking of the massive, comprehensive, and permanent organizing of people in every realm and domain of society.

> But mass nonviolent demonstrations will not be enough. They must be supplemented by a continuing job of organization. To produce change, people must be organized to work together in units of power. These units may be political, as in the case of voters' leagues and political parties; they may be economic, as in the case of groups of tenants who join forces to form a union, or groups of the unemployed and underemployed who organize to get jobs and better wages. More and more, the civil rights movement will have to engage in the task of organizing people into permanent groups to protect their own interests and produce change in their behalf.[56]

The above statement reveals that, for King, organizing was more foundational than the political actions of demonstrations, marches, and civil disobedience. Among his many achievements, King also left a legacy of community organizing. His last word for people was "organize."

Impact

Through the success of the Civil Rights Movement, African Americans shed their psychological fatalism, defeatism, inferiority, and despair. It woke them from the spiritual and moral slumber of resignation, cynicism, and hopelessness.

Under his leadership millions of black Americans emerged from spiritual imprisonment, from fear, from apathy, and took to the streets to proclaim their freedom . . . Martin Luther King, the peaceful warrior, revealed to his people their latent power; nonviolent mass protest, firmly disciplined, enabled them to move against their oppressors in effective and bloodless combat.[57]

Through his organizing work and the success of the movement, King assisted in the moral awakening of people (conscientization), enhancing their collective agency and sense of confidence. As a result, African Americans changed the ways they dealt with whites in interpersonal encounters, which in turn had a big effect on the perceptions and behavior of many whites, leading to mutual respect. It helped people participate in civic life and release their creative energy for justice, democracy, and peace.

Under King's leadership, participants were motivated not only by self-interest, but also by passion for God's shalom and justice. King inspired people to dream a different world from the current one, that a different, a better, world was indeed possible. Such an impact was possible because his was a victory against all political odds. He showed the oppressed that victory was possible through efficient organizing that harnessed moral commitment and spiritual dedication. The Civil Rights Movement and its innovative experiments in community organizing had a huge impact on community organizing and social movements within and without the United States, empowering the struggle for justice and proving the power of organizing. It inspired the resurgence of faith-based activism and progressive political agendas in both local and national levels. Several major community organizations, such as SCUPE, PICO, and CCDA, have their historical roots in the Civil Rights Movement and its transformative experiences.

Conclusion

The biblical idea of covenant served as the latent moral framework for King's Civil Rights Movement. Covenant enabled his ministry to overcome the tripartite evils and to build the beloved community. King's heavy reliance on the Exodus-Sinai story, the gospel of Jesus, and appeal to US democratic traditions (the Declaration of Independence, the Constitution, and the Emancipation Proclamation) as spiritual and moral resources revealed his natural affinity with the covenantal moral vision and practices. The success of King's movement and people's response to the Civil Rights Movement demonstrate the vibrancy and resiliency of the covenantal tradition in America as a principle of organizing in political life. Although brief and insufficient, Americans indicated their willingness to embrace more fundamental principles of justice in the nation's life.[58]

King's approach is not so different from the previous three community organizing movements, as King relied on the Exodus-Sinai story as the base story (a moral prototype) and on its pattern of judgment-restoration, and pursued a moral society (the beloved community) through the transformation of existing racial, economic, and international relationships. What is distinctive in comparison to the three other movements was that he creatively synthesized all three historical traditions in a modern, pluralistic, and globalizing social context. Also, through his wholehearted embrace of Jesus' Sermon on the Mount, King not only theologically justified nonviolence, but elevated it to a faith-informed political practice.

Similarly, the triad of love, justice, and power (which are organically interrelated and integral to the biblical idea of covenant) was systematically articulated in theological and philosophical terms, and practically applied for organizing in his public campaigns for civil rights, voting rights, and economic rights. This synthesis was not only motivated by the contextual requisite to adapt to a new situation but also aided and deepened by his African American church tradition of organizing and passion for justice. Through King, covenantal organizing obtained theological and philosophical clarity and coherence, moral focus, and practical relevance (tying together theory and praxis, words and deeds), while retaining theological convictions and religious identity.

Having surveyed four different expressions of covenantal organizing, the following chapter will engage these insights and findings with Saul Alinsky and explore what covenantal organizing means for our own social-political situations, as well as how Christian covenantal organizing can creatively incorporate Alinsky's method in developing a more capacious and politically effective covenant ethics of community organizing.

6

Saul Alinsky's Community Organizing

A Brief Overview

"Change comes from power, and power comes from organization."[1]

In the last four chapters, we have examined the organizing power of covenant through the study of examples in the Bible and in Christian history: the Exodus event, Jesus' ministry, the Puritan movement, and Martin Luther King Jr.'s Civil Rights Movement. Although the biblical symbol of covenant was differently employed in different social-historical contexts (in tackling different social issues and political challenges such as power differences and social status), there is a certain historical continuity among them: They commonly shared the conviction that God is a moral God who judges the unjust social system (Pharaoh, Roman Empire, Old England, white racism, classism, militarism) and works to bring about a new just society (the promised land, the new creation, the new Israel, the beloved community); covenantal organizing is grassroots-oriented (not elitists), bottom-up (not top-down), organic/dynamic (not abstract or bureaucratic) in nature; it evokes and releases the radical impulses of justice and social renewal and reconstruction for people.

All four examples, explicitly and implicitly, follow a covenantal narrative pattern of liberation-restoration as the organizing principle of a new community. In the last three cases, the Exodus-Sinai narrative played a formative role as the paradigmatic organizing for the covenantal renewal. In applying the Exodus-Sinai paradigm, Jesus, the Puritans, and King appropriated different aspects of the Exodus-Covenant motif. Jesus revised the Sinai Covenant in espousing his own eschatological New Covenant, while Puritans engaged the Exodus-Sinai Covenant with Enlightenment humanism and other philosophical sources to build a systematic political philosophy for the early modern democracy. Martin Luther King Jr., on the other hand, utilized the biblical resources of the Exodus and Jesus as well as Puritan covenant tradition in the United States to forge his own global vision of the beloved community and praxis of nonviolence in order to confront the evils of racism, classism, and militarism.

The study of these examples demonstrates a deep contextual sensibility and wide applicability of covenantal organizing in different social situations. That is, the examples show that covenant can serve as the organizing principle for a theocratic society (ancient Israel), a local community under imperial occupation (Jesus and the early church), a newly established community (New England Puritans), or a religiously pluralistic society (African Americans in the United States). This wide applicability demonstrates the fecundity, capaciousness, and resilience of covenant as a key principle of a community organizing.[2]

In light of our survey, then, what is the meaning and significance of covenantal organizing today? How can we reactualize it today in a way faithful to the Bible but relevant to our political situations? Where do we see its manifestation today in the United States? I ask these questions because, given the covenantal origin (genealogy) of US democracy, one may claim that the current malaise (a crisis of democracy and civil society) has something to do with the loss or demise of commonwealth tradition. So a challenge for us in the context of this study is to ask: How can covenantal organizing be reactualized and what form of covenant is appropriate and relevant for our society today? At the same time, through history, though the explicitly religious character of covenant has been dissipated, diluted, or hidden along the way to embrace diverse religious views and cultural communities, its flame of liberative impetus, core values, and organizing motifs has not been completely extinguished. The covenantal motif (more specifically the Exodus-Sinai impulse) is still alive here and there in the nation, if not necessarily in a religious form. I identify Saul Alinsky's community organizing as one of those secular manifestations of a covenantal tradition. Consequently, the following two chapters study Saul Alinsky's community organizing from a covenantal perspective. Chapter 6 discusses Alinsky's community organizing, providing—a brief historical background of its rise and summary of its core principles, values, strategies, and its distinctive contributions to democratic politics, while chapter 7 engages Alinsky with the covenantal organizing we have studied in the previous chapters. My objective is to explore a possible recontextualization or reactualization of God's covenantal organizing in our own social context through a dialogue with Saul Alinsky, in particular through confronting the four interlocked crises of our civilization. This task is relevant and even exciting because Alinsky's method is making important contributions to local grassroots politics and social justice today in many parts of the nation.

Saul Alinsky is regarded as a father of modern community organizing; he is credited with inventing and spreading community organizing as a staple of modern grassroots democratic politics. With his focus on improving living conditions of the poor and marginalized, Alinsky championed new ways to organize the underprivileged for a democratic change. His community organizing is uniquely American in a sense, through its tie to American democratic tradition and with its emphasis on the local participation and extensive involvement of religious communities.

Alinsky inspired the rise of many other broad-based community organizations in the United States and the world. Numerous professional community organizers, labor, and civic leaders have been trained through Industrial Areas Foundation (IAF) workshops, including Fred Ross, a principal mentor of César Chávez and Dolores Huerta. It is said that various grassroots organizations (e.g., SNCC) and political activism in the 1960s are indebted to him. He made a profound impact on democratic politics by popularizing core methods and practices of organizing such as one-on-one, power analysis, confrontation, and agitation. For example, *Time* magazine wrote in 1970: "It is not too much to argue that American democracy is being altered by Alinsky's ideas."[3] Alinsky's groundbreaking methods, deep insights of operation of power, and provocative tactics have left indelible marks in American politics and the practice of community organizing. As mentioned in the introduction, Alinsky's community organizing is now receiving wider public and scholarly attention in the wake of the rise of neoliberal oligarchy and the crisis of Western democracy.

Saul Alinsky (1909–1972)

Born to immigrant Jewish parents in Chicago in 1909, Alinsky grew up in a time of political and economic upheavals, watching the devastating impact of the Great Depression (1929) on ordinary people. He saw how the poor were abused and exploited by local governments, slum landlords, and corporations. His time was also the era of the active labor movement, domestically and internationally, in response to the abuse of corporate powers.

Alinsky's interest in community organizing budded with his graduate study of criminology at the University of Chicago, a bastion of urban studies at that time. Natural to his discipline, he had an interest in urban pathologies, including organized crimes in Chicago, notably the Al Capone gang. Through his social studies, Alinsky noticed that the poor and the powerless typically suffer from various dysfunctions and pathologies within their communities such as drug addiction, juvenile delinquency, domestic violence, and so on. He learned that many of these pathologies were neither merely personal nor hereditary but rather social and environmental, and could be undone only by transforming their environments. One of Alinsky's sociological insights was that humans are social animals who constantly interact with their environments. Humans are never merely passive or adaptive; they are also subjects who work to improve their social conditions. Hence, his goal was to build neither an ideal healthy community in separation from society (like a sectarian religious community) nor an internal moral transformation, but to change the environments surrounding a community by developing the political power and collective agency of a community through organizing of people. Alinsky's primary concern was how the marginalized could build their own power base to overcome hostile conditions.

Among various sources,[4] organized crimes offered some precious insights on community organizing. Through his ethnographic study, Alinsky learned that gangs provide an alternative form of community (a place to belong) that imparts a sense of membership, trust, care, and economic means. Alinsky saw the importance of personal trust and loyalty among gang members for organizational survival and business enactment. As a secretive organization that operates outside the law, organized crime always requires unity, allegiance, and commitment among its members to protect their interests from external threats. Loyalty is highly valued to protect self-interest. Gang leaders use carrots and sticks—rewards for loyalty and threats of violent punishment against disloyalty.

After finishing his study of criminology, Alinsky went on to work as a government criminologist while working as a part-time organizer with the Congress of Industrial Organizations (CIO). Through his fieldwork, Alinsky learned the historical experiences and hardheaded tactics of the labor movement (relationship of unions with corporate management) and applied these lessons to local grassroots politics (relationship of citizens to public officials) and his organizing of the "Back of the Yards," an industrial and ethnic community area on the southwest side of Chicago. Based on his experience in the "Back of the Yards," in 1940 Alinsky established the Industrial Areas Foundation (IAF) to systematically work on community organizing.

During the 1960s, Alinsky's methods and tactics were adopted by college students and social activists in promoting their social agendas and issues. In particular, Alinsky was influential in LBJ's War on Poverty, the labor movement, and the Civil Rights Movement. As a result of his innovative vision and effective work through the IAF, other community organizing networks were established by his early associates (e.g., Tom Gaudette, Fred Ross) and others who were inspired by his vision and practices.[5] These networks include: ACORN, Direct Action Research & Training (DART), Gamaliel Foundation, Industrial Areas Foundation (IAF), Midwest Academy, National Training & Information Center (NTIC), PICO, and regional groupings such as InterValley Project (IVP) and Western Organization of Resource Councils (WORC). Claiming several million members combined, these organizations have trained numerous community organizers and activists, and popularized the ideas and methods of community organizing both domestically and internationally.[6]

Areas of community organizing are now vast, including the subjects of: poverty, domestic violence, job training, juvenile support, stopping toxic waste sites in communities, alternative school, local health center, housing plan for the poor and the elderly, anti-crime, anti-police brutality, senior citizen programs, anti-discrimination in the workplace, services for the mentally ill, promotion for corporate accountability, advocating for human rights and social justice, etc. As this list demonstrates, all major urban problems and issues of injustices could be areas and targets of community organizing, revealing the potency and wide applicability of Alinsky's method.

However, whatever the starting point or immediate focus of a local organization, Alinsky believed that an issue cannot be approached individually apart from a larger problem of a society; each is only a facet of a general social pathology and disorganization.[7]

Alinsky's Community Organizing:
Main Ideas, Core Principles, and Practices

In general, community organizing is the collaborative work of people to organize themselves into a collective body (i.e., organization) to address common problems in their community. They do so by building unified grassroots power that brings meaningful solutions to these problems. The participants democratically engage with each other to identify the problems, seek solutions, and use persuasion and/or confrontation to achieve their goals. Pursuing a radical form of democracy where citizens are the subjects, Alinsky's approach was people-centered (populist), grassroots oriented, empirical, and pragmatic, while predicated on the unity-in-diversity principle.

Unity in Diversity

Like covenantal organizing, Alinsky's method relies on some form of the unity-in-diversity principle in building and maintaining an organization. Organizing is a process that coordinates diverse self-interests among participants (individuals and organizations),[8] while building common interest and a common good, and the principle of unity in diversity functions as a dialectic mechanism of balancing and harmonizing individuality and solidarity. Alinsky compares organizing to a chemical process in which different elements (hydrogen and oxygen) are brought together in proper proportions and under the right conditions to make a new product (e.g., water).[9] The image is very organic, which is reminiscent of Paul's image of the church as the body of Christ in which different parts collaborate under the lordship of Jesus.

This principle is also reflected in Alinsky's vision of democracy and civil society as a system of multiple spheres and organizations (political, economic, and social) organized by people. Resonant with a covenantal vision of a complex, differentiated society, Alinsky conceives of a democratic society as a complex, organic, interactive system in which multiple organizations are voluntarily formed and maintained through people's free consent and contributions, rather than by a top-down, uninformative, hierarchal structure. A democratic society should legally guarantee people's participation in multiple organizations together with their basic rights.

> The best insurance of an open society is a whole complex of voluntary organizations, each with a large following and each so involved in action that they deserve and derive strong loyalty from large sectors of the population. Such powerful organizations would resist the surrendering of their power and of the loyalties of their followers to a central power. Therefore strengthening your organization becomes a high priority for the reinforcement of the political openness of our society.[10]

Participation in multiple organizations and multiple loyalties are not only natural to human lives in a modern society, but also necessary for the fulfillment of their potentials and democratic values. Deprived of this institutional affiliation, individuals become vulnerable to the brutal, massive power of the state and corporations, and without the counter-vailing power of mediating institutions, the state and corporations turn authoritarian and dictatorial.

People-Centered

Alinsky's community organizing is thoroughly people-centered. The foundational principle of community organizing is the belief in the free-dom, self-determination, and wisdom of people in governing their own social lives and enhancing democracy. Organizing starts and ends with people—taking seriously where they are, what they have, to what they aspire. In addressing problems, community organizing respects people and their wisdom and inherent power to solve problems.[11] The first rule of organizing is to respect the subjectivity and agency of people: never do for people what they can do for themselves.

> A people can participate only if they have both the opportunity to formulate their program, which is their reason for participation, and a medium through which they can express and achieve their program. This can be done only through the building of real People's Orga-nizations in which people band together, get to know one another, exchange points of view, and ultimately reach a common agreement which is the People's Program.[12]

In his emphasis of people's power, Alinsky was very critical of elit-ism, charismatic leadership, super-heroism that champions specialized knowledge, and extraordinary individuals and their talents at the expense of the power of ordinary people, in one form or another. Organizers take people's own experiences as a textbook and help them to develop their own capabilities to accomplish solutions. Such an approach is based on the belief that change will not happen if people do not own their issues and if they are not willing to work for it. Alinsky's approach is empirical; it begins where people are. He said,

> As an organizer I start from where the world is, as it is, not as I would like it to be. That we accept the world as it is does not in any sense weaken our desire to change it into what we believe it should be—it

is necessary to begin where the world is if we are going to change it to what we think it should be. That means working in the system.[13]

Alinsky taps into accumulated grievance and discontent, and organizes people for collective action around commonly identified problems. This grievance could come from the current state (e.g., poverty, racism, and sexism), which is inconsistent with the professed goals and ideals (such as the Constitution) of society. Perhaps ordinary people's basic needs and legitimate concerns are not being addressed, or politicians and government officials are beholden to special interests and lobbyists rather than public interests.

Once gathered, participants share their dissatisfaction and discontent and experiences of injustices, collectively identify the problems that affect their community, and then seek solutions together by deciding on courses of actions and strategies. That is, people ask questions: What is going on in the community? Why is it not solved? Who is responsible for it? Who are beneficiaries and victims of these problems, and why? What are the consequences of these problems in their current lives and what are future consequences if the current status quo continues? What would it take to change the situation? Who are our current or potential allies and friends? These questions are useful to identify common problems and motivate people.

Organizing equips and empowers ordinary citizens to control their political future and community life. An organizer cannot do more than what people actually can do. An organizer's role is not to lead but to assist people in organizing and leading themselves. They serve as a resource person. People's opinions, ideas, and passions should be respected, and any new idea or insight from an organizer needs to be first checked out with people. A program is important, but empowerment of people and their ownership of process are even more so. Program follows people, never the other way around. The specifics of a people's program are contextually worked out and determined by people themselves.

In the same spirit of empowering people, Alinsky respected local wisdom, tradition, and experiences. He noted:

> The foundation of a People's Organization is in the communal life of the local people. Therefore the first stage in the building of a People's Organization is the understanding of a community, not only in terms of the individual's experiences, habits, values, and objectives, but also from the point of view of the collective habits, experiences, customs, controls, and values of the whole group—the *community traditions*.[14]

He added:

> The foundation of a People's Organization is the community, and the foundation of conflict tactics is community traditions. Just as knowledge of the terrain is of the utmost importance for military tactics in actual warfare, so too is the knowledge, the full understanding and appreciation of the power of local traditions.[15]

Contrary to secular advocates of liberal democracy, he did not dismiss local traditions, religion, or culture as obsolete or as hindering forces to social progress, but rather used them as indispensable resources for community organizing because they present built-in social and cultural capital, namely, a community's capabilities to solve its problems.

Alinsky emphasized that organizing is not a one-time campaign to get a concession on a certain issue from politicians and government officials, but an organic, ongoing process requiring a sustained effort to solve community problems. The success of democracy requires ongoing practices of organizing in which people directly participate and exercise their power on matters of their community. In this sense, community organizing is contextual in nature; thus, no one process is exactly the same. One has to constantly adjust or invent their tactics, methods, and strategies depending on social contexts.[16] Hence, people need to always be alert and responsive to a new or changing social situation.

Because of its people-centeredness, community organizing is different from electoral campaigns (which happen through the elected power of a few representatives or government officials) and philanthropy (which relies on the charity or almsgiving of a few rich individuals). Rather, it seeks a lasting change in the condition of social life as well as people's self-perception of their capabilities and moral agency. Alinsky was critical of philanthropy, because philanthropy corrodes people's moral agency by turning them into passive receivers, creating perpetual dependency. In its consequence, it is no different from the "welfare colonialism" of a big government. He declared that "the people are the motor, the organizations of the people are the gears. The power of the people is transmitted through the gears of their own organizations, and democracy moves forward."[17]

Grassroots Orientation

Alinsky's people-centeredness reflects his deep respect of and commitment to grassroots democracy. He was deeply rooted in the rich democratic tradition of the US; he was intellectually inspired by Patrick Henry, Thomas Paine, Walt Whitman, Henry Thoreau, and Frederick Douglass. The first chapter of his *Rules for Radicals* begins: "What follows is for those who want to change the world from what it is to what they believe it should be. Whereas *The Prince* was written by Machiavelli for the Haves on how to hold power, *Rules for Radicals* is written for the Have-Nots on how to take it away."[18]

A local, grassroots focus of community organizing is found in Alinsky's aversion to social movements. His maxim for community organizers was "build organizations, not movements."[19] His aim was to incrementally build enduring, long-term "people's organizations" in local communities, not a onetime, sensationally driven social movement. The comment of Edward Chambers, Alinsky's successor at the IAF, is telling regarding this point:

> We play to win. That's one of the distinctive features of the IAF: We don't lead everyday, ordinary people into public failures, and we're not building movements. Movements go in and out of existence. As good as they are, you can't sustain them. Everyday people need incremental success over months and sometimes years.[20]

Why would a person like Alinsky, who was passionate for social change, be wary of a social movement? As a social movement seeks a quick solution, its approach is antithetical to organizing because it tends to focus on a charismatic leader rather than the ordinary people and the enhancement of their organizing capability; in addition, its national scope distracts people's ownership and attention from local problems.

Alinsky understood politics as the art of crafting a common life. For him, democracy was a political system based on the self-ordering, self-governing power of people. Democracy by definition is a system based on the organized power of people; as Abraham Lincoln declared, it is the rule "of the people, by the people, and for the people." One may say that democracy is a morally informed organization of political power for the common good of people. Hence, for its survival and sustainability, democracy relies on the works of ordinary citizens; when people refuse to participate and contribute, real democracy is not possible, and only pseudo-democracy (in which ruling elites constantly devise ideas and excuses to justify their control of power at the expense of ordinary people) prevails in its place. The heart of democracy is the sovereignty of people (the belief that power comes from people), and community organizing is a method to actualize this ideal. In Alinsky's view, although the principles of public accountability and non-arbitrariness (rule of law) are important, the sovereignty of ordinary people is central to democracy that contrasts itself from monarchy, dictatorship, and oligarchy.

Democracy

One of Alinsky's central insights was that democracy lives and thrives on voluntary organizing of people. Democracy is a dynamic political system that requires the ongoing participation of a large number of citizens who are committed to civic services and the common good, in addition to well-defined and transparent procedures and an established system of accountability based on the rule of law, a structure of checks and balances, and the free flow and accessibility of information. Democracy is as much a practice as a theory.

> Democracy is a way of life, not formula to be 'preserved' like jelly. It is a process—a vibrant, living sweep of hope and progress which constantly strives for the fulfillment of its objective in life—the search for truth, justice, and the dignity of man. There can be no democracy unless it is a dynamic democracy.[21]

In other words, liberal ideas of constitutionalism and the rule of law are far from sufficient to guarantee a proper function of democracy. Democracy is sustained by constant organizing of people. Without organizing there is no demand of accountability to ruling elites and power holders and democracy becomes corrupted or hollowed. As Stout notes, community organizing is the only measure to prevent "robbery and scoundrelism" of the elites.[22] Organizing is indispensable in democracy in order to protect people's basic rights and fairness and transparency in political processes, and to make democracy meaningful. Only when people are organized and participate in its political process are its ideals of freedom and justice actualized. Without popular, educated, virtuous citizen commitment and sustained public participation, democracy cannot but crumble.

Alinsky offered community organization as such a means for people to grow and assert their collective agency, power, and democratic will. Organizing is a tedious work that requires time, patience, and endurance—the nitty-gritty work of meetings, talks, and trust building. Organizing is a concrete grassroots method that enacts and actualizes the democratic ideals of freedom, justice, and equality in the complex and changing social reality of competing ambitions, interests, egoism, and power struggles. The ethos of community organizing is anti-elitist and anti-establishment; it appeals to the sense of people's powerlessness under the control of the expert and managerial class and corporate power. It offers a method to channel popular collective discontent into a sustained force of collective action.

Civil Society

As previously mentioned, civil society is essential to the integrity and vitality of democracy. Civil society serves as a buffer between the state and citizens, protecting individuals from abuses of the state and the market, providing social spaces for personal expressions and leadership, and operating as a social system of checks and balances.

Alinsky's community organizing presupposes and relies on the existence of civil society. Civil society is the furnace of common life and the underpinning of democracy. In civil society, people learn the art of symbiosis (life together) and practice democracy. Through their participation in various organizations, people learn to be responsible citizens, asserting themselves and listening to others as they debate and deliberate on the matters that commonly concern them.

Most importantly, civil society is the locus of community organizing. Consisting of the myriad of mediating organizations, civil society offers a rich soil where various kinds of social associations, including community organizing, take place and the multiple loyalties of individuals are acknowledged and freely exercised through these organizations.[23]

Democratic Values

Although many discussions of community organizing tend to focus on a social process or method of organizing (such as one-on-one or confrontation) to accumulate power, community organizing envisions a democratic society and commits to its core assumptions and values in its practices. Despite its emphasis on pragmatics of power, tactics, and victory, community organizing is a value-driven activity based on commitment to democracy and principles of justice. Alinsky subscribed to the liberal democratic values of freedom, equality, and solidarity (the French Revolution), which originated from the Judeo-Christian belief that all humans are bearer of the *imago Dei*.[24]

> Certain universally accepted moral principles will inevitably find their places as cornerstones of any real People's Organization. The very

character of the organization will be a social incarnation of that flaming call of the French Revolution, "Liberty, Equality, Fraternity," or what the world's great religions describe as respect for "the dignity of man."[25]

Hence, from Alinsky's perspective, organizing should serve democracy, and not all organizing is good organizing. This point is important in distinguishing Alinsky's method from other forms of organizing that are anti-democratic in nature. Fascists and communists also organize their bases to undo or overthrow democracy or to retain undemocratic regimes. Demagogues are effective in stirring up broad emotion, but such populism is not to be confused for organizing.

Power

One of Alinsky's distinctive and enduring contributions to democratic politics is his insight on power: Power is the ability to accomplish one's intention, and it is at the heart of one's agency. Free exercise of power is what defines moral agency. A core premise of his method is that power arises from organized people, its accumulation and mobilization is critical in achieving social justice, and power analysis is necessary to achieve a desired social change. At the bottom line, injustice is caused by the imbalance or concentration of power. This concentrated and unchecked power is inevitably abusive. The poor and the marginalized are suffering because they lack power to protect themselves from the abuses of the powerful. Positive social change means to alter the existing unjust, unbalanced power relations and establish new social relations by redistributing power and resources.

For example, racism is not just a personal bias or cultural prejudice; it is an issue of social power ("social" here meaning in social relationships). In the United States, existing racial relations between whites and people of color operate according to rules, choices, and preferences made by whites. Community organizing in this context means to upset this power relationship and arrange new terms of relationship based on fairness and equality between races. The desire for change begins with power analysis. Together people study: Who has power? How is power used in social relationships? Whose interests and desires are served and why? What is the best means to change a power relationship in a given situation?

Since lack of power is a major cause of injustice, moral persuasion and social criticism alone are usually not sufficient for change to occur. He frequently cited African American abolitionist Frederick Douglass:

"Power concedes nothing without a demand. It never did and it never will." The production of meaningful countervailing power is indispensable to bringing about necessary social change. Without the use of countervailing power, victimization cannot but continue.

If power is necessary to build justice, then where does power come from? Based on his empirical observations, Alinsky believed that power has two primary sources: organized people and organized money. Political parties and social institutions exercise power because they have organized people and/or money. However, since the poor do not have money, their only source of power is through organizing themselves. From his study of organized crime, Alinsky identified a new source of power: relational power that comes from longstanding personal relationships. People individually may be powerless, but when organized, particularly in large numbers, they definitively gain power, which makes change possible. The wisdom is that there is power in numbers. Alinsky declared, "Change comes from power, and power comes from organization."[26] An individual who is not part of an organization is vulnerable to the abusive power and arbitrary decision of the powerful. Alinsky's message to the distraught people was: "If you want justice, organize." To generate and mobilize power, people need to build an organization and develop shared goals and strategies. Organizing is the only way for the poor to protect themselves from abusive power.

Self-Interest

While people-centered and people-initiating, community organizing begins with where local people feel their self-interests lie. Community organizing does not propagate a social utopia or moral purism. It appeals to the self-interest of individuals rather than lofty moral ideals. Organizers teach on the benefits of organizing for participants: what community organizing can achieve for them and what benefits it brings to people and their families. Community organizing is not possible when it fails to motivate people to actively participate, and such motivation only arises when people find that organizers respect and attend to the issues that they really care about.

Alinsky's notion of self-interest is a constant source of misunderstanding, especially among religious people. It is different from egoism or selfishness; it rather refers to the enlightened idea of one's legitimate interests or rights. While sounding individualistic, it is relational. The word "interest" comes from the composite of two Latin words, *inter* and *esse*, "between" and "being," and literally means "to be between." It carries the connotations of "To be concerned with or engaged in; to affect; to concern; to excite."[27] Self-interest presupposes a social or relational nature of human life. Hence self-interest, following this Latin etymology, can be described as a self's conscious engagement or concern with others on the matters of a community that affect them. Dennis Jacobsen's following statement reveals a relational assumption of self-interest in community organizing:

> Organizers view self-interest as the only true way of relating to another person because self-interest respects the two sides of the relationship. Selfishness denies the "other" in the relationship. Selflessness denies the "self" in the relationship. Self-interest honors both the "self" and the "other" in the relationship. Organizers say that to know your self-interest, to declare your self-interest, and to act on your self-interest is an act of political courage.[28]

Self-interest is not a private interest, just as the public good is not an abstract or general good that excludes self-interest. Self-interest is the shared interest of people in the sense that it is the interest that is shared among individual members of a community. Promotion of common interests (e.g., health, education, job, income, living wages, street safety, and water) does not contradict the needs and self-interest of individual people. For example, parents know that the personal safety and academic success of their children are not separate from the collective interest of neighborhood problems, such as drugs, street safety, and so on.

In community organizing, knowing people's self-interest has the effect of building solidarity and finding common ground. The insight found here is that enlightened self-interest naturally leads people to participate in collaborative work to meet their self-interests.

Specifically, in the process of organizing, one's self-interest is identified and pursued in reference to that of others. Collaboration is also prompted when individuals become aware that a collective pursuit of self-interest has a better chance of success than an individual one. In other words, overlapping self-interest forms a common interest that motivates people toward collective political action. Such a process of mutual learning and collaboration occurs through a series of one-on-one encounters, small group meetings, and self-education. Mutual interactions throughout the organizing process help to enlighten individuals' self-interest and open them to collaboration in the pursuit of common good. In community organizing, one may say, the common good is a long-term oriented self-interest.[29]

In close association with Alinsky's appeal to self-interest, one method that community organizers use to increase people's participation is multi-issue organizing. Multi-issue organizing is a strategy that respects people's self-interest while at the same time building a power base in community organizing.

> Multi-issue organizing is required because different people experience different problems with different degrees of intensity at different points in their lives. The single working mother without extended family supports is interested in child care; the homemaker mom with teenagers is interested in the local middle or high school. The retiree who depends on public transportation has yet a different concern. The organization that wants to involve all of them has to offer the possibility of addressing all their concerns in the not-too-distant future. A believable picture of what people power can accomplish must be painted; the initial painter is a professional community organizer.[30]

Multi-issue organizing adds institutional sustainability to organizations. An organization formed on a single social issue dies quickly when the issue loses its social relevance or potency.

Summary

Our discussion exhibits that Alinsky's community organizing, like covenantal organizing, is the attempt to bridge the gap between "the world as it is" and "the world as it should be." "The world as it is" describes the world that the poor and the marginalized experience on a daily basis, while the world as it should be is the world we desire (or the world promised by the Constitution) and long for; it is the world where justice, fairness, and truth reign, thus indicating the future vision of a society. We need this vision because "the world as it is" alone breeds cynicism, hopelessness, compromise, and co-optation, and the brutal will to power, *realpolitik*, reigns. Conversely, "the world as it should be" alone leads to utopianism. Hence, any human drive toward a new society must be based on an empirical analysis of "the world as it is."

Methods/Practices

Organizing takes place through myriad processes of getting to know people, building solidarity, and accumulating power.

One-On-One

Among several practices of community organizing, one-on-one meeting is a foundational practice. Typically a thirty-minute conversation, it is a face-to-face, informal, personal conversation without any prescribed rules. It is instrumental in building and facilitating trust, network, and reciprocity between the participants. As organizing is essentially an ongoing relationship-building enterprise, one-on-one relationships are the building block of organizing. It is different from online chatting that happens casually among anonymous participants without any shared purpose or direction of conversations.

One-on-one serves as a crucial tool to build trust and relationship within a group. It helps to discover common, overlapping areas of self-concern, interest, passion, gifts, and talents among the members of a community. However, the one-on-one is more than rational analysis, but affectionate interaction. It sends a message that an organizer values the worth of each person and respects his or her concerns. One-on-one offers a precious opportunity "to set aside the pressures and tasks and deadlines of the day and to probe another person, to look for their talent, interest, energy, and vision. The other person's perspective is of primary value. Their stories and insights and memories are more important than a name on a petition or contribution to a cause."[31]

Self-Education

Building organization includes a self-initiated educational process by people on the ground. The process of education is necessary because, according to Alinsky, people are naturally fearful of change. They usually feel "so frustrated, so defeated, so lost, so futureless in the prevailing system that they are not willing to let go of the past and chance the future." Without education, revolution would not happen.

Education in community organizing is practical, people-centered, and problem-solving, rather than technical, abstract, and instructor-oriented. Education focuses on building the capacity of both individual members and the group as a whole. Using various techniques and methods, organizers help individual members to grow and expand their individual capabilities, skills, knowledge, leadership, communication, and self-care. Education is based on the daily lives and experiences of people. It takes place "in the fields, in City Halls and housing agencies, in state legislatures and back board rooms, in T.V. studios and editorial boards.

The materials that we and our fellow leaders use are the unlimited examples of failure in our cities: the bankrupt programs and grounded pilot projects, the political fixes and insider deals. We don't have to look far for issues. They surround us."[32]

Education is not separate from the process of organizing, but rather integral to it. One-on-one meetings, small groups, and other participatory events offer the opportunity of self-education to learn leadership skills, self-assertion, decision-making, and communication, because building and operating an organization requires many skills—recruiting, relationship building, raising funds, power analysis, framing issues, strategizing, mobilizing for political actions, and negotiating. Community organizing follows the action-praxis model of learning. People take initiative in studying the causes of their oppression and suffering.[33] People become the subjects, not the objects, of the process. Education is praxeological in community organizing; people learn through participation, critically reflecting on their real-life situations, family, job, school, children's safety, etc.[34] For example, committee members soon find that they must become informed and knowledgeable about their assigned tasks. To be capable of carrying out their own responsibilities, they must know about the problems and activities related to their committee's work. Similarly, they have to learn various political skills to successfully carry out collective actions, such as making public demands, putting pressure on the powerful by employing different means and strategies of provocation and confrontation (including the savvy use of the mass media and SNS), mobilizing a community through public persuasion and events, building coalitions with other groups for a common cause, and negotiating with adversaries. Through these processes, ordinary people are transformed into change agents for their community.

Coalition

Community organizing typically takes place in a local community. However, a social issue is far from local in its nature and effect; it is inextricably related to a larger social system, public policies, and laws. From his early years, it was Alinsky's strategy to build broad-based and mass-based community organizing. In order to be politically effective, therefore, it is necessary to build collaboration among groups that share similar concerns. Alinsky observes:

People's Organization has two major objectives: first, to organize and do what can be done on the local scene, and second, to utilize the organization as a springboard for the development of other People's Organizations throughout the nation. They recognize that only through engaging in a national organizational program amongst millions of other working people can they ever hope to break loose from their shackles and their misery. They know that the people elsewhere are the same kind of people, their problems are the same, their needs, their hopes, and their aspirations are the same. A people's program is therefore predicated upon the thesis that only through the combined strength of many such organizations as their own can they ever hope to cope effectively with those major destructive forces which pervade the entire social order and converge upon their communities and themselves to establish the blight both of the area and of their lives.[35]

For example, the IAF is the organized body of multiple organizations. A membership in it does not threaten a local organization (agency). It brings diverse organizations to cope with a social issue that no single organization is able to address. Coalition arises in the place where the interests of diverse groups converge. Coalition is built around the common concerns and issues of a community that different groups share despite different religious affiliations and cultural backgrounds.

Coalition building is the actual practice of the aforementioned unity in diversity. Coalition does not threat the integrity or autonomy of each individual agency. Within coalition, "Each agency will continue to carry out its own program, but all are being banded together to achieve sufficient strength to cope with issues that are so vast and deep that no one or two community agencies would ever consider tackling them."[36] That is, within a coalition, each organization, while maintaining its distinctive autonomy, has a cooperative relationship with others. Collaborating with other grassroots organizations has the effect of expanding a power base by bringing together further information, people, networks, and resources. It breaks down "the wall of isolation separating the various agencies" by removing prejudices and suspicions and competitions, and instead builds intimate association and frank conversations.[37]

Agitation, Confrontation, and Conflict

While upholding the norms of freedom, equality, and human rights, Alinsky believed that these values could be actualized (approximated) in social relationships only when the balance of power is achieved. To achieve the power balance, confrontations with power holders are inevitable. He defines "people's organization" in very straightforward, militant terms.

> The building of a People's Organization is the building of a new power group. The creation of any new power group automatically becomes an intrusion and a threat to the existing power arrangement. It carries with it the menacing implication of displacement and disorganization of the status quo.[38]

This means that a people's organization is not a social club of shared hobbies, but of shared self-interest. It functions as a social power group. Its existence upsets the existing power relationships in a society. It exists to fight off menacing threats to people's well-being. A people's organization's sole purpose is to disrupt and displace the current status quo in order to ensure the basic rights and well-being of ordinary people. Hence, its operation is inevitably conflictual. He noted:

> The first step in community organization is community disorganization. The disruption of the present organization is the first step toward community organization. Present arrangements must be disorganized if they are to be displaced by new patterns. . . . All change means disorganization of the old and organization of the new.[39]

To disorganize the current status quo, various tactics of agitation, disruption, confrontation, and collective actions (e.g., public agitation, polarization, marches, sit-ins, nonviolent disruption, public shaming, strikes, greenlining, and boycotts, etc.) are used to achieve political objectives.[40] For Alinsky, Machiavellian tactics are not the goals themselves, but necessary ways to upset and deorganize the unjust power structure and restore justice.

Given the entrenched nature of power, Alinsky recognized that the change of power relationship is not an easy task at all; moral persuasion (rhetoric) alone can never achieve this goal. Using creative, militant, ruthless tactics, while remaining nonviolent, is necessary for an intended change. He explains the necessity and importance of conflict tactics and agitations as follows:

> [S]ince most attempts at the building of People's Organizations have been broken by the attacks of an opposition which knows no rules of fair play or so-called ethics, it is imperative that the organizers and leaders of a People's Organization not only understand the necessity

for and the nature and purpose of conflict tactics, but become familiar with and skillful in the use of such tactics.[41]

Put simply, his point is that there is no Mother Theresa in politics, so to speak. In politics, conflicts are inevitable, and agitation and confrontation are forms of asserting power to get the attention of the rich and powerful.

Alinsky urged people to be creative with the tactics of agitation and confrontation. Rather than imposing rigid rules for campaigning or repeating the same tactics, different organizations may invent different strategies and tactics that fit their situations. People can use their limited power by effectively employing the tactics of confrontation, agitation, and disruption. Power is a matter of perception, as it is psychological as much as rational: "Power is not only what you have but what the enemy thinks you have."[42] There are creative ways to increase one's power base by using this emotional and psychological dimension of power. To create the perception of power, exaggerated threats are sometimes necessary. Alinsky noticed that "[t]he threat is usually more terrifying than the thing itself."[43] Equally effective are public ridicule and embarrassment of adversaries. In order to energize a campaign, and move public opinion to one's own side, it is sometimes necessary to provoke popular sentiments and anger. As Alinsky put it, this is accomplished by "rubbing raw the resentments of the people . . . fanning [their] latent hostilities to the point of overt expression. [The organizer] must search out controversy and issues, rather than avoid them, for unless there is controversy people are not concerned enough to act."[44] Such tactics are effective in emotionally unsettling power holders, thus making them vulnerable to mistakes out of fear, confusion, or shame, or discouraging them from using their power resources.

Similarly, Alinsky believed that an initial victory is crucial for the psychology of the participants in community organizing. Why is an initial victory important? Winning has a psychological benefit in boosting morale and keeping participants committed. It helps overcome any sense of self-doubt and brings unity and a sense of confidence, thus increasing power and commitment, keeping people in the organizing movement: "Success can be used to convince the skeptics on the sidelines to participate. When more people participate, more people power is built and more recalcitrant issues can be addressed."[45]

While pursuing the actualization of a democratic society, Alinsky rejected moral idealism (or an ideological doctrinaire) and did not hesitate to adopt Machiavellian tactics in achieving real, tangible political results. He commented:

> The man of action views the issue of means and ends in pragmatic and strategic terms. He has no other problem; he thinks only of his actual resources and the possibilities of various choices of action. He asks of ends only whether they are achievable and worth the cost; of means, only whether they will work. To say that corrupt means corrupt the ends is to believe in the immaculate conception of ends and principles.[46]

Accordingly, Alinsky detested those who are only talking without any doing, who possess high moral rhetoric without concrete actions. Hence, he believed that the morality of political actions should be judged not in itself but always "weighed against the morality of inaction."[47] Without remaining private or aloof, people need to participate in political actions that serve the common end (i.e., social change). In other words, spectators do not understand the challenges and complexities that the underdogs face in the political process of changing a power relationship. At times, Alinsky sounds extremely utilitarian to the extent of claiming that ethics exists to justify politics, not the other way around: "You do what you can with what you have and clothe it with moral garments."[48] Such a Machiavellian rhetoric has to do with the goal of winning the power game against the powerful.

Conclusion

Alinsky identified himself as a permanent voice of the underdogs, "the poor man's Machiavelli."[49] Alinsky was democratic in his political vision, but radical in his political engagement. His method was deliberately grassroots-based, actional, pragmatic, and contextual. He developed community organizing as a political method that simultaneously addresses the ideal of democracy and the reality of power, human aspiration for a just society and dogged human brokenness (e.g., self-protection, egoism).[50]

At the heart of Alinsky's method is civic associationalism. His method is built upon a long tradition and spirit of civic associationalism in the United States, and expanded into a method of political resistance. Alinsky aimed at organizing and mobilizing the power of people for the actualization of democratic ideals. Community organizing takes democracy to the grassroots level and grounds it in the daily lives of the ordinary citizens. It helps people to have the ownership of democracy and its processes as citizens. His method complements electoral politics in an important way by filling the gap that the representative democracy (the republican system) inevitably creates between the government and citizens. Its emphasis on the grassroots organizing of people is indispensable for the success of democracy, because formal, electoral politics can never replace daily democratic practices, nor nurture citizenship and political agency of people.

Despite his advocacy for radical democracy, interestingly, Alinsky was not a typical hot-headed revolutionary. Instead of a violent revolution, Alinsky advocated for incremental political changes through organizing in local communities. He did so out of his assumption that changes cannot surpass the power and capability that people actually possess. Despite his radical rhetoric, he operated out of democratic assumptions: although conflicts are inevitable in politics, citizens should rely on nonviolent means to resolve them; one should not underestimate the reforming potentials within a democratic system; negotiation and compromise with the opponents are an indispensable part of democracy. That is, citizens should find ways to work together even when they disagree.

Alinsky was a democratic realist and pragmatist who endeavored to bring about changes within a democratic system. He stressed a careful balance between confrontation and compromise, always considering the amount of power that people have. Equally, he warned about tactical excesses that could invite backlashes from opponents.[51] Alinsky believed that ideological purity and revolutionary utopianism are not so helpful in a pluralistic society made of diverse racial and ethnic communities and ideological groups and networks.[52]

Alinsky's unconventional wisdom, provocative insights, and iconoclastic approaches with concrete, tangible results have made a lasting impact on American democratic politics. Alinsky's contribution to community organizing is enduring, especially his method of broad-based community organizing (BBCO) exemplified by Industrial Areas Foundation (IAF), and the concept of the professional community organizer.

Having studied Alinsky's community organizing, the next chapter will compare covenantal organizing with Alinsky's method in detail. In this chapter, we have seen that Alinsky's core moral convictions (freedom, justice, equality) and political orientation (grassroots) are commensurate with a covenantal tradition (commonwealth). Some motifs and insights of his work are very similar to those of covenantal organizing: grassroots orientation, horizontal organizing, passion for justice, the unity-in-diversity principle, and so on. The two are not identical but they are closely associated. Hence, I will examine where the two agree and disagree, how they are related to each other, and the meaning and implication of their relationship for the reactualization (recontextualization) of covenantal organizing today.

7

Covenantal Organizing and Community Organizing

A Comparison

"[I]n order to change an existing imagined order, we must first believe in an alternative imagined order."[1]

Organizing community is what characterizes humanity. According to Yuval Noah Harari, what made *Homo sapiens* the most successful human being, ousting Neanderthals, was his ability to collaborate and organize on a massive scale, for example, in the cases of religions, nations, and money.[2] Humans always organize themselves, formally or informally, to meet their deep needs for intimacy, relationship, and security. Organization is a stable structure that organizing produces for the efficiency, order, stability, and productivity of collaboration.

This chapter compares covenantal organizing with Saul Alinsky's community organizing method by examining their similarities and differences. The two might initially seem to have no relationship at all, since one is secular and political while the other is religious and particular. However, the two are intimately related, sharing several core moral-political thrusts, dynamics, and features. I claim that covenant theology and Alinsky's community organizing are not only compatible but also complementary; each can benefit and be strengthened by incorporating the insights of the other. Covenantal organizing is broader in its vision and scope, and theoretically (philosophically) coherent in its own theological logic and conceptualization. Alinsky's community organizing is pragmatic, actional, and populist, with the rich pragmatic wisdom,

tactics, and strategies of real politics. Their mutual affinity and complementarity are beneficial for both in order to develop a more expansive,
capacious, and pragmatic (politically effective) model of community
organizing.

Similarities

Although certainly not identical, covenantal and community organizing
share several striking ethical objectives, motifs, and characteristics.

Organizing

Both covenantalism and Alinsky see organizing as a mechanism of voluntary bonding around a commonly shared goal on the basis of mutual
trust, loyalty, and justice. They share several assumptions, core values,
and mechanisms of organizing. First, both take "organizing" as a key to a
common life. They assume that human life is different from other species
by virtue of the conscious, intentional effort of human beings to organize
themselves as enduring political and moral entities. Their starting point
is based on the sociological insight that an organization (small and large,
including society) is made through organizing. Such organizing serves
two purposes: formation of an organization and resistance to unjust powers and social systems. Organizing includes the process of gathering and
binding people together and empowering them toward a common purpose in order to correct unjust power relationships and abuses.

There are diverse ways of arranging social relationships and distrib-
uting resources and power: monarchy, aristocracy, oligarchy, and caste.[3]
However, covenantal organizing and Alinsky's idea of organizing are different from these forms of organizing, as they focus on voluntary participation, mutual trust, and commitment to common objectives; they are
aware that collaboration best serves the interests of all concerned, including by providing protection from the abuse and misuse of power. By
taking ordinary people (more precisely, the marginalized) as the subjects
of organizing, they stress the grassroots, subversive, and transformative
nature of organizing.

Justice

It is immediately obvious that covenantal organizing and Alinsky share
a deep passion for justice. That is, both aspire to a just and egalitarian
society. Covenantalism and Alinsky tie organizing to the achievement of

a just society. They operate in roughly the same terms of the dynamic of liberation (resistance) and reconstruction (alternative), and they use organizing as the primary means to fill the gap between "what is" and "what should be," that is, deconstructing old relationships and constructing new ones. They agree that justice forms the basic architecture of a common life. Both covenantalism and Alinsky explicitly and implicitly accept the idea of natural law or natural rights: they agree that there are certain norms and values, such as dignity, freedom, equality, and human rights, that are universal in nature and authority, even though their historical interpretations may vary. Society cannot survive without a well-established sense of justice. Justice secures a minimal order from the threats of chaos and disorder, establishes the cooperation of society by protecting the weak and the marginalized, and serves as the basis of ongoing adjudications.

Organizing is intimately associated with justice. Justice is concerned with right individual, institutional, and social arrangements and their distribution. That is, just organizing has to do with arranging just social relationships and ensuing just distributions of authority, positions, responsibilities, and resources. One's conception of justice is deeply rooted in one's moral commitments—what one thinks the social world ought to be like.

Covenant and Alinsky alike condemn the concentration of power and unjust social arrangements. They share the observations that social injustice results from an imbalance of power, and that unchecked power inevitably becomes abusive and exploitative. Hence checks and balances are necessary to limit power and maintain a minimal standard of justice in society. Both deeply recognize that organizing is necessary to correct power imbalances, to achieve social justice, and to create the conditions for human flourishing. In their organizing, both are grassroots oriented, empowering and organizing the oppressed and downtrodden (ordinary citizens) into collective political agency.

Power Realism

In their deep awareness of human brokenness and depravity (the entrenched nature of a power structure and the selfish nature of the rich and powerful), covenantal organizing and Alinsky share a certain sense of political realism that the powerful never voluntarily give up or share their power, and hence, that some form of confrontation and conflict is inevitable to change current unjust power relationships and achieve justice (although not every form of conflict is desirable).[4]

Politics

Both understand politics as the art of life together through a fair and just organization (arrangement and distribution) of people, resources, and rights. Organizing is the heart of politics because politics is essentially concerned with the question of how to form and maintain a common life among diverse members by adjudicating their different views, interests, and claims according to the standards of justice in pursuit of the common good. Luke Bretherton notes:

> What the rules and principles of organizing define is the space of politics: that is the process through which to maintain commonality and recognize and conciliate conflict with others in the mutual pursuit of shared goods.[5]

Both covenantalism and Alinsky agree that a fair and just organizing of society is critical for human flourishing, and politics takes on that responsibility.

Democracy

Among diverse political systems, both covenantalism and Alinsky uphold (or lean toward) a democratic form of governance. This shared passion for justice, political realism, recognition of self-interest, role of communication, and grassroots orientation points toward or explicitly affirms the features and characteristics of modern democracy. As we discussed in previous chapters, the biblical idea of covenant contains radical democratic ideas and ethical motifs, and thus has made a substantial contribution to the rise of modern democracy in a creative synthesis which includes Enlightenment philosophies. Some of the covenantal ideals, in particular economic justice, are even more radical and egalitarian than modern democracy.

Covenantalism and Alinsky embrace democratic principles and values. They attempt to organize a community that is grounded in the free consent of people and by the rule of law. Both emphasize the democratic values of human dignity, freedom, and equality, while respecting associational pluralism and separation of powers. They also use dialogue and negotiation as the primary means of organizing a society. Covenantalism and Alinsky share a belief that the resolution of conflicts and differences in a democratic society should be nonviolent—a contest of ideas through persuasion and negotiation. Although Christians have often used covenant to exclude others and stooped to violence to achieve their goals, covenant, as a general principle, advocates a nonviolent means of political change.[6] Indeed, covenant institutionalizes and normalizes nonviolent resolution of conflicts through communicative exchanges, negotiations, and agreements.

Empowerment

Empowering marginalized people is central to both covenantal organizing and Alinsky's method. Their focus is on empowering people to organize themselves into a collective change agent. Organizing is employed as the mechanism of empowering the marginalized—through enhancing their internal capabilities and agencies as they organize themselves into an organization, as well as accumulating and applying collective power to confront injustices.

In addition to resistance against an unjust system, both covenantalism and Alinsky address the formation and nurturing of the agency of individuals. In covenantal and community organizing, the poor and the oppressed are not the objects of pity and charity, but the subjects of decision-making and action. Organizing offers individuals the opportunity for self-empowerment. Organizing and related activities create social capital for a community and enhance the civic capability (democratic agency) of each citizen. The gathering of people with similar concerns helps set individuals free from isolation; forming an organization toward a common purpose protects them against abusive power. Through the organizations they form, people experience a sense of empowerment as they find mutual trust and shared interests with others; they are enabled to be less dependent on experts, elites, and professionals as they stand up for their rights.

Participants learn actual democracy through various, often messy, processes of self-governance—debating their own ideas, writing their own rules, electing their own leaders, and selecting their own agendas through negotiation. People are not passive recipients of orders, aids, and services from supposed superiors, but become active subjects in their own right. They take ownership of the organization and its rules and procedures. Democratic education naturally occurs in their life in the organization. Participants learn and appreciate the role of community rules and procedures in resolving conflicts and adjudicating disputes. Through organizing they learn symbiosis, civic virtues, self-dignity, and democratic leadership.

Empowerment relies on various moral and psychological means. As we saw in previous chapters, for Christians, God plays a dramatic role in empowering people through the demonstration of God's power in exorcism and miracles. For the empowerment of people, covenantalism and Alinsky rely on a certain collective educational process that frees people from self-blame, guilt, and false consciousness (a process which Paulo Freire called "conscientization").[7] Jesus' Beatitudes and King's first speech at Holt Street Baptist Church played such an educational role, just as Alinsky relied on power analysis and social criticism. To empower people, they appeal to and bring to mind the universal values of the intrinsic worth, freedom, and equality of every person. But its goal is the same—to free people from the self-blame and guilt which typically results from their long-term internalization of oppression.

The "relational politics" of covenant and Alinsky's grassroots organizing stand in good contrast to "impersonal politics" centered on experts or technocrats.[8] While the latter is delivered from above and outside a community, the former is initiated by local people from below and inside a community. Our current malaise, along with many social pathologies, results from the displacement of relational politics by impersonal politics, which disempowers citizens.

Unity in Diversity

Both covenant and community organizing rely, implicitly or explicitly, on the principle of unity in diversity as a key mechanism in building an organization. That is, both covenant and community organizing are understood as a process of developing some form of unity out of diversity. Covenant and community organizing involve a process of coordinating the different interests of individuals to search for common interests and a common good. For covenantal organizing and Alinsky's community organizing method, respect for human dignity (basic human rights), mutual trust, reciprocity, dialogue (communication), and consensus (agreement) are important values for building an organization. While consensus and trust pertain to unity, respect for dignity and human rights helps to protect the particularity of each party. Dialogue and reciprocity are the values that mediate unity and diversity.

Unity is not understood as something externally imposed from above, but rather as something that emerges organically through a pact among members. Both models assume that genuine unity is impossible without respecting the freedom and particularity of each member as individual freedom is actualized in a society (more so for covenant). Both understand that a healthy community or organization is located within and structured by the inevitable tension between diversity and unity.

Diversity without unity is divisive and chaotic, while unity without diversity is suffocating and suppressive, typically maintained through the use of violence. Organizing balances the two and acknowledges genuine differences while searching for a workable compromise.[9] Both models understand the organizing of a community as a crucial means of overcoming the dangers of individualism and collectivism, anarchy and tyranny. That is, organizing helps control the anarchic tendency inherent in individualism even as it helps assuage the hierarchal tendency inherent in collectivism.

Civil Society

The organizing principle of unity in diversity is reflected in covenantalism's and Alinsky's embrace of the idea of civil society. Covenant, as we saw with the free-church Puritans, contributed to the rise of civil society. Given its genealogy in covenantalism, modern civil society has a federal structure. Alinsky also adopts a federalist understanding of civil society. He views civil society as the plurality and interconnection of associations competing and collaborating with each other in fulfilling a democratic vision of checks and balances.

Closely associated with their vision of civil society (and the principle of unity in diversity) is the principle of subsidiarity: a larger social organization or political body, such as the state, should not intrude on the autonomy of a smaller organization or community, but should empower and encourage their participation and contributions. Subsidiarity entails that both power and responsibility are shared among different organizations and social bodies.[10] To promote the common good, it is important for larger organizations not to negate the participation and contribution of the smaller organizations that comprise it. In covenantalism, the autonomy of smaller organizations is intrinsic and integral. That is, each consociation has sovereignty to fulfill the purpose of its creation. Although the autonomy of each organization or group should be protected, it should always be in coordination with others to enhance the common good. Society should be organized in a way to protect the smallest and lowest body from the domination of the largest. As we saw in the twelve tribes of ancient Israel, each small community has its own sovereignty and its unique contribution toward the common good.

However, thanks to its theological vision, philosophical capaciousness and balance between community building and political action, a
covenantal view of civil society (associational pluralism) and common
good is theoretically more elaborate and coherent than that of Alinsky.
It offers not only a compelling theological account of the federal structure of civil society and its institutions, but also a holistic ethical vision
for conceptualizing inter-institutional relationships in civil society—the
good of each particular institution in relation to the others in pursuing
the common good.

The common good is realized through the contributions of individual members and various institutions. The good of each sphere and
the good of society as a whole are not necessarily contradictory but cor-
roborating. The common good is partially realized through the advance
of the good of each institution. Indeed, the common good increases
through the well-being of each institution, as well as unity among diverse
social institutions, which organizing work mediates. Covenant respects
this pluralistic but harmonious nature of the common good; it affirms
"competing loyalties with the greatest possible harmony."[11]

Communication

Covenantalism and Alinsky share the insight that a community is built
upon and maintained by mutual trust and loyalty, which serves as its
glue. They take communication to be the primary means of building
trust and relationship—thus as a constitutive part of the process of organizing. This assumption is based on the premise that a good community
is built upon trusted relationships, and that trust arises through transparent communication.

There are several reasons for their shared emphasis on communication: as the basic mode of human social exchange, communication is the
most essential means of social collaboration; communication is a nonviolent means of sociopolitical engagement, which is consistent with a democratic vision of a society; and communication presumes the recognition
of the individuality and alterity of each party. At the same time, communication is a process to coordinate different ideas and interests in pursuing the common good. In other words, communication is an important
ongoing process that mediates and harmonizes unity and diversity,
binding and loosing. On the one hand, it clarifies what the respective
rights and responsibilities of each party are; on the other hand, it has
the effect of building trust and unifying partners into deeper fellowship.

Through communication, life in a community or organization becomes a reciprocal and cooperative enterprise, and that community is renewed and revitalized,[12] continuously bestowed with new energy and insight. Communication is an ongoing and open-ended process of organizing. Finally, communication embodies a democratic ethos; it rejects control and domination in interactions among the members.

Self-Interest

Both covenantalism and Alinsky recognize and affirm self-interest as an important motivating element for entering a trusted relationship with others. Following Enlightenment utilitarian rationality, Alinsky takes self-interest as a prime incentive for human political actions, while covenantalism affirms self-interest because it is a natural, indispensable aspect of human existence (since humanity as a species is inevitably concerned with survival and self-fulfillment).[13] In fact, covenant indicates a form of relationship built upon a just and fair exchange of interests between participants under God's supervision. Covenant attends to the legitimate concerns (basic rights) of each partner entering the agreement.

In covenantal organizing, the idea of self-interest and self-protection is intimately associated with the intrinsic worth and dignity of each person. It refers to a legitimate claim of persons as God's image bearers. Self-interest (or self-love) is the foundation of one's agency (a healthy exercise of selfhood) and the basis of a genuine, reciprocal relationship that covenant seeks to build. But it never endorses any attempt to seek self-interest at the expense of others. Hence, a covenantal relationship is neither excessively resistant nor excessively submissive.[14]

However, both covenantalism and Alinsky, in the final analysis, attempt to balance and negotiate the interest of self and of others according to the principles of justice; they encourage and teach people to think of self-interest in reference to others' interests in building solidarity and power base. Both assume that enduring community is possible in the context of fair, just, and reciprocal relationships. However, covenant places self-interest in a far more relational, communal, and moral framework because its ultimate goal is friendship with others.

Contextuality

Both covenantalism and Alinsky respect particular historical and social contexts where organizing takes place, because creative adaption to the vicissitudes of history and the changes of society is necessary for any effective organizing. In other words, every meaningful organizing is adaptive and contextual, while pursuing the same goal and maintaining the basic principles. Our survey in chapters 2–6 reveals that covenant adapts to different social and political contexts. God's people have interpreted and applied covenant differently in different historical and social contexts without losing its identity and theological convictions; they have addressed the question of justice in their own contexts under the same vision of shalom.[15] God's people are called to always be alert and responsive to God's voice as well as to new or changing social situations as they organize.

Similarly, Alinsky's community organizing is contextual in nature, as it attends to a particular local history, people's past experiences, community traditions, and available resources. There is no one-size-fits-all solution to human problems because each community situation is unique. Thus, organization is never a fixed entity, but requires ongoing revision and renewal. Likewise, power analysis and interpretations of justice (freedom, equality, and human rights) are never absolutely fixed, but need to be constantly discerned in specific contexts through collective deliberation among members. Hence, people always need to be alert and responsive to new or changing social situations, constantly adjusting or reinventing their tactics, methods, and strategies.[16]

Coalition

Coalition refers to diverse groups working together for their common purposes while maintaining their own distinctive identities. Alinsky welcomed the idea of coalition from the beginning and designed the IVF as a broad-based organization of multiple local organizations, because coalition is a necessary way of building and expanding the power base for people. It took a longer time for covenantalism to embrace a religious-cultural coalition.

Although some early Calvinists, modeling the theocracy of ancient Israel, rejected entering a relationship with different religious and racial groups, later generations of covenantal theologians and Martin Luther King Jr. had no difficulty in embracing the idea of coalition (or collaboration with other religious groups) on the basis of compact. Such embrace is more faithful to and consistent with the covenantal vision itself. For example, the idea of confederacy or federalism is not so different from coalition in its dynamics because both rely on the principle of unity in diversity, bonding, and bridging.[17] In coalition, a local organization is connected with other organizations while maintaining its own distinctive vocation. Community organizing relies on coalition building as one major strategy in accumulating power and enhancing political effectiveness. That is, based on covenantal theology, Puritans developed a sophisticated, pluralistic vision of a society, which gradually matured to embrace the idea of coalition with other cultural and denominational groups for the enhancement of the common good. In the work of Martin Luther King Jr., we see a mature form of such coalition building.

Compact offered a theological ground to enter a moral agreement/coalition with others. From a covenantal perspective, the Creation Covenant and the Noahic Covenant offer theological grounds for compact and coalition with non-Christians; both are inclusive covenants that God made with the representatives of all humanity (Adam and Eve, and Noah, respectively), binding the entire human population regardless of faith-response, beyond particular religious communities. The natural law refers to the stipulating norms of these covenants.[18]

On the basis of our discussion in chapter 1, one may say that coalition is theologically acceptable when recognizing that God's organizing work, His reign, takes place beyond the walls of the church. That is, the triune God is working among other religious and civic groups as well as with Christians. In building coalitions, Christians rely on the natural law and natural rights and may build a quasi-form of covenant, or compact, with different religious groups.

Summary

The discussions above show that various moral emphases and political dynamics of Alinsky's community organizing are congruent with the ethos and dynamics of covenantal organizing. Covenant and community organizing share similar political passions, moral concerns, and key features despite their different philosophical backgrounds and ideologies (one secular, the other religious).

These similarities become even more striking given the fact that Alinsky implicitly relies on the idea of pact as the core process of organizing. That is, Alinsky's community organizing is a kind of pact making, namely compacting, as his emphasis on free human consent implies. The following statement of Luke Bretherton demonstrates a striking similarity between community organizing and covenant (more accurately, a covenantal nature of community organizing), even though he never specifies "covenant" as the historical origin and framework of community organizing for Christians as this work does.

> I take the term *community* in the term "community organizing" to denote a coming together by mutual agreement of distinct institutions for a common purpose without loss of each of their specific identities or beliefs and practices. As an organization, it is consociational in structure: that is, it is a federated alliance of institutions with often divergent and conflicting beliefs and practices that nevertheless form a single union and in which authority is constituted from the consent of each participating institution rather being derived either from some preexisting or superior authority or aggregated from the votes of individuals.[19]

As we have seen, the notions of "consociation" and "federated alliance" belong to a covenantal vocabulary,[20] thus disclosing the striking similarity between community organizing and covenant. This similarity comes from the foundational insight that organizing is an indispensable aspect of a common life and politics, and the task of politics is to organize a common life according to the principles of justice.

Pacting is a democratic way of organizing a group or a community, which is implicitly presupposed in community organizing as well. Bretherton's account reveals a certain implicit covenantal thinking operating in Alinsky. Alinsky presumed some form of social contract between political leaders and citizens; the former is elected to serve the latter and thus should be held accountable by the latter. Bretherton's account also points toward the fact (possibility) that community organizing is a quasi-form of covenant.

Where does this similarity come from, then? The striking similarity between covenant and community organizing is far from coincidental. In light of the historical origins of democracy, constitutionalism, and civil society in the US, one can see a historical connection between Puritan covenantalism and Alinsky's community organizing. Harry Boyte's comment is helpful for tracing this historical connection:

> [T]he IAF melds several strands of political language and culture— populism, republicanism, and religious concerns for social justice—in a distinctive mix that helps revive the commonwealth tradition of pragmatic citizen politics, a tradition that forms a practical antidote to the abstract and idealized discussions about public life, civic virtue, and citizenship widespread today.[21]

In American history, "the commonwealth tradition" is an *alias* for a covenantal tradition that streams down from Puritan politics. As we saw in chapters 6 and 7, this affinity explains why the idea of covenant has played an important role in the rise of democracy, constitutionalism, civil society, and human rights in the modern West through the work of Puritans and free church movements, and how it influenced the rise of community organizing in the United States.

In light of the extensive kinship between covenant and community organizing, I may say that Puritan covenantalism explains the historical genealogy of community organizing. One may say that Alinsky's community organizing is a historical effect of covenantal politics in the United States (through Puritans and the free church tradition).[22] Covenantalism, in its secular form, lives to this day through community organizing, and Alinsky's community organizing is a secular, populist manifestation of covenantal politics.

Differences

While covenantalism and community organizing share many political insights and moral ideas, there are considerable differences in their respective emphases and nuances, as well as in certain assumptions of their approaches to organizing. Covenant, as the primary vehicle of God's organizing, is quintessentially theological in its foundation and approach, while Alinsky conceives organizing in a liberal democratic framework— rooted in a modernistic understanding of freedom, rationality, and self-interest. As a change-oriented pragmatic practice, community organizing does not bring any a priori metaphysical or theological assumption to politics.[23] It stresses the temporary nature of human action and decisions in changing political and social contexts.

Unlike Alinsky's view, in covenantal organizing, God is involved either as a direct partner (divine-human covenant) or an overseer (human-human covenant). Because of the theocentric basis of the covenant, human moral consensus may change but the foundational moral purpose of God remains constant.[24] While equally valuing voluntary human participation and consent, covenant is distinguished from contract by virtue of its ground in God and God's law (revealed in the Bible and the natural law). Every form of human covenant, for example, such as a Christian marriage, is limited and conditioned by the divine law; it must be consistent with and fulfill the purpose of the divine law.[25] This implies that human covenantal agreement is constrained and guided by God's law.

Hence covenant is morally far more demanding in its emphasis on and commitment to justice, sincerity, and loyalty to the newly organized relationship.[26] Technically speaking, from a covenantal perspective, community organizing (of democratic organizations and society) is an aspect of a human-human covenant under God, and in the Bible the ethics of a human-human covenant is the outworking of the divine-human covenant. That is, the divine-human covenant precedes, embeds, and guides human-human covenants. In covenant, fidelity and obligation to God is inseparably tied to fidelity and obligation to other humans and creatures; Christians are called to treat others in the way that a loving, truthful, and righteous God has treated them in Jesus Christ. God's character and actions offer a model for relating to each other. With God as overseer, covenantal partners are accountable to each other beyond their immediate interests. In covenant, one's moral obligations are specified in the stipulations of the law, but not exhausted by them. It is larger than the letter of the law. Nor is obligation confined to the immediate partners of transaction, but indirectly includes people outside the covenant. This means that public interest (or the common good) is always presupposed in covenant. The source for this care for the public is the gifted nature of our life; humans are indebted to God, other creatures, and the resources that the earth provides.

Similarly, while Alinsky focuses organizing on power accumulation to resist injustices, covenant does not stop with political interests alone. Covenant grounds organizing far more deeply and broadly than Alinsky by emphasizing the moral purpose and moral values in organizing and enactment. While in Alinsky's model people are organized around shared self-interest, in covenant people are organized not only out of self-interest, but also around shared moral values (while not excluding self-interest), in particular, love for God and care for others. In other words, in the covenant, love, along with justice, is equally a motivator for Christian participation in community organizing, because love for others is an appropriate moral response to God's initiating, unconditional love (*hesed*).

In his suspicion of grand theories and moral idealism, Alinsky was anti-ideological, and refused to offer any comprehensive vision of social organizing; his primary focus was on the change of a local community and its power relationship with ruling elites. Given its pragmatic nature, his method is useful for producing local political power, but not so much for achieving broader cultural change.[27] Boyte's observation is poignant in pointing out the limitation of democratic interest politics, including Alinsky's community organizing:

> But like conventional politics, much of grass-roots activism has spoken a thin, sometimes cynical language of narrow interests and protest detached from any enlarged social and political vision. This kind of activism also neglects the ways in which citizen politics is an art, requiring such abilities as good judgment, skillful use of power, critical thinking, imagination, and rhetoric. Interest-organizing often succeeds in particular issue fights or local struggles, but it does little to change the wider pattern of power relations in communities, nor does it affect to any significant degree the political culture. In fact citizens organizing without larger purpose simply reflect the terms of politics-as-usual.[28]

It is an open question to what extent Alinsky's method is free from the traps of narrow interests and cynicism which reproduce politics as usual, and how effective it is in transforming the broad utilitarian ethos undergirding democratic politics today.

Scope and Intensity of Community

Covenant also attends to a far broader scope, and with a far greater intensity in organizing work. Alinsky did not pay any attention to ecological concerns; his approach was anthropocentric under the influence of modernity. Yet, in the face of a deepening ecological crisis, the agenda of community organizing cannot be decided on a merely anthropocentric basis for human self-interest; it should include the wider biotic community—the sanctity of other species and their habitats.

The meaning of community in covenant is comprehensive (indeed, eschatological) and includes other species and their interests and concerns as fellow members of God's creation community. In its organizing vision, covenant includes other creatures as well (Gen 9:12–17). God's organizing expands to the earth and all its creatures.[29] In the Creator, all creatures are morally bound toward each other.

> All life on earth is kin and born to belonging. Humankind and other-kinds live into one another's lives and die into one another's deaths in relationships. Nothing is, without the other. Such is the way of "covenant." Covenantal bonds—between God and Earth, between God and humankind, between humans and one another and the rest of

life—establish, order, and sustain creation as we know it. The way of covenant, for better and worse, is the way things are.[30]

A biblical worldview contends that the human world and the natural world are interdependent. Creation is the cosmic context of human covenants; therefore, any form of community organizing that searches for a just society should take into account ecology as the biological and foundational basis of human existence. Each creature has an intrinsic value, a certain right, as a member of God's creation; such rights include access to space and resources for survival and thriving. Hence, every transaction must be examined in light of the solidarity of the entire creation in God. In the long run, this awareness makes a huge difference in our treatment of others and in building an eco-friendly community.

Balance between Community Organizing and Organizing Community

In light of our study, community organizing, broadly speaking, has two dimensions: the communal and the political, or community building and political action (political advocacy).[31] Covenant integrates these two dimensions in a more coherent manner and dialectical balance than Alinsky. The goal of covenantal organizing is not only to achieve just and fair relationships but to also build a moral community and a distinctive peoplehood among its members. This means that liberation from oppression, though necessary, is not the ultimate goal. Rather, it is just the beginning of the task of building a just, righteous, and peaceful community that fulfills God's original intention for humanity.

For Alinsky, community organizing focuses on political action—the strategic activity of organizing and mobilizing people for political change. The goal is to correct unjust power relationships by organizing and building up people to enhance collective agency and power. In other words, organizing of community is more instrumental than intrinsic; the political triumphs over the communal. Alinsky understands "community" primarily as a sociological (empirical) entity, a local neighborhood rather than a normative one. However, this community dimension is more crucial today to counter the erosive effects of neoliberalism, the mobility of globalization, and the fluidity of communication technology, as we discussed in the introduction. In this highly mobile, fragmenting, contractual society, this communal dimension (along with the formation of moral character and virtue of community members) cannot be taken for granted anymore. While Alinsky imagined local community organizing as the backbone of a vibrant democracy, Alinsky's community organizing, for its success, requires healthy, enduring communities and viable civic institutions. Local communities and civic organizations serve as the primary loci and means of Alinsky's political organizing. As discussed above, local communities and civic organizations are indispensable for democracy. All successful community organizing presupposes the existence of some functional communities, or their networks, together with individual members who are concerned for justice and the well-being of their communities.

To put it plainly, while it may sound tautological, the organizing of a community is the foundation for community organizing. A community provides many things for individuals—a sense of belonging and identity, basic care, and a sense of security and protection. A normative, communal dimension of a community is important not only to expand the ethical scope of organizing, but also to increase the effectiveness of community organizing. A communal vision, such as the beloved community or shalom, may play a crucial role in organizing people as it provides a common goal and moral reference point for participants. It is useful to facilitate and strengthen coalitions with other groups for the common good, as we saw in King's Civil Rights Movement. Since the various social pathologies (e.g., addiction, suicide, depression, anxiety) that we experience today make organizing a far more challenging task, the organizing or renewal of a community is a primary, antecedent task of political organizing (as in Jesus' time).

Love, Justice, Power

This communal nature of covenantal organizing is better elaborated in terms of the triad of love, justice, and power. Covenantal organizing is different from Alinsky's organizing because of its harmonizing balance of love, justice, and power. That is, while Alinsky stresses justice and power in his community organizing, covenant emphasizes love as much as justice and power. Covenant seeks not only a just order through a system of checks and balances, but also a community of love.

Alinsky did not emphasize love as the explicit goal or value of community organizing because he was wary of the dangers of moral idealism and romanticism associated with love, which often confuses issues of justice and undermines the militancy of struggle.[32] Although he did not understand community organizing in a purely utilitarian, tactical, and pragmatic manner (as community organizing operates within a democratic framework and upholds the freedom, dignity, and equality of each person), this moral dimension was not always adequately emphasized, but it was overshadowed by its pragmatic concerns and interests.[33]

There is tension and ambiguity between morality (democratic values) and political utilitarianism in Alinsky's work, which becomes more evident in his later years. For example, in his book *The Rule of Radicals*, Alinsky tends to glorify victory, without any hesitancy about the utilitarian usage of power tactics to achieve it.[34] An instrumental view of power triumphs over a relational dimension. It is difficult to find moral coherence between antagonizing and compromising with adversaries. While committed to democratic values and principles, his tactics are mostly utilitarian in nature, which is further amplified when winning a political struggle is upheld as the final goal of organizing.

Why is "love" important? It has to do with basic human nature and desire: humans are social in nature and seek not only self-interest but also enduring relationship, trust, and affection with others. Organizing people (formation of a community) is political in nature. It includes the recognition and distribution of power; it requires certain rules for the use of power and interactions among people. However, organizing a community entails more than the just distribution and arrangement of power and the rule of justice. It pursues a shared goal, a common identity, and unity—a form of love. While immediately expressed in the form of compassion and care for others, in one way or another, the question of love is always involved in politics. A good organization or community has both enforceable (laws, community procedures, and standards) and unenforceable (trust, affection, and care among the members) dimensions. Alinsky does not disregard the latter dimension in internal organizing, but neither does he elaborate on it any further.

With love, covenant is more than a fair exchange or respect of rights; it calls for unlimited commitment and self-sacrifice. Love specifies, deepens, and solidifies this reciprocal, cooperative relationship to a new level. When a society loses this quality, it becomes litigious, competitive, indifferent, impatient, and cruel.

One major difference between Alinsky and covenantalism is the latter's scope of political imagination, with love at its heart. Justice is necessary but not sufficient for the proper functioning of a political community. While correcting injustices (putting things right) is crucial, love is also needed to make righted relationships more wholesome in mutual respect and care. Only love and forgiveness can bring restoration to previously alienated relationships.[35] The norm of love is politically relevant because love makes everyday relationships more than cold transactions.

As Reinhold Niebuhr espoused, it is a permanent moral challenge to bring the dimension of love to politics. One cannot be naïve about the reality of power and human nature, but love is still relevant to politics. Politics as the art of symbiosis requires the recognition and adjudication of diverse claims of self-interest as well as some form of self-sacrifice for the causes of justice and the common good, which are not separable from self-interest (in the form of deferred long-term self-interest). To link self-interest to self-sacrifice requires a creative moral imagination. Many community organizers in the post-Alinsky era are aware of this limitation of Alinsky's protest-based, populist orientation. Harry Boyte observes:

> IAF groups believe that it is not sufficient to simply protest; to 'move into power' on a continuing basis in the modern world, citizens must also assume an important measure of responsibility for the basic public goods of their community.[36]

Hence, even in the process of confrontation and struggle, love for others should never be forgotten or forfeited, but must always guide every action. As King's movement demonstrated, love changes the tone of protest and prevents participants from overly relying on instrumentalism and violence. God's demand of love prevents us from uncritically resorting to instrumentalization of others for self-success. If democracy is a system that normalizes nonviolence over violence through voting, discourse, and negotiation, then love and justice are crucial in dealing with power. Without a deep concern for others and the common good, self-interest (even if "enlightened") results in a highly litigious, contentious democracy, as we see in US politics today. Jesus' love ethic, often dismissed as unrealistic, has political relevance as it transcends the binary of the oppressor and the oppressed.[37]

Justice includes punishment for violations and retribution for harms and damages, but because of its intrinsic relation to love, justice also restores, reconciles, and redeems in a covenantal framework. It aims at community building rather than sheer assertion of individual rights. Without love, justice can be legalistic, contractual, and ultimately divisive and conflictual.

In today's individualistic and competitive cultural environment, it is not so easy to maintain the dialectic balance between love, justice, and power. That is why a clear social vision and sophisticated ethic such as covenantalism—that connects vision, values, and actions—is important. In covenantal organizing, power becomes relational rather than instrumental, love is communal rather than sentimental, philanthropic, or paternal, justice is relational and restorative rather than monolithic and punitive. Embedded in a covenantal framework, a Christian exercise of power is communal rather than instrumental in nature. Communal power strives toward building a just community. It presupposes the fundamental solidarity of humanity and the dignity of each person, including one's enemies. It is neither unilateral nor coercive; it is characterized by its good will and active openness toward the other (thus keeping the conditions of communication open to others) without being naïve or romantic, or compromising the principle of justice.[38]

Moral Agency and Organizing

The organizing of moral agency is an urgent concern today in order to confront and address metastasizing injustices as well as the fragmenting power of "liquid modernity."[39] While rightly credited for developing a method for citizen protest and political change, Alinsky faces limitations in addressing widespread democratic impoverishment in a neoliberal society, visible in the erosion of community, agency, and character.[40] Covenantal organizing addresses this challenge of eroding agency and wider democratic impoverishment more effectively than Alinsky. Thanks to its thoroughly relational orientation, it touches on not only the behavioral but also the psychological and emotional aspects of organizing. For example, God's love experienced in one's life frees one from the fear, insecurity, and anxiety that impacts one's use of power. Jesus' ministry of exorcism and healing offers a necessary window into the psychological and emotional impact of oppression on individual lives. To sustain one's struggle against injustice, inner freedom from the long-standing damage of oppression is necessary. Worship rituals and communal practices contribute to the formation of a community and the agency of its people.

In various ways, one's covenant relationship with God has identity-shaping power. One's identity is less a matter of some underlying substance (what one is) than a characteristic of one's relationships with others (who one is).[41] The ideas of election and calling, which are closely associated with covenant in the Bible, are directly related to a person's identity formation. Being elected means being called, and being called includes finding a new missional identity in God. To state it differently, personal identity and vocation are largely a function of one's covenantal response to the God who elects and calls. Likewise, for Christians, worship, fellowship, and communal practices are occasions where identity, agency, and virtue are formed and nurtured.

Value Orientation

Because of its balance between communal and political orientations, covenant is more value-oriented than Alinsky, emphasizing the value of the education of its members. Alinsky tends to focus on skill-based education, such as power analysis, mapping local communal traditions, studying community issues, articulation of self-interest, agitation, and protest. Boyte speaks of the limitation of Alinsky's pragmatic orientation:

> The mistake of the first forty years of Alinsky's organizing was the absence of political education. We were very good at the action, very clever and imaginative, but we didn't make a commitment to the growth process of the people. We never forced people to reflect. We never took retreats, or did extensive evaluation.[42]

One new development in the post-Alinskian generation of community organizers is the awareness and necessity of ongoing self-reflection and education about the basic principles and foundations of democracy—the theory of popular sovereignty, rights, accountability in the use of power, civil society and mediating structures, justice, the nature of public life, diversity, participation, civic actions, concern for the poor, governance—in short, the theory of democratic life.[43] This development points toward the increasing convergence and complementarity of Alinsky's community organizing and covenantal organizing around democracy, human rights, citizenship, and responsible governance.

Balance between Protest and Governance

In its balance between community organizing and political organizing, covenant offers a far more conceptually coherent and organic understanding of the relationship between governance and grassroots organizing, while Alinsky tends to emphasize the latter far more than the former.

As a comprehensive philosophy of organizing, covenant offers a plausible, encompassing theoretical framework that integrates this grassroots resistance and the just governance of democracy—the work of justice from below and from above—in balance.[44] Covenant not only engages in a liberative endeavor toward a just society, but also offers a just structure of governance. As we saw in the example of the Puritans, covenant ethics developed a plausible, sophisticated theory of governance including the rule of law, constitution, republicanism, and proper distribution of authority, power, and resources.

Governance is an integral part of the enactment and implementation of covenant and its stipulations. As we studied, covenant includes a liberative attempt to correct injustices and to create more just and egalitarian social conditions for a common life; however, once imbalances are corrected and a new community is formed (or renewed), then the members of a community are called to live out their obligations as responsible parties of the covenant. Both members and their governmental representatives are held equally accountable for the implementation of the agreed-upon obligations.

One topic on which covenantal organizing differs from Alinsky is its emphasis on the rule of law. Alinsky, while, considering democracy to be the best available political system, did not offer much discussion on the rule of law and the question of how to maintain a good social order. Rather than offering any elaborated theory of the rule of law, Alinsky just accepted the rule of law as a given, integral part of democracy. His concern was far more on how to change the law—the subversive, grassroots side of democracy—rather than governance. However, this strength is also his weakness. Democracy relies on the rule of law, and good governance solves many problems. In real politics, we cannot underestimate the importance of just legislation, as we saw in the Civil and Voting Rights bills in the United States.

In covenantal organizing, grassroots organizations are not the only forces that exercise checks and balances against the potential abuse of power. The Constitution and the rule of law in a democratic legal system also play a crucial role in democracy by restricting concentrated power. In a democratic society, it would be ludicrous, even irresponsible, not to use established democratic processes, legal systems, and electoral politics to achieve better justice. The ultimate goal of organizing is to build a sustained, just society, which occurs through the organizing of fair regulations, the just restructuring of social relationships, and the clear communication of rights, goods, and services under the rule of law.

The emphasis on the rule of law in covenant is closely associated with justice; the rule of law is supposed to embody concretely the principle of justice as the regulative basis of social relationships. Humans organize and order their personal and social lives guided by certain rules and principles of justice.

The rule of law is indispensable to maintaining a democratic system. Under the rubric of covenantal organizing, it institutionalizes the structured restraints on rulers when achieving and implementing justice. A good democratic structure offers a legal basis for preventing tyranny and removing an abusive or incompetent ruler (president) by the representatives of the people (Congress), when needed. Serving as the minimal requirement of justice and social order, the rule of law is necessary for the stability and predictability of social interactions; it prevents mutual destruction and procures minimal conditions for self-fulfillment.

Summary

A covenantal political imagination is more comprehensive and encompassing than Alinsky's method of community organizing. Its understanding of self-interest, its triad of power, justice, and love, its attention to civil society, and its dialectic emphasis on the relationship of resistance and governance are more nuanced and balanced, just as its scope is broader and more ecologically sensitive. Also, in dealing with the concentration of power, covenant offers a far more comprehensive and deeper understanding of the abuse of power by locating it in human fallenness, and offers a mechanism to address it through religious rituals (repentance and confession of sins). It compels us to wrestle with the dark side of humanity. From this covenantal social imagination, democracy, civil society, human rights, and justice receive a deeper moral ground, an expansive democratic vision, and an inexhaustible source of organizing motivation and energy.

Given its extensive affinity, covenant has no major difficulty in embracing the methods of community organizing,[45] such as power analysis, one-on-one meetings, small group discussion, co-deliberation, and confrontation. The specific application of these practices simply needs to be carefully discerned in terms of its consistency with the moral vision and norms of the covenant. Various techniques of community organizing can be adopted in a Christian context for the church's prophetic ministry. The example of Martin Luther King Jr.'s campaign compellingly demonstrates that covenant can embrace Alinsky's pragmatic tactics without compromising its covenantal convictions and principles. King worked within a democratic system and extensively used organizing methods similar to Alinsky's while appealing to the Bible and the norms and values of the nation's foundational documents. This affinity between covenant and Alinsky's methods also explains why a disproportionately large number of churches have been attracted to community organizing.

The two are not only compatible but also complementary to a large extent. While community organizing adds to covenant theology political practicality and pragmatism, covenant provides a comprehensive social vision, a high moral purpose, and deep, enduring moral values and communal practices for forming and nurturing moral agency. Covenant theology can help clarify and reconceptualize the values, strategies, and methods of community organizing; community organizing can be strengthened in the framework of covenant. Covenant offers a social vision that helps to place Alinsky's community organizing in a broader, deeper, and more enduring theistic basis. Community organizing may find in the covenant a clearer vision and more coherent tie between the goal and the method.

On the other hand, Alinsky's method can bring street wisdom and practicality in handling power players such as government officials and corporate managers. Alinsky's methods of one-on-one, power analysis, small group deliberation, coalition building, and tactics of agitations and confrontations are much-needed skills for actual grassroots political activists seeking to implement the vision of the kingdom and its justice. It offers a pragmatic method to translate the kingdom organizing of Jesus into democratic practices of building trust, confrontation, negotiation, disruption, and compromise for the progress of a common life.

Alinsky challenges Christians to take their prophetic criticism to a next level, that of concrete political actions. As John Bowlin, ethics professor at Princeton Theological Seminary, comments, community organizing helps future pastors recognize that

> [C]harismatic leadership and sermonic performance require actual organizing to be effective. The popular, if mistaken notion, is that prophetic preaching can generate social change on its own, that rhetorical power is sufficient and gets things done . . . [detached from an actual community organizing work and agenda] the words generate good feelings, but nothing changes in the world.[46]

Developed against the grain of political realism and corruptible human nature, Alinsky's method compels Christians to think seriously about power analysis and civic engagement, and to address the hidden or ongoing injustices (notably racism, sexism, and classism) in society, with which churches themselves are complicit. Alinsky's method reminds us of the grassroots nature of the church's ministry.

Alinsky urges Christians to think beyond the walls of the sanctuary, and to confront the real concerns and issues of their community. It is Alinsky's key insight that charity and prophetic criticism alone are not sufficient. Collective actions make a difference in forcing the powerful to change. Alinsky challenges Christians not only to speak against the powerful, but also to act collectively against them, to move beyond individual pietism and sectarianism, speculative theology, and actionless prophetic social criticism in order to engage in the actual lives of the poor, confront abusive powers, and be part of a community newly emerging from the grassroots. This is not a small contribution.

The incorporation of Alinsky's method into covenantal organizing can be productive for the Christian ministry of social change, as it enhances political effectiveness. With this incorporation, covenantal organizing is equipped to integrate a cosmic vision with a practical method of political praxis. From a Christian perspective, Alinsky's community organizing is a secular form of the grassroots praxis of covenantal organizing, which is useful in righting unjust relationships in a local community, while covenant is a theological ethic of community organizing. Put differently, Alinsky's method can be understood as a Christian ministry practice that applies covenant organizing on a daily grassroots level—working closely with local people by watching and assessing how corporations, political elites, and elected officials live up to their pledges and responsibilities.

This compatibility and complementarity do not mean that Christians will not experience any tension with Alinsky's method. The tension between the Christian moral ideal of love and the political pragmatism of Alinsky (including his confrontational tactics and strategies) is inevitable. Hence, it is necessary for Christians to discern carefully in every concrete situation what is acceptable and what is not based on the gospel.

8

Covenantal Organizing Today

The Fight against Neoliberal Capitalism

"If money is the bond binding me to human life, binding society to me, binding me and nature and man, is not money the bond of all bonds? Can it not dissolve and bind all ties? Is it not, therefore, the universal agent of separation?"[1]

This book has studied covenant as a comprehensive Christian philosophy of social organizing, presenting the triune God as a grand organizer who uses covenant in organizing creation into the shalom community. Covenant embodies God's organizing vision most perfectly, directly bearing upon God's *oikonomia*—the management of God's *oikos*, the planet.

Organizing creation and the people of God is the running motif of the Bible. It is always associated with covenant, with the Exodus-Sinai story as its prototype. In particular, this book identified liberation-reconstruction as the overarching narrative pattern of covenant in God's organizing of His people. In general, God's covenantal organizing has three distinct stages: judgment (deliverance/liberation from chaos or injustice), formal consent, and building an alternative community. Inextricably interrelated, the three stages constitute the overarching paradigm of God's organizing of a community of shalom.

God organizes God's people (community) through God's love, justice, and power, and covenant constitutes a structure of relationship where one's exercise of power is delineated (channeled) under the moral guidance of justice (embodied in the divine and moral law) in seeking fellowship with God and others. Relying on this pattern, we examined the role of covenant as an organizing principle against various oppressive forces in different historical and social contexts: Egypt, Roman Empire, Old England, and the segregated South of the United States (two in biblical contexts, two in the post-biblical era). These four examples of covenantal organizing demonstrate the plausibility and attractiveness of God's covenantal organizing. This survey demonstrates the potency (efficacy) of covenant as the theologically informed practical principle of community organizing. Closely connected with God's moral character, work, and agency (deliverance of the oppressed and the needy), covenant evokes and discharges strong egalitarian and liberative ethos and energy. Through its liberative impetus and embedded remembrance of God's deliverance, covenant constantly calls for the reworking of social relationships and the redistribution of power and resources.

Our survey proves that covenant is the "firm but flexible framework for political change."[2] It is creatively adaptive to different social and political contexts; it acts as an organizing principle for a theocratic society (such as ancient Israel, in which one religion dominated), for a minority religious community (as in the early church), or a religiously pluralistic society (as in Martin Luther King Jr.'s movement) where democratic ideals and values are not actualized. These different adaptations (applications) reflect the power-difference (political realism) and theological agenda of a covenantal community in particular historical and social situations. We need to carefully discern what is possible and what is realistic as well as what is normative. In this context, the book also studied the affinity, difference, and complementariness between covenantal organizing and Alinsky's community organizing, while suggesting the latter as a secular manifestation of a covenantal tradition in the United States.

What are the implications of this study for a current society in desperate need of major reorganizing today? What would covenantal organizing look like today? How does covenantal organizing address current social, political, and economic situations? How could it address the four interlocked crises of community, agency, democracy (justice), and global order? How does it equip Christians to address current challenges? To address all these questions in a thorough manner would require another book.[3] And there could be several different ways to approach these challenges. However, at least for Christians, it is my claim that covenantal organizing, especially by incorporating Alinsky's pragmatic insights and techniques, points toward a plausible direction to fight neoliberal oligarchy and address the four interlocked challenges without imposing its religious view upon others.[4] In a creative and synthetic way, covenantal organizing addresses the challenge of organizing at multiple levels.

The Effects of Neoliberalism

As mentioned in the introduction, a major threat to democracy and human rights comes from unrestrained neoliberalism that utilizes globalization and the advance of communication technology for its own advantage. Neoliberalism is "a theory of political economic practices that proposes that human wellbeing can best be advanced by liberating individual entrepreneurial freedoms and skills within an institutional framework characterized by strong private property rights, free markets, and free trade."[5]

Over the last several decades, defying national boundaries and political ideologies (democracy, socialism) and transcending religious-cultural differences, neoliberal capitalism has globally expanded its reign. Through its ideology of endless material success (and the promise of all accompanying pleasures), neoliberalism has been successful in legitimating its control and political agenda not only as a dominating economic system but also as a new global metanarrative ("there is no alternative" [TINA]) in place of socialism and Keynesianism. Neoliberals use various non-economic methods and tactics (e.g., political, ideological, and psychological) to promote their agenda. Beyond its sheer economic genius and potency, much of the neoliberal agenda's success has come through influencing legislation through lobbying, maneuvering policy making, manipulating human desires, and controlling media that has become available due to the deregulation of telecommunication laws. For example, cross-selling, cross-promotion, and privileged access to information at the exclusion of others have been standard operating procedures.[6]

> We are not dealing with a paper tiger. Tremendous power is concentrated in the hands of an unaccountable few. Capital's mobility destroys neighborhoods and regions by disinvestment or gentrification; undermines union organization with threats to relocate and barely regulated intimidation; fosters destructive competition between ethnic, racial, native, immigrant, age, and gender groups; and plays local, state, and national governments against one another in efforts to create "union-free" low wage, low tax, low regulation environments. The Reagan revolution made government and the civil service enemies rather than tools for the common good.[7]

The neoliberal reign has become increasingly totalizing with its tentacles on every realm of our social life—politics, education, media, academia, family, and so on.

Thus, the four crises are closely, if not exclusively, associated with the operation and destructive effects of neoliberal capitalism riding on the shoulders of globalization and advance of communication and transportation technologies. Its crude materialism (hedonism) contributes to the erosion of agency and community and the decaying of democracy; it has been moving resources and power to the rich few by taking advantage of the mobility of communication technology (the Internet) and is void of the checks and balances needed in a global society. Let's examine the contribution of the neoliberal economy to the four crises in further detail.

Democracy

Corporations exercise enormous influence on political processes (e.g., policies, debates, and elections) and control over the media, resulting in the demise of democratic values and institutions. Under its oligarchic control, the democratic system of checks and balances has broken down over the years. People know that liberal democracy, turned into a house maiden of neoliberalism, is now controlled by money. More and more important decisions are made without the participation of people who are excluded from big decision-making processes, their voices shut out on matters affecting their survival and livelihoods.

Neoliberalism is increasingly monopolistic and even anti-meritocratic, serving the rich rather than the middle class and the poor; it has failed to produce fair outcomes for most people. If we carefully examine the operation of neoliberalism, we recognize that it has craftily removed various checks and balances, bent laws for its benefit, and created loopholes. It has bought experts, technocrats, and scholars to perpetuate its ideology of freedom and meritocracy. Using their enhanced power, neoliberals have changed the laws of the nation and international society to their advantage, making fair competition and social mobility difficult, and resulting in an enormous concentration of power in a remarkably few rich people. Rules are skewed and bent for the rich and their children. The actual income of the middle class has stagnated or declined over the decades; most young people do not think their future will be better than their parents'.

The triumph of neoliberalism has led to the loss of the autonomy and credibility of various liberal institutions (academia, media, churches, unions, think tanks, etc.), and their experts, professionals, and institutional leaders.[8] The profit motif, competition for success, and professional careerism which is attracted to or rewarded by wealth, power, and pleasure, have severely undermined the integrity and mission of institutions as well as the professionalism and vocation of individuals. Out of self-preservation or careerism, these institutions bought into the neoliberal promises of material wealth, comfort, and security. As a result, they have lost their power to check and balance corporate power.

> [I]nequality is dangerous for liberal democracy. And the dangers are self-perpetuating: disparities of wealth make it difficult to organize countervailing powers, and the absence of countervailing powers makes for increasingly radical disparities. The long-term effect of this process, the characteristic product of radical inequality, is tyranny in everyday life: the arrogance of the wealthy, the humbling of the poor.[9]

As a result, liberal democracy and its institutions (such as the rule of law and the free media), together with economic meritocracy, are now being discredited, and more and more ordinary citizens feel alienated, abandoned, and angry. People are restless and angry and want a major change in our political system.

Community and Agency

The ideology and practices of neoliberalism have a huge disintegrating effect on community and individuals. Institutions are market-centered (by adopting a corporate management style), and relationships are contractualized; every entity is commodified, and every major decision calculated in monetary terms. It turns citizens into consumers, establishes techniques to create new habits of self-indulgence, promotes individual material achievements and self-gratification, and contributes to the undermining of political agency and civic virtue. Karl Marx seems right in saying that capitalism melts everything that it touches. Hence, neoliberalism makes the tasks of organizing and sustaining long-term relationships difficult.

Global Order

The opening of national borders after the collapse of the Soviet Union and popular availability of communication and transportation technologies have allowed corporations not only to move their financial capital instantaneously at various market speculations but to coordinate and integrate their businesses activities in multiple sites and locations. However, the mobility of financial capital and corporations means the weakening of the negotiating power of the state and labor unions against corporations.

Exploiting the fixity of the state whose jurisdiction is restricted to its territory, corporations, in particular financial banks and Multi-National Corporations (MNCs), are defeating the best efforts of many governments to regulate them. That is, relying on their mobility, corporations have increased negotiating power and exercise their veto power over state policies on taxation, environment, and labor. Corporations look for countries and locations with little or no environmental and labor regulation in addition to high tax breaks. They threaten to relocate their factories and offices when their demands are not met. Unfortunately, states comply and make deregulatory concessions to corporations. Corporations now compete to the top for market control and to the bottom for more profits.[10]

With the spread of globalization, the past several decades have witnessed a shift toward global corporate oligarchy, in which a select number of corporate leaders and policymakers of rich nations are endowed with decision-making power over the common matters of humanity and transnational affairs without any transparency or accountability to the public.

We need to rearrange the current political economy in a far more equitable and just way. The current liberal democratic form of globalization is skewed to protect MNCs, and benefits the rich at the expense of billions of ordinary people and non-human species. Its vision is so thin and abstract and individualistic that it cannot offer any meaningful structure or worldview of life together. Humanity has already experienced the devastating consequences of such unfair international arrangements through two world wars. We are hitting the same wall again. Without our innovating and enhancing grassroots democracy in the global community, this elitist, oligarchic practice will continue wreaking havoc on the biotic world and poor countries.

In summary, the four crises we experience today are closely associated with neoliberal capitalism. Hence, addressing the four interlocked crises is necessary to fight back against the neoliberal oligarchy reigning in our society.

Responses to the Four Crises

The current status quo cannot be sustained. It is clear that we need to radically resist neoliberalism and develop a different, alternative political economy and social system. Politics are never separate from economy. If economy (competition and meritocracy) is not fair, then the politics that support the economy are also unfair. It is naïve for politicians to believe democracy will remain intact under this unfair arrangement of economy.

It seems that our political system cannot reform itself. We cannot sit around or assume that things will get better. In fact, things could get worse if we do not take action, as we have done in the past decades. We need more than criticism and populist anger. Jeffrey Stout observes:

> Loosely grouped liberals are doing some good. They express their qualms about the status quo mainly by casting votes, attending occasional rallies, signing petitions, and donating money to agencies like Oxfam and Amnesty International. Such acts have good effect. But they will never succeed in overturning plutocracy and militarism. The liberals' aversion for strong ties hampers them.[11]

Going one step beyond criticism, we need grassroots organizing. Only massive public pressure can coerce politicians to listen to the voice of Main Street, not Wall Street. We need democratic renewal and the reweaving of civil society. We need democracy in the economic realm as well as in the political.

What can we do? It becomes evident that only grassroots organizing that resists neoliberalism and builds a new alternative society is the answer to the current crisis. Toward this end, I believe that covenantal organizing offers valuable insights and constructive directives to fight against neoliberalism. Covenantal organizing offers an empowering vision, complex social imagination, and effective political tools for the struggle. The organizing power of covenant is not only in its vision, rules, and values, but its coherence and comprehensiveness (encompassing nature), which addresses organizing at multiple levels (personal, communal or institutional, societal, global). That is to say, covenantal organizing offers a comprehensive vision and method of organizing—both for individual institutions and society as a whole. Specifically, in coping with the totalistic power of neoliberalism, covenantal organizing is capable of addressing the four crises mentioned in the introduction: the renewal of community and individuals, democracy (reweaving of civil society and its institutions), and global ordering. This point is important, because as neoliberalism's reign is totalistic, the answer or the alternative should be comprehensive without being totalistic, addressing the four realms of agency, community, democracy (politics), and global order.

First and foremost, covenantal organizing aims at a systematic change of political economy, not a change of political leaders alone. Covenantal organizing envisions radical democracy and inclusive politics not only in electoral politics but also in the economic realm. Covenantalism pays constant attention to the poor (widows, orphans) in organizing a social system. The biblical vision of Jubilee and Sabbath economics defends economic rights. Covenantalism claims that every member of humanity deserves basic material benefits to protect their dignity. Meeting the basic needs of covenant members was God's fundamental demand to those in a covenantal relationship with God. Scripture teaches that without basic economic security, justice and the beloved community are impossible. Scripture strongly condemns the system that perpetuates poverty and inequality. Protection of basic economic rights is the precondition of citizenship and democratic participation. Cancellation of debts offers a fresh start for the indebted and restores them as meaningful members of a community. Acts 4:34-35 speaks of, if not common possession, then some kind of common fund to subsidize the poor, pay for the burial of members, and/or buy freedom from slavery.[12]

The pattern of judgment and reconstruction (resistance-alternative) found in covenantal organizing is fruitful in critiquing neoliberalism and in casting an alternative—a more just and compassionate vision of a society. In organizing a new community, covenantal organizing operates through the two-phase pattern of deorganizing and reorganizing, liberation and reconstruction, resistance and alternative. The former has to do with the criticism of injustice, exploitation, and oppression, while the latter has to do with the just ordering of a new society by introducing new laws, rituals, and communal practices. As the former necessarily includes grassroots political organizing and collective struggles against oppressive forces, a new peoplehood and polity arises as the result of reorganizing. In summary, various principles and methods of covenantal organizing—grassroots organizing (including coalition building based on the principle of unity in diversity), commitment to justice, human dignity, democracy, power analysis, and various tactics of confrontations and agitations—are useful in our fight against neoliberal oligarchy.

Community

As our local communities, institutions, and civil society undergo fragmentation under the pressure of distrust, egoism, and mobility, a covenantal approach of organizing is useful in reorganizing them. Covenant is a collaborative, artful work that intends to build a just community according to the principle of unity in diversity. Inherently critical of the concentration of power into one person or one class, covenant denotes a just and righteous structure of a community built upon mutual trust and fairness with shalom as its goal. It is not grounded in biological affinity but in the free consent of people. Covenant envisions a society where people "live free while being bound together in appropriate relationships."[13] It offers several critical ethical parameters of organizing: gratitude as a default disposition of life (recognition of the gifted nature of human existence), compassion that flows from such a disposition, transparent, truthful, and active communication among members, commitment to the principles of justice, and nonviolent engagement and consent (agreement) as a tool of community formation. Covenantal organizing, in my view, uniquely and seamlessly combines these elements and implements them through its communal practices.

Covenantal organizing (and Alinsky) reminds us that a good and vibrant community requires the constant work of organizing and ordering of a social life through inclusive, truthful, transparent, and caring communication and exchanges among its members. Covenant offers the enduring structure and channel for such communications and exchanges and the practices of renewal for a community.

Various practices of covenant and community organizing help to thicken our sociality and strengthen the relational fabric of society. Alinsky's techniques of one-on-one, small group meetings, and praxis of education contribute to nurture trust and strengthen ties and bonds among participants, which leads to the building of an organization. Some of Alinsky's practices are helpful for community building within the church as they enhance trust, intimacy, and relationship building among the members. These methods aim at strengthening the bond among the members. Getting to know each other, sharing personal stories (passion, pain, anger, and desires), and learning how to identify common objectives and potential areas of conflict are useful and necessary skills for a healthy church, and applicable to members' families and work places as well.

As well-known in liturgical studies and anthropology, liturgy, or *leitourgia*, has organizing power; it serves as the means to transform individuals into a new corporate entity. For Christians, the Eucharist together with baptism, as the central liturgical practice of the Church, contribute to the organizing of a community by interweaving individuals into the same body of Christ with the same story, memory (*anamnesis*), and mission. His broken body and shed blood symbolize God's kingdom community that Jesus organized around his life, death, and resurrection. Gathered around the one table, people are united by participating in his body. Reminding us of our new identity and membership in God's community (bonded in the blood of Jesus Christ), the Eucharist nurtures the communal spirit by reversing our tendency to ruthless competition, endless accumulation/possession, and stratifying of people according to power, privilege, and status. By sitting at one table together, participants are reminded that they are all free, equal, and one with each other. David Fitch writes, "We must tend to [Christ's] presence because his presence always brings reordering of our lives together into his kingdom. This is what makes this table so revolutionary at the core; here God shapes a people to be his kingdom in the world."[14]

Ongoing fellowship and discursive practices in a covenant community can refurbish community with new moral energy and cultivate social capital by gradually turning a contractual relationship into a covenantal one. Covenantal organizing (or something similar, like compactual organizing) is promising today in response to the demise of traditional communities and weakening of the nation-state and spread of materialism. Many people are experimenting with small, open forms of community centered on diverse issues, interests, and concerns, and are organized out of practical necessity (saving resources) or relational aspirations. These new communities are not purely natural (blood-oriented), but artificial, with some enduring bonds and commitments. They tend to be organizationally horizontal, democratic, grassroots-based, ecologically conscious, and globally minded.

Formed with the habits of organizing (entrusting, truthful communication, and compassion) in their own churches and homes, Christians may engage their own workplaces and neighbors. However, in organizing a community, we should not work in a tribalistic, ethnocentric way, but in an open, inclusive way that fits with the reality of global interconnectedness and interdependence.

Agency

Covenantal organizing helps to restore agency through various means of communal practices, such as worship, fellowship, and community actions. Among its several mechanisms of agency-formation, I want to briefly discuss the role of worship in organizing Christian lives and shaping agency.

Worship personally and communally connects people to God's organizing work. Although not solely restricted to it, Christian communion/communication with God occurs in the most explicit, focused manner in worship. Divine intimacy experienced through worship and prayer matters for political activism and struggles. Worship and political action (justice work) are not contradictory. They are simply different sites of God's organizing. Worship is a political act of kingdom. It has immense political potential and implications.

Worship as an integral aspect of covenantal organizing addresses the structural and psychological (objective and subjective) conditions of the oppressed. As we see in examples from the early followers of Jesus or African American churches, through worship, people experience self-affirmation of worth and healing in personal and interpersonal relationships. For Christians, the struggle for justice is rooted in intimate, mystical communion with the triune God.[15] The struggle for justice is empowered by God's love and grace. Worship enhances the sense of unity among the participants, renewing their sense of purpose, hope, and solidarity. Worship has power to renew and empower moral agency. It is the occasion of the reorienting and reorganizing of people by the triune God. Worship helps to redirect people's energies for higher moral purposes and causes.

Covenantal organizing does not separate worship and ethics. The biblical narratives of the Exodus, the crucifixion, and the resurrection inspire people to envision a just society. Sermons, rituals, and aesthetics excite, energize, and sustain people in a political struggle with deep religious imaginations, dramatic stimulation, and motivating power. Whenever worship happens, the memory of God's deliverance (such as the Exodus and the death and resurrection of Jesus) and the hope of shalom are refreshed and rekindled; people are challenged and empowered for the organizing work of love and justice.

Worship offers an opportunity for personal, intimate, and mystic communication (fellowship and union) with God and others in the power of the Spirit. Christians drink from the deep well of the Trinity (Fellowship of the Fountain), sustained by the sweet communion of their brothers and sisters. Through worship, people continue to draw sustenance and support from God to grow and mature to their fullest potential as God's kingdom organizers in the various spheres of life where they are called to serve. However, such agency does not have to be myopic or ethnocentric or narrowly fundamentalist. It could also expand vision and deepen convictions, civility, and compassion toward others. Personal moral convictions and imaginations nurtured in Christian communities matter for social change. As we see in numerous historical examples, such as Dorothy Day, Iris Wells, Martin Luther King Jr., César Chávez, and Hannah More's work of abolitionism, Christian conviction could be vital for sustaining a social struggle and building a democratic society.

Democracy

Covenantal organizing presents a comprehensive Christian moral vision and practical methods to renew and strengthen democracy, human rights, and civil society. Covenant affirms basic rights such as fundamental freedom and equality, as well as the unity of humanity. Through its emphasis on justice, the separation of powers, and the rule of law, covenantal organizing, through its complex, pluralistic vision of society, promotes democracy and protects individuals and civil society and its institutions from the domination of the state.

Covenantal organizing institutionalizes critique and confrontation (liberation) against the oppressive, unjust status quo, and reconstructs a desperately needed new society, while its emphasis on the rule of law is indispensable for a good, just governance. Its emphasis on the sacredness of human life and human rights offers the minimum basis of justice.

In fighting against neoliberalism, covenantal organizing restores the checks and balances needed at domestic and global levels. The rule of law should reflect the principles of justice (freedom, equality, the sanctity and solidarity of all lives) instead of serving special interests. In politics, we should make sure that our elected politicians represent the people, not corporations. Toward this end, we need a radical restructuring of campaign finance law to limit the influence of money in campaigns and elections, and we need to turn elections into public campaigns rather than ones swamped in corporate money. New laws should strengthen transparency and accountability. Similarly, we should seriously consider requiring enhanced transparency and accountability in online transactions and interactions.

Covenantal organizing is critical of concentrated power and resources such as those occurring in neoliberal social arrangements. Extreme economic inequality undermines trust and unity, breeding social cynicism and violence. Poverty is unjust and a threat to the community—an invisible but real form of violence that causes the slow death of the poor. In their book, *The Spirit Level*, Richard Wilkinson and Kate Pickett argue that economic inequality not only damages social relationships and trust among people, but also contributes to the rise of mental and physical illness among the members of a society, both the poor and the rich.[16] A covenantal idea of Jubilee emphasizes the redistribution of resources, including forgiveness of student loans and debts of poor countries.

Covenantal organizing strives toward a free, egalitarian, and solidaric society. God's covenant has a leveling effect. In covenant, the poor are empowered, the excluded are included, unjust social structures are resisted, and traditional boundaries of status (race, sex, class) are redefined.[17] The covenant brings people together under God's reign and the solidarity of God's love; it cares for and values every member and shares the goods (produce) of the earth according to God's justice. No one is expendable in a covenantal community.

Covenantal organizing is instrumental in reconstituting and interweaving civil society:

> The body politic is a constructed, fractious, and fragile artifice that requires something like the practices of community organizing in order to constitute and reconstitute it out of its disparate elements. It is a constant work in progress rather than a spontaneous, natural phenomenon.[18]

As we see in the Puritan covenant, covenantal organizing's vision and practices affirm and strengthen the intermediate structure of civil society. Likewise, as we see in King's work, covenant refurbishes society with new energy by activating organizations and citizenship. Civil society is a living, symbiotic, social organism that needs to be constantly renewed; it receives new members (immigrants, newborns) and requires adaptation to ongoing political and cultural changes.

The renewal of civic organizations and primary institutions is important for democracy. Democratic renewal is tied to the renewal of each institution. As Stout mentions, "Democratic change will happen on a large scale only if many organizations that are themselves democratically structured cooperate in bringing it about."[19] The repair of civic society and its institutions is vital and significant not only for democracy but also for the formation of moral agency, for civil society and its institutions play an important role in moral education and the development of democratic citizenship and moral agency. A more detailed discussion of covenantal organizing and democracy will follow shortly.

Global Organizing

Covenantal organizing is much needed in our current situation because our global society needs reorganizing beyond its post-World War II arrangement. Globalization's expanding contact among different races, cultures, and religions instigates ongoing competition and even antagonism. It seems that humanity faces two stark options: mutual destruction or a just structure and agreement of mutual interactions.

We cannot completely undo globalization given the level of technological and economic integration that we have today, with its constantly shifting nature. However, we have no option other than the long, patient, ongoing work of grassroots organizing, including global collaboration that addresses pressing concerns such as global warming, nuclear proliferation, skyrocketing military spending, immigration, human trafficking, etc. Through resilient community organizing, we may achieve relative justice and a better quality of life for ordinary people.

We need to harness globalization with a clear moral vision, direction, institutional structure, and law informed by shared moral values and principles of justice. Otherwise, people will reject globalization and readily resort to nationalism and authoritarianism when they do not see economic and moral congruence between globalization and local community.

Alongside the reinvention of democracy in domestic realms, we need to innovate and enhance grassroots democracy in the global community and newly establish the rules, systems, and practices of democracy in the global realm by creatively combining direct democracy and the representative system.[20] To organize the global society is to bring the rule of law and the system of checks and balances to the global market in a manner that guarantees transparency, fairness, and accountability. The globalization of finance or commerce and popular culture without institutional structures of mutual accountability and justice is unsustainable; it condones exploitation, a culture of hedonism/corruption (pornography, sex trafficking), and pollutes and destroys the planet.

A new global organizing cannot exclude the biotic world and other species. We should not integrate the global market and give free reign to MNCs without recognizing the ecological and human cost of their business activities. In this era of ecocide and global warming, one cannot approach community organizing anthropocentrically. As we studied, covenantal organizing offers an inclusive moral vision of the commonness of life, including the planet itself and other species. The exact form of a new society could take several different forms. However, such a society, in light of our discussion in the previous chapters, should have the following moral emphases and characteristics.

Covenantal organizing transcends the scope of ordinary secular politics and their anthropocentrism. Covenantal organizing is not a merely human historical activity but is part of God's cosmic organizing work in history. As aforementioned, covenant bears upon God's *oikos*—the entire creation. This theological insight expands community organizing to be inclusive of non-human species (creatures)—respecting their intrinsic values and rights. Covenant offers a refreshing vision for the renewal of our society and our relationship with other creatures.[21]

At the core of covenant is the voluntary joint participation of free and equal individuals toward common ends. Covenant expresses a deep desire for peaceful coexistence and a quest for self-fulfillment within the boundary of structured accountability. It recognizes that a certain sense of structure or order is indispensable for common survival, self-fulfillment, and flourishing. Its principle of unity in diversity offers a way to connect the local and the global. Its organizing principle of federalism applies to local, societal, and global levels.

Our globalizing society desperately needs a deep covenantal model of polity and structure. It increasingly becomes clear that communication (including online) without covenantal trust will be not reliable; morality without a transhistorical ground is not sustainable; neoliberal economies without institutional checks and balances are unjust and oppressive, serving only the rich few; and globalization without covenantal organizing will be chaotic and unstable.[22]

To organize global society in a covenantal way is a huge task, but there is no other option. Fortunately, the idea of covenant is not unique to Israel and Christians. Daniel Elazar's research shows the existence of covenantal or quasi-covenantal forms across cultures.[23] We may all utilize an indigenous tradition of covenant for a just organizing of a global society. From a Christian theological perspective, this implies that the ability to form covenant is given to humanity with the creation, but this ability, like other abilities, has been corrupted and distorted. Instead of mutually liberating and empowering each other, we oppress and exploit others or isolate ourselves from others.

Summary

To undo neoliberal oligarchy and reconstruct political economy in a more just and fair way, we need a massive social movement. Electoral politics and judicial power alone are no longer reliable for meaningful social changes. This undoing in turn is impossible without reinvigorating grassroots democracy that works through community organizing and the mobilization of a wide range of individuals and organizations, especially women, people of color, and diverse religious and civic groups.

The brief engagement above of covenantal organizing with the four crises exhibits the comprehensive and practical nature of covenantal organizing in fighting against neoliberalism. Since the control of neoliberalism is totalistic, any meaningful political-moral response to it should also be comprehensive, and covenantal organizing meets this demand. With its double edges of liberation and reconstruction, covenantal organizing offers the urgent push of resistance and the pull of the vision (common flourishing; shalom), and invites humanity to the common work of liberation and reconstruction by overcoming the division among different groups and communities.

Likewise, when we simultaneously need organizing at multiple levels—personal, communal, national, and global—covenantal organizing offers a comprehensive theoretical and practical paradigm for such a task. In covenantal organizing, these levels are not mutually exclusive, especially when guided by the global vision of humanity and the planet. Realistically, our fight against neoliberalism may begin with local organizing that assists the reorganizing of a community and formation of individuals. But local organizing itself is not the goal; it should always be aware of the impact the global aspect has on our lives. Otherwise, our local organizing may be myopic and short-term.

It is my claim that we need locally grounded community organizing that prepares for a social movement like the Civil Rights Movement. Through organizing, we are made ready for a movement to renew and reorganize our society and political economy. Major social movements, such as the movements of Martin Luther King Jr., César Chávez, and anti-apartheid movements in South Africa, began with local organizing. Rooted in strong local organizations, they changed the course of history, injected new meaning into common human life, and transformed human moral imaginations and values.

The ultimate goal of a social movement is the renewal of the national covenant. Today, the United States needs a national covenantal renewal in a multicultural, multiracial context. Secular liberal democracy, human rights, constitutionalism, and capitalism need a deeper moral ground, and covenantal organizing can play a role in national renewal similar to what Jesus and King attempted in their respective contexts. Otherwise, current cultural malaise and mistrust may worsen, leading to the demise of the republic itself. This renewal cannot be a technical adaptation of the current political economy of liberal democracy and neoliberal capitalism, but must be its radical reinvention through a new moral imagination that casts a new moral vision that is genuinely inclusive, ecological, egalitarian, and solidaric. The renewal should not only strengthen core democratic values and norms (such as constitutionalism, rule of law, and justice) and human rights, but also expand them to include economic rights. As mentioned above, a liberal democracy that does not protect economic rights and enhance the power of labor is unable to protect basic human dignity and restrain the destructive power of neoliberalism. Again, toward this end, covenantal organizing offers an appropriate philosophy and methods for such a renewal of the nation and social change.

Then what are the roles of Christians in fighting against neoliberalism and rebuilding civil society in domestic and global realms?

The Church's Calling

Covenant organizing challenges Christians to rethink the nature and mission of the church and its political engagement. Covenantal organizing prompts a different kind of theological imagination on being the Church, doing ministry, and engaging in society. It offers a fresh and creative perspective on a dynamic relationship between God's reign and the Church's identity and mission. Reimagined, the Church exists in the modality and movement of God's organizing of creation.

The Church is the sacrament of God's kingdom-organizing power, a foretaste of His shalom. As the fruit of the collaborative organizing of the Father, Son, and Spirit, the Church is a permanent organizing event and station of the triune God for the renewal of creation. In other words, the Church is an organized community for the advance of God's reign of shalom on earth as it is in heaven.

The Church is God's organizing in action. It repeatedly reorganizes itself anew in the power of the Spirit. God forms and organizes those whom He called into a community—the body of Christ in conformity to the life of the triune God. Church as a living organism is never static or self-enclosed but is constantly organizing itself by adjusting and interacting with its environment. Organizing does not end with building an institution, but always leads to mission. God organizes God's people to reorganize the world; the Church's organizing exists for the reorganizing of the world.

In light of God's organizing work in history, Christians cannot remain individualistic or indifferent to massive economic inequality and injustices inflicted upon their members. God's covenantal organizing challenges Christians to go beyond individual pietism, sectarianism, speculative theology, and ecclesiastical structure and engage in the actual lives of the poor by confronting abusive powers. Importantly, covenantal organizing takes prophetic criticism (ministry) of the Church to a next level: political action. It recognizes that charity and prophetic criticism alone are not sufficient. We need organized actions.

The Church can no longer ignore or disregard the political economy of its own society, because to enter God's reign (which the Christ event indicates) is to embrace a covenantal form of political economy in its life, one way or another.

In this era of neoliberal ascendance, Christians need to recover the biblical vision of God's covenantal political economy (Jubilee, Sabbath economics, the Lord's Prayer) and enact such a community life among themselves at a local level and in its prophetic ministry in society. The question of a political economic system is neither value neutral nor irrelevant for Christians. Life in a Christian community should reflect core covenantal values and its way of life, importantly, including the covenantal political economy: how power and resources are shared in the church, how social relationships are arranged, and how fellowship and communal activities are practiced. The Church, as the visible domain of God's reign, is different from other reigns by the distinctive nature of its political economy that reflects and embodies God's reign. Specifically, Christians today cannot ignore the difference between democracy and authoritarianism, neoliberalism and democratic socialism, just as they cannot practice both Pharaoh's system and the covenant economics of ancient Israel.

To develop and enact covenantal organizing and its strategies in our own distinctive cultural contexts, we need to creatively appropriate and combine the organizing lessons of the Exodus event, Jesus, the Puritans, and Martin Luther King Jr., because our historical and social situations differ from theirs. Gleaning insights from their community organizing and covenant politics, Christians in various places may come up with creative ways to fight neoliberal oligarchy in their own contexts. For example, Jesus' community organizing was effective in preserving and empowering distressed, dislocated, and disempowered people, exploring the alternative egalitarian community life of mutual care, solidarity, and support; some may learn from Jesus' ministry in Galilee that covenant is instrumental in bringing isolated, vulnerable individuals together and forming a new community among them. Christians may seriously think of and experiment with an intentional community of local shared production and consumption to protect the vulnerable and sustain basic subsistence (free from complete dependence on corporations and market forces) and practice an ecological life style.

We may learn from the Puritans' institutional imagination in building civil society and apply it to our global contexts in order to rein in global capitalism and implement justice. Similarly, we need Martin Luther King Jr.'s wisdom and imagination to build a movement of large-scale organizing on the basis of community organizing. As King did, Christians may build coalitions with local civic organizations that share the same concerns and commitments and support or join existing movements such as "reclaiming the commons," "multitude in motion," "fifty years is enough," etc.

Baptism and Eucharist

The discussion above on the Church's renewed identity and mission prompts us to rethink the sacraments: Baptism and Eucharist. The two are symbolic, performative actions that God uses to organize God's people as we express our covenantal identity and organizing mission as God's partners. A Christian community is a covenant-organized community of the kingdom, born in water and nurtured by Jesus' sacrificial blood and flesh. The sacraments have the power to reconstitute, restore, level, and bond diverse people into a new community.

Baptism is a sacrament of initiation into God's covenantal community. Christians are endowed with a new identity in baptism—the children and organizing partners of the triune God. To be baptized is to enter the covenant and be grafted into the body of Christ. It indicates the beginning of a new life (with a new identity) through solidarity with God and others in Christ. Migliore notes:

> There can be no baptism into Christ without a deepening of the sense
> of solidarity with fellow [human and non-human] creatures and with

> all their needs and yearnings . . . Baptism creates a solidarity that defies
> and shatters the divisions and barriers that sinful human beings have
> created.[24]

Hence, racism, sexism, classism, anthropocentrism, and other divisions have no place in light of this solidarity. As the sign of life, water symbolizes our new identity in Christ in solidarity with all creatures in a clean, pure, and transparent way.

Together with Baptism, the Eucharist was the key emblem of God's community organizing, now embodied in the crucified and risen body of Christ. The Eucharist is the symbol of the New Covenant with God (the creator, parent of humanity), a new people (a global tribe), and a new creation (the future of the world). The Eucharist was the culmination and climax of this covenantal social practice of Jesus. Echoing the Passover meal of the Exodus-Sinai story, and ritualizing Jesus' table fellowship, it symbolically institutionalizes resistance against oppression and the shared life among God's people.

The Eucharist embodies the spirit of the Jubilee as it emphasizes the practice of mutual sharing and forgiveness. The sharing of a meal and building of a community overlap with the declaration of a new covenant in his body and blood, symbolized by bread and drink. The Church needs to explicitly and uncompromisingly embody and practice this Eucharist vision of God's organizing by including everyone, sharing resources, confronting injustices, and building an alternative community.

> Christians cannot eat and drink at this table—where all are welcome
> and none goes hungry or thirsty—and continue to condone any form
> of discrimination or any social or economic policy that results in hunger or other forms of deprivation. The Lord's Supper is the practice
> of 'eucharistic hospitality,' in which strangers are welcomed into the
> household of God. Christians cannot share this bread and wine while
> refusing to share their daily bread and wine with the millions of hungry people around the world. There is an intrinsic connection between
> responsible participation in the Lord's Supper and commitment to a
> fairer distribution of the goods of the earth to all its people.[25]

The Eucharist connects the story of Jesus' life, death (sacrifice), and resurrection with the story and practice of solidarity and the daily sharing of basic subsistence (bread and wine). The Spirit renews and strengthens faith and the mutual bond among God's people when they partake in the same body—God's gift and promise for humanity.

Baptism and Eucharist serve as the visible symbols (icons) of a new, global eschatological tribe of God. They permanently institutionalize Jesus' vision of a community and his organizing in liturgical performances. In a rich, condensed symbolic way, both tell us what the community is like and how it is organized. Hence, Baptism and Eucharist are the starting points of our local organizing as well as the horizon of our global organizing. The future of humanity and the earth depends on how we organize ourselves and the planet in justice and righteousness in light of Baptism and Eucharist, and for this task, the biblical idea of covenant offers the way for Christians.

Summary

I hope that our conversation demonstrates how a biblical vision of covenant as a community-building and organizing mechanism is plausible and relevant to our current political and social situations in renewing church, democracy, and civil society. In particular, covenantal organizing (incorporating Alinsky's practical methods) offers Christians a practical political method to fight neoliberal agendas in local communities without compromising their religious identity and convictions. Covenantal organizing offers a coherent vision and feasible method that equips Christians for community organizing. It sets Christians free from the temptations of fearmongering, violence, scapegoating, despair, cynicism, and resignation, and enables them to stand against or subvert the unjust political-economic system and reinvigorate the decaying cultural patterns of our society.[26] Equipped with covenantal organizing, Christians may engage in local organizing, national coalition building, and global alliance-making in order to undo neoliberal oligarchy.

Community organizing is not a mere practical application of Christian theology and ethics to civic life and politics, but rather describes the intrinsic aspect of the gospel that echoes and fulfills the Exodus-Sinai story in Jesus Christ. In a deep resounding echo of the Exodus-Sinai story, the biblical idea of covenant reminds Christians of God's bottom-up organizing in history and God's demand of a Jubilee form of political economy. Detached from the echoes of the Exodus in the Bible, the idea of covenant could degenerate into individualistic contractualism or abstract proceduralism.

For Christians, covenantal organizing is not optional, but integral to Christian discipleship—the kingdom work for the common flourishing of God's creation. Covenantal organizing indicates the act of discipleship that aims to actualize shalom through the work of justice and reconciliation. Working together with other organizations and local community organizers, Christians may organize the poor and the marginalized into a community of moral agents who support each other through care and aid, and confront an unjust political and economic system.

The struggle for justice and organizing of a new community should be rooted in intimate, mystical communion with the triune God to continuously sustain and refresh us in the struggle. The potency and positive impact of worship and rituals for community organizing and social change can never be underestimated. We see numerous examples in the case of Mahatma Gandhi, Martin Luther King Jr., Dietrich Bonhoeffer, César Chávez, and so on. Whenever we gather, pray and praise, break bread, and drink a cup together, we remind ourselves to be God's covenanted people who are called for the organizing of God's beautiful world into shalom.

This chapter briefly studied the meaning and implications of covenant organizing and tested its feasibility in this era of neoliberal ascendance. The final chapter will examine the plausibility of covenant organizing as a social philosophy in comparison with current prominent models of social philosophy: liberal democracy, communitarianism, identity politics, and postmodern philosophy.

Conclusion

"Come, let us go up to the mountain of the Lord,
to the house of the God of Jacob;
that he may teach us his ways
and that we may walk in his paths."
For out of Zion shall go forth instruction,
and the word of the Lord from Jerusalem.
He shall judge between many peoples,
and shall arbitrate between strong nations far away;
they shall beat their swords into plowshares,
and their spears into pruning hooks;
nation shall not lift up sword against nation,
neither shall they learn war any more;
but they shall all sit under their own vines and under their own fig trees,
and no one shall make them afraid;
for the mouth of the Lord of hosts has spoken.

Micah 2:2-4

Since the Enlightenment and the Industrial Revolution, the West has made impressive strides in reorganizing society from a feudal system to a capitalist democratic one. Relying on organizing efficiency and productive forces (represented by science, technology, and the military), it has succeeded in remaking the world in its own image (in terms of popular culture, fashion, arts, music, food), to the extent that Francis Fukuyama declared "the end of history"[1]—the permanent triumph of the Western political economy! As mentioned in the last chapter, liberal democracy's uncritical embrace of globally ascendant neoliberalism and globalization has led to the discrediting of liberal democracy and its ruling elites. Today, at the apex of its ascendancy, liberal democracy is losing its credibility in the United States and other parts of the world. As a result, many are reverting to authoritarianism, nativist chauvinism, anarchism, and identity politics. Politically and socially, the demise of liberal democracy as a dominant political system is engendering an ideological vacuum, social anomie, and anxious confusion in domestic and international relations. However, distrust of liberal democracy is not restricted to its functional competence; for decades, communitarianism and postmodernism have been challenging its philosophical (metaphysical, epistemological, and ethical) basis, including its ideas of rationality, neutrality, individualism, and human rights.

Our society is turning into an ideological jungle. Diverse social philosophies and ideologies are competing against each other, making the task of justice and organizing more complicated and challenging. The erosion of community and civil society, the spread of fake news, and the ruthless logic of the market are worsening anomic situations.

Critical evaluations of these philosophies are important because human social life is impossible without some form of organizing. Such organizing is guided by certain social philosophies and often informed by religion. In addition, in our current globalizing situation, humanity may not survive without a radical reorganization. The fierce urgency of our global crises, in particular global warming (which may soon be irreversible, with devastating consequences), does not allow humanity to waste any more time. We need to collectively mobilize all our energies, resources, and wisdom to address these crises. Otherwise, we may perish together. A good social philosophy is indispensable in bringing people together around a common vision, procedure, norms, and methods of achieving the purpose.

In this final chapter, I briefly engage covenantalism with major current social philosophies: liberal democracy, communitarianism, postmodernism, and identity politics.[2] I demonstrate how covenantalism offers a more coherent and relevant social philosophy of organizing than liberal democracy, communitarianism, nationalism, postmodernism and various kinds of identity politics. It attends to the key concerns of identity politics (identity), communitarianism (community, virtuous agency), postmodernism (hegemony, historicity), and liberal democracy (constitution, rule of law, basic rights, fair procedure), while avoiding the extremes (weaknesses) of each in dealing with the four crises. These philosophies either deny the necessity of organizing itself (postmodernism) or focus on only one dimension of organizing, such as the local (communitarianism) or legal (liberal democracy) levels.[3] Most are either inefficient or irrelevant for dismantling the regnant neoliberal oligarchy. Covenantalism offers an alternative to these ideologies by organizing our society and global community while undoing neoliberal power.

Liberal Democracy

As briefly mentioned above, democracy is undergoing a major crisis in the West. The rise of illiberal democracy and identity politics, as well as the spread of postmodernism in various parts of the West, is threatening its validity. We can discern several limitations of liberal democracy. The crisis has to do with the philosophical limitation of liberal democracy itself and the loss of its credibility through its corrupt enmeshment with neoliberal capitalism.

(1) Electoral politics in the United States today are rigged by money and special interests rather than the tested moral values of humanity. Technical expertise, which no longer questions the purpose, meaning, and vision of the common good, is preferred.[4] The impoverishment of civil society and primary organizations, under the erosive power of neoliberal capitalism and globalization, has resulted in the erosion of the credibility of our democratic institutions and structures such as Congress, the free press, and the electoral process, which are fundamental to democracy.

The preoccupation with partisanship and sensationalism (including hyperactive media and character assassination) increasingly turns politics into a utilitarian game, detaching politics from the common good, a long-term social vision, and a holistic understanding of public life itself. The neoliberal economic ethos of winning by any means has spilled over to the public realm as well; many assertions lack empirical evidences and validity, and many politicians and lobbyists intentionally mislead and maliciously deceive for their political interests. Sensational content scores more than facts. The formal structure of democracy may remain the same, but its moral content and ethos have been eviscerated.

Humility in allegiance to truth and concession to facts are no longer prevailing norms in the public realm (especially on social media).

As a result of this evisceration and erosion, our society is about to lose even its basic minimalist virtues of democratic survival—tolerance and public reasoning. Our democratic capabilities of adjudication and tolerance have declined, and the result is dangerous fragmentation that festers antagonism, conflict, and violence. People are increasingly intolerant of different political opinions and parties, and one's disagreement on an issue is treated as cause for suspicion about one's moral integrity or patriotism. Opponents are frequently attacked and demonized; people are less trustful of the possibility of adjudication through the use of public reasoning; and public discourse is losing efficacy. Instead of trusting the redemptive possibility of public discourse through the test of validity claims, fake news, alternative facts, and moral absolutism abound.

President Trump has been especially dangerous in accelerating this process of norm erosion with his attacks on the free press, the judicial system, and public discourse. By breaking the democratic norms of civility, respect, and tolerance, he is trivializing the very institution of democracy itself and undermining its moral foundation. We cannot foresee the long-term consequences of his attacks because he is more the symptom of deep cultural malaise than its cause. This is a sad and frightening result of the erosion of the common good and sense of solidarity to which the policies of neoliberal capitalism and individualism have contributed.

(2) The moral framework of liberal democracy is judicial and contractual. This thin contractualism and individualism contribute to the corrosion of ties among human beings. Liberal democracy treats individuals as the bearers of rights. Hence, it tends to cultivate defensive and protective attitudes toward neighbors and society rather than proactively engaging with others to build communal bonds and enhance the common interests of a community. With its preoccupation with rights (especially of those who have been traditionally marginalized), it tends to reduce politics to a contest of narrow self-interest. Its focus on distributive justice (i.e., who gets what from the government) and individual rights, while necessary, is insufficient to empower the marginalized and their communities (i.e., to empower their ownership and control of their political life).

However, the assertion of individual rights alone does not build an organization or a community. A liberal emphasis on individual freedom, equality, and justice is limited in addressing the questions of moral forma-tion, agency, and community. Seeing democratic politics as the expression of individual rights, liberal democracy does not recognize the responsible and respectful exercise of the rights that depend on the support of vari-ous local communities and intermediating organizations, which cultivate such a sense of respect and responsibility. Individuals need more than freedom for their fulfillment; they also need a community and institu-tions that support and facilitate their fulfillment.

Democracy is far from a pure legal structure comprising the Con-stitution, the rule of law, and elections; it is a complex, living organism that is sustained through the commitment of citizens to ideals, norms, and values that are broader and higher than any legal structure. A legal structure alone can never fully guide citizens' behavior.[5] This is shaped in the non-legal realm through primary institutions and civic organiza-tions, as citizens imbibe, learn, and practice the shared ideals, norms, and values of society that serve as informal but still binding authorities.

A political community requires coordination; while the law does play such a role, it is not sufficient. For the survival of democracy and the republic, we need not only the equality of members before the law, but also a commitment to the same ideals, values, and norms. A democratic system cannot function properly without a democratic culture support-ing it; to believe otherwise is to put the cart before the horse. Culture is the root while the system is its flower. As the root atrophies, the flower withers.

> The reinvigoration of the written checks in the American Constitution depends on the reinvigoration of the unwritten checks in American society. The great institutions—Congress, the courts, the executive establishment, the press, the universities, public opinion—have to reclaim their own dignity and meet their own responsibilities. As Mad-ison said long ago, the country cannot trust to "parchment barriers" to halt the encroaching spirit of power. In the end, the Constitution will live only if it embodies the spirit of the American people.[6]

The culture of voluntary participation and care for others enhances the quality of the community. Solidarity arises from trust, and trust is vital to make social exchange nonviolent and efficient.

Covenantal organizing is crucial for restoring a viable democracy by reinventing and empowering the informal authorities of a society to build or restore trust among its members. Through its balance between "community organizing" and "political organizing," covenant offers a far broader vision, deeper basis, and more practical method of community organizing than communitarianism, identity politics, and liberal democracy. While sharing the same concerns for democracy, human rights, and discursive reasoning, covenant is different from liberal democracy in its commitment to community, the value of character, associational pluralism, and the public role of religious communities. Covenant is more communal and thicker than liberal democracy while taking the basic rights of people far more seriously than communitarianism.

Freedom in the covenant is federal or relational freedom. All creatures have moral obligations toward each other in their interdependence and in their exercise of freedom. Without those communities, individual rights could become empty, reduced to legal codes and detached from communal practices. A good political community requires more than freedom and individual rights; it needs something that binds the members together in mutual care, sharing, and compassion. These affectional dimensions are important for coordination.

Covenantal organizing challenges liberal democracy's allegedly natural tie with neoliberal capitalism. The current crisis demonstrates that democracy is not functional without the protection of basic economic rights. As human dignity is integral to democracy, politics and economy can never be completely separated. In terms of its value orientation and moral emphases, covenantalism reveals a closer affinity with democratic socialism than neoliberal capitalism. Scandinavian and northwestern European nations that have adopted democratic socialism have enjoyed a better quality of social life and social harmony.

Covenantal organizing presents a value-oriented, not merely technical (pragmatic or utilitarian), approach to politics. Politics cannot disregard value questions. The question of value has to do with culture. A democratic change without a cultural change is short-lived. Democracy needs a deeper moral and cultural basis. In American history, major democratic progress was possible when democratic politics were combined with grassroots organizing, inspired by a noble religious vision, values, and practices, and forming a larger public whole.[7] Covenantal organizing today aims at a broad social-cultural reorganizing—a moral, epistemological conversion to a different way of seeing ourselves, others, and reality, which empowers people with a new vision, a new sense of self-dignity, and a new moral purpose.

Communitarianism

The combined forces of global mobility, individualism, communication technology, the coercive power of the market, and postmodern ideologies have contributed to the demise of community (expressed through primary institutions). Today, under the rubric of communitarianism, the importance of good community receives extensive attention from educators, psychologists, policymakers, and ethicists who, to a certain extent, realize the crisis impinging upon Western civilization. Growing scholarly interest in virtue ethics, community, and identity reflects urgent concerns about the demise of community and its impact on agency.[8]

Ultimately, however, communitarianism takes the opposite direction. With its strong emphasis on a community's particular history and tradition, in general communitarians tend to take a sectarian, parochial posture. They doubt or deny the necessity of (intra-communal) common morality and the possibility of adjudicating conflicting moral claims in public. Thus, they are unable to address the major difficulties of global governance in a pluralistic society.

However, as we have seen in the United States, without addressing structural injustices, communitarianism may end up as romantic nostalgia, or worse, become vulnerable to populism, nativism, and ethnocentrism. One may even go so far as to say that nationalism (state authoritarianism), ethnocentrism (white nationalism), and other exclusionary forms of identity politics (including religious fundamentalism with a racist streak) are distorted expressions of communitarianism when biological affinities (race, ethnicity, gender, nationality) serve as the boundary markers of a community and its collective identity. They appeal to the communal tradition, history, and identity of a particular race, religion, or nation, offering an outlet for people seeking a deeper ground for their identity and the meaning of their life in the midst of jostling economic and cultural powers. For example, state authoritarianism, advocated and embodied by the leaders of some nation-states (e.g., Russia, China, Singapore, Cuba), relies on a particular national history, tradition, ideology, or collective sentiment in order to secure social integration and identity formation for the purposes of promoting national economic and military interests in competition with other nation-states in the global economy. Its agenda is similar to that of religious radicals (only in a nationalist form), resulting in the oppression of ethnic and religious minorities and political dissent.

Religious fundamentalism (e.g., ISIS, the Taliban, and Hindu, Buddhist, Christian, and Jewish radicals) denies a pluralistic sociocultural reality and the basic rights of humanity, and tries to control or impose its particular religious viewpoint and morality through political, physical, and legislative means. This inevitably results in the marginalization of religious minorities and the suppression of religious freedom, which can often escalate into violent religious conflicts.

Covenantalism is different from a natural, biological, ethnocentric community, or a liberal contractual society. A covenantal community is built upon mutual trust rather than biological affinity. It is communally oriented while communicatively engaged. It is solidaric as well as reciprocal. Its relationships are built upon open and reflective mutual engagements in justice and love.

Postmodernism

Postmodernism, countering the modernist epistemology and understanding of truth, morality, and reason, claims that all realities we know and all methods of knowing them are socially constructed; they are embedded in particular intellectual traditions as the artifacts of long-term linguistic and social practices.[9] The truth that Western institutions propagate is ultimately the function of power, and the sets of disciplinary practices of modern institutions are bio-powers that are designed to control citizens using the regime of knowledge.

Although postmodernism offers an excellent critique of various forms of hegemony, it is not so helpful in building alternative forms of social institutions and communities. The suspicion that reduces all ideas of truth and reason to ideology or rhetoric of privilege and power has the effect of making all social relationships into a pure power play. Rhetoric triumphs over truth, self-assertion over adjudication, and suspicion over collaboration. The result is moral relativism, in which every claim is equally legitimate and valid. Its hermeneutics of suspicion, a necessary tool for criticism, is not sufficient to build trust and ground the public. In particular, its rejection of any possible adjudication or any redemption of validity claims makes meaningful public discourse impossible, resulting in detrimental effects on civil society. It is true that as postmodern philosophy claims, all knowledge is historically embedded, and ruling ideologies are complicit with dominant powers. However, not all knowledge is arbitrary, not every truth claim is equally valid, and truth is not completely reducible to power and interest.

Postmodernism has resulted in a misunderstanding in which institutions themselves are intrinsically problematic. This discourages participation in institutions rather than working for their revitalization or reformation. Postmodern disregard for truth and reason impedes the basics of organizing such as dialogue, coalition building, and public engagement. A common life cannot be built upon or sustained by endless regression, deconstruction, and suspicion.

Postmodernism ultimately succumbs to expedient utilitarianism and power, erodes our social fabric, and creates a context for the rise of authoritarianism and fake news/alternative facts. Many do not mind manipulating and bending facts to fit an ideological agenda or selfish interests because there is no longer such a thing as truth. Its micropolitical focus easily loses sight of the massive structural force impinging upon all of us, often easily compromising with cultural fetishism.[10] The inflated negativity and suspicion that characterizes postmodernism is inadequate for guiding a complex world of global inequality, interdependence, ecological degradation, and exchange.

Postmodern relativistic philosophies deny any shared narrative and referential values or transcultural authority of moral norms by reducing them to social practices or habits of a particular tradition. Its moral relativism makes it extremely difficult to gain social consensus on major issues, since meaningful governance requires, at minimum, a shared moral ground and vision. It is increasingly forgotten that past achievements against fascism, Nazism, and communism in Europe, and segregation in the United States, were made possible through basic, shared morals and norms such as the sacredness of life. Postmodern moral relativism and its celebration of irony and contingency foster neo-tribalism, skepticism, and privatism, ultimately succumbing to instrumental rationality, utilitarian economism, and Nietzschean worship of the will to power.

A covenantal community is not purely historical but ontotheological; it is grounded in the economy of the triune God in history and the moral structure of the universe. Covenantal organizing is based on the recognition that morality is not a sheer artificial human construct; it carries in itself authority and binding power. Natural law is not completely fictional, because every society has proverbs, moral wisdom, and witticisms that transcend its original community. From a Christian perspective, natural law is attributed to God's ongoing organizing work in history through the Creation Covenant and the Noahic Covenant. Although it is true that

natural law has sometimes been used to maintain the hegemony of
the ruling elites, natural law (or something similar to it) is necessary
to protect marginalized people and to assist in adjudicating conflicting
opinions and ideas in the public sphere. Otherwise, with an overwhelming overflow of information, our common realm will be further eroded,
and our public life will be further divided, with potentially devastating
results. This common-sense wisdom applies to online communication.
We need a certain normative structure—yes, covenant—for online communication. How to build covenantal relationships online is a challenging task. We need to listen to H. R. Niebuhr's point: "Is freedom of
speech a right that could have been maintained in society where there
was no prior implicit and unlimited promise among the members that
they would be loyal to truth as they saw it and not bear false witness
against their neighbor?"[11]

Zygmunt Bauman notes: "Norms enable as they disable; anomie
augurs disablement pure and simple. Once the troops of normative regulation vacate the battlefields of life, only doubt and fear are left."[12] Richard Sennet's observation is also on target: "Routine can demean, but it
can also protect."[13] Cynicism, suspicion, and endless deconstruction that
deny the provisional role of public reasoning and public morality will
never solve the problems that we face.

> Political scientists tell us that democracies require a little faith. To
> engage with others, you have to believe that if you lose a contest or a
> debate, the winner will treat you equitably; that if the other side wins,
> it will act within the law and not send its opponents off to jail. You
> have to assume that institutions will be fair and that leaders will act in
> the country's best interest.[14]

Covenantal values of freedom, equality, trust, reciprocity, solidarity, and justice are foundational for any viable human relationship—
interpersonal, institutional, or social. The denial or loss of these values
poses a grave threat to the well-being of both its members and society
because every society, for its survival and functioning, needs basic levels
of trust and commitment to the rules, norms, and vision of a good life
that the members share. Otherwise, a common life is inconceivable,
and only chaos awaits. Covenant offers this provisional ground of truth
and morality that operates through the work of communicative reasoning in forming, improving, correcting, and adjusting communities. Its
operating epistemology is neither completely objectivist nor relativist,
but critical realist.

Identity Politics

Another distinctive phenomenon of democracy in the postmodern era, one closely associated with communitarianism, is the rise of identity politics. Though not the only reason, the crisis of agency has to do with the rise of identity politics in the United States. Isolated and disembedded from their communities, individuals feel lonely and vulnerable due to corporate or governmental neglect, manipulation, misinformation, and abuse. In this social milieu, identity is an acute concern, and identity politics offers individuals a sure ground for their identities and even a community of like-minded (or lookalike) individuals. By providing an immediate, tangible ground of belongingness (race, ethnicity, gender, religion, nationality), identity politics appeals to many who feel vulnerable in this era of loneliness, deep suspicion of others/otherness, and hyper-competition (winner takes all), reflecting the highly divisive and frenzied state of our politics.

However, identity politics also shows a tendency to be fragmentary and divisive, even to the point of rejecting public reasoning. The narrow, dogmatic expression of identity politics cannot properly address the major ecological, economic, and educational challenges we face in our common humanity. It "emphasizes recognition by the prevailing structure of power rather than the need to change the power structure as such."[15] A reified form of identity politics leads to the balkanization of civil society and endless division and conflict, thus undermining the public sphere and its functions of adjudication, negotiation, and collaboration.

Identity politics is susceptible to the tactic of divide-and-conquer used by ruling elites who will do anything to frustrate any kind of resistance in order to protect their own privilege and current status quo. Racism, sexism, and environmental anthropocentrism are real, powerful, and destructive. Thus, they need to be dismantled. However, we should not demonize others; not only does this make communication more difficult, but it also creates a deep sense of distrust, antipathy, and enmity. As Martin Luther King Jr. said, the goal is not to defeat and humiliate others but to persuade, obtain understanding, and build a new community.[16]

Covenantal politics distinguishes itself from narrow racial identity politics. Covenant is neither color-blind nor culture-blind. The core insights of covenantal organizing apply to racial relationships as well. That is, one may conceive of interracial relationships as covenantal, in that each racial group interacts with others under the strictures of justice, and freely participates in and shares power for the advance of mutual well-being. Its principle of unity in diversity offers a way to coordinate group identity and self-determination for the common good and solidarity.

Covenantal organizing embraces and celebrates the diversity of race, ethnicity, and culture while incorporating unflinching prophetic confrontation and uncompromising solidarity with people on the margins. It distances itself from separatism and black nationalist ideology. Covenantal organizing addresses the question of self-determination and self-identity while avoiding the lure of separatism or postmodern fideism. While respecting the particularities of race, ethnicity, and culture (including "white" ethnicities), it constantly seeks the common good of society and the planet.

Interethnic relationships can be formed and deepened in a covenantal framework. Covenantal organizing harmonizes unity and particularity, the common good and group identity. Each group, without compromising their identity, respects the rule of law, practices democratic negotiation and persuasion, and imagines intergroup relationships as a federal (covenantal; unity-in-diversity) relationship in a way similar to the constitution of civil society. Good, truthful communication serves as a means of both deepening relationships and clarifying differences, for communication is the process that holds the relational polarities of uniqueness and unity together.

Summary

We compared covenantal organizing to several models of social philosophy regnant today. However, I doubt that any of these philosophies are adequate for fighting neoliberal oligarchy or capacious enough to address the quadruple crises of agency, community, democracy, and global governance in an integral way. One cannot deny that the democratic future of the nation will be bleak if we continue to choose individual rights over community, tribal identity over communicative reasoning, sensational populism over democracy, postmodern moral relativism over public ethics, and partisan interest over the common good.

On the contrary, covenantal organizing offers a capacious social philosophy of organizing that is encompassing in its scope (as it includes a biotic world) while practical in its application. As our fight against neoliberal oligarchy is urgent, covenantal organizing, through the double edges of liberation and reconstruction, offers the urgent push of resistance and the urgent pull of the vision of common flourishing, and invites humanity to the common work of liberation and reconstruction by overcoming the divides among different groups and communities.

Covenant as a Way of Life

Covenant is the art of association for God's people. Covenant reminds us that we are created to be loving, associational animals. Covenant gives a theological and moral basis for an egalitarian form of social arrangement that protects basic human rights. Its emphasis on the indebted nature of human life to God, the rights of every member of creation, care for the marginalized and oppressed, and inclusiveness invigorates the human work of justice, liberation, and community building. Its various practices help to nurture mutual networking through care and support as its members pursue common flourishing.

Covenant represents a deep human aspiration for a just, righteous, and peaceful society where every creature flourishes. In the Bible, covenant is not a purely religious idea, but a subversive, even revolutionary vision for a just and peaceful society.[17] However, it is not utopian; it is given to us as God's gift and promise. It invites constant human exertion, commitment, and collaboration toward a better society.

Covenant distances itself from utopian idealism, Machiavellian realism, erosive individualism, and suffocating tyranny. A covenantal vision of a just, egalitarian, supportive community may never be perfectly realized in history, but its organizing has the effect of undercutting privilege and inequality by counteracting the exploitative and dehumanizing tendencies of society. Covenant constantly calls for redefinition, the reworking of social relationships, and the redistribution of power and resources. Renowned biblical theologian Walter Brueggemann articulates the social-political meaning and significance of covenant in following words:

> [C]ovenanting becomes a way to think about the nations and kingdoms of the earth, a way requiring risk, emotion, and solidarity. Covenanting . . . is the way all of society is intended to be with its markings of justice, freedom, abundance, and compassion. And the people . . . are to work toward that transformation and not give up on the world.[18]

With shalom as its ultimate goal, covenantal organizing is eschatological in nature. In God, organizing is a constant process of creative innovation and resilient exertion to approximate shalom. Its vision of a new community is never perfectly realized in history, but it has the potency to undercut the privilege and power of the elites and to correct social inequality. Therefore, tyrants and ruling elites are afraid of the liberating power of the story; they suppress its dangerous memory or distort it by selecting a partial aspect of it to promote. I want to conclude this work with Brueggemann's observation about the nature of covenant and how it represents a dream of a just society to which we all aspire:

> [T]he world is intended by God to be a community that covenants, that distributes its produce equally, that values all its members, and that brings the strong and the weak together in common work and common joy. Though it is not yet that kind of community, we are assured that soon or later it will be (see Rev. 11:15). And the mission of the believing community is to articulate, anticipate, and practice the transformation that is sure to come.[19]

Hence, as Elazar notes, "The covenantal-federal way is not dogma but rather a direction, a path"[20] in dealing with questions of how we all justly live together for common flourishing. Covenantal organizing, either in a theological or secularized form (i.e., compact theory) has appeared in different ways in different times of history, but its regular manifestation is "one of the fundamentals of politics."[21] Hence, today the restoration and expansion of covenantal organizing (as we examined in a critical conversation with Alinsky) in our own social-political context is necessary for dismantling neoliberal oligarchy, reweaving our civil society and institutions out of their state of fragmentation and division, and rebuilding our citizenship free from rampant egoism and indulgence. Our global society waits for the rise of another creative expression of covenantal polity.

As long as covenant represents human aspirations for a free, just, and interconnected society, it will not disappear; later generations will rediscover it as King Josiah of Judah did (2 Kgs 22–23; 2 Chr 34–35) and the prophets preached. Whenever God's organizing pattern of liberation-reconstruction is proclaimed by the church, covenant will be instrumental in gathering people and empowering them to renew our passion.

God is still organizing. God is moving and working in history to reorganize broken humanity and creation again and again. This movement of God, latent or manifested, invisible or visible, never stops and cannot be permanently stalled. In order to inject new meaning into history, and to transform human moral imaginations and values toward a common life, God is preparing God's people for a massive movement moment. No one knows when or where the next movement will arise; however, if we do not prepare ourselves through organizing, we may miss the opportunity to act. We neither create nor determine *kairos*, but we may contribute to its advance and fulfillment.

Hence, now is the time to organize!

Notes

Preface

1 Jeffrey Stout, *Blessed Are the Organized: Grassroots Democracy in America* (Princeton: Princeton University Press, 2010), 18–19.

Introduction

1 Larry L. Rasmussen, *Moral Fragments and Moral Community: A Proposal for Church in Society* (Minneapolis: Fortress, 1993), 11.

2 On a popular cultural level in the United States, individualism reinforces and justifies this habit of detachment and contractualism. The liberal emphasis on autonomy and self-fulfillment has led to nurture individuals who are focused on self-care and personal fulfillment, creating a narcissistic culture.

3 According to David Kinnaman, "Young adults are more likely than their predecessors to believe that sometimes the rules have to be bent to get by in life." See David Kinnaman, *unChristian: What a New Generation Really Thinks about Christianity . . . and Why It Matters* (Grand Rapids: Baker, 2007), 44.

4 For example, the ratio of CEO pay to worker pay was 42:1 in 1982, but 354:1 in 2012. See Finance Degree Center, "Skewed: Income Inequality in America," Global Research, December 11, 2013, http://www.globalresearch.ca/skewed -income-inequality-in-america/5361223.

5 Anthony Giddens warns that the danger of "manufactured risk" is growing today—the risk created by the advance and popularization of technology and science (e.g., proliferation of nuclear and biological warfare and technologies). He says, "We started worrying less about what nature can do to us, and more

about what we have done to nature" (Anthony Giddens, *Runaway World: How Globalization Is Reshaping Our Lives* [New York: Routledge, 2003], 26).

6 Larry L. Rasmussen, *Earth-Honoring Faith: Religious Ethics in a New Key* (New York: Oxford University Press, 2013), 358.

7 Donald S. Lutz, *The Origin of American Constitutionalism* (Baton Rouge: Louisiana State University Press, 1988), 6.

8 Bryan D. Estelle, *Echoes of Exodus: Tracing a Biblical Motif* (Downers Grove, Ill.: IVP Academic, 2018), 1–2.

9 Estelle, *Echoes of Exodus*, 2.

10 Anthropologically, this fact attests to a living nature of any vital religious tradition. Theologically, it testifies to the work of the Holy Spirit, who particularizes God's covenantal reign in different historical and social contexts.

11 Hak Joon Lee, "Public Theology," in *The Cambridge Companion to Christian Political Theology*, ed. Craig Hovey and Elizabeth Phillips (New York: Cambridge University Press, 2016), 44.

12 Lee, "Public Theology," 44.

13 One sees a similar attempt and historical examples in the social teachings of the Roman Catholic Church.

14 For the sake of our discussion, it is necessary to distinguish covenant from contract and compact, as they are often used interchangeably. A contract is private in nature, describing an agreement with a restricted commitment, such as in a business matter. A compact is not as specific as a contract; it is a mutual agreement based on generally accepted or recognized norms. A compactual relationship is more comprehensive and lasting than a contract, but less so than a covenant. Its moral and legal authority rests on the general will of the people as the collective body. Compared to compact, covenant is more serious, solemn in its nature, witnessed by the highest authority (God or a king) as the final guarantor or supervisor. Accompanied by oath-taking, covenantal obligations do not derive from consent alone but also from the highest authority who authenticates them.

15 Robert Bellah, in his *The Broken Covenant: American Civil Religion in Time of Trial* (Chicago: University of Chicago Press, 1998), ix, also offers his observation regarding this point:

> It is one of the oldest of sociological generalizations that any coherent and viable society rests on a common set of moral understandings about good and bad, right and wrong, in the realm of individual and social action. It is almost as widely held that these common moral understandings must also in turn rest upon a common set of religious understandings that provide a picture of the universe in terms of which the moral understandings make sense.

1 God

1 I regard other distinctive acts of God, such as liberation, atonement, reconciliation, justification, and sanctification as the aspects of God's organizing clustered around covenant.

2 The idea of organizing captures the dynamic process and ongoing nature of God's reign more effectively than a Reformed theological idea of divine order.

3 At the heart of the Christian doctrine of God is the Trinity. The triune God is the originating as well as finalizing power and reality. The idea of the Trinity serves as the organizing principle of the entire Christian theology. In explicating God's self-organizing, this chapter is built upon the social analogy of the Trinity. However, this analogy is not without its critics. For a detailed discussion of the social analogy and its critics, see John L. Gresham Jr., "The Social Model of the Trinity and its Critics," *Scottish Journal of Theology* 46, no. 3 (1993): 325–43.

4 Daniel L. Migliore, *Faith Seeking Understanding: An Introduction to Christian Theology* (Grand Rapids: Eerdmans, 2014), 79.

5 John D. Zizioulas, *Communion and Otherness: Further Studies in Personhood and the Church* (New York: T&T Clark, 2006), 107.

6 Trinity is averse to a monistic thinking; it has developed as a safeguard against a simplistic, reductionistic understanding of God. The Trinity is a theological concept devised to explain both spatial (transcendental and immanent) and temporal (eternal and historical) dimensions in human experiences of God in Jesus Christ through the power of the Spirit. According to Paul Tillich, the Trinity is a theological symbol which resolves a tension experienced between the universal and the historical, the personal and the impersonal, the transcendental and the immanent, the hidden and the manifested. See Paul Tillich, *Systematic Theology*, vol. 1 (Chicago: University of Chicago Press, 1951), 228.

7 James Perman Eglinton, *Trinity and Organism: Toward a New Reading of Herman Bavinck's Organic Motif* (New York: T&T Clark, 2012), 80.

8 Clark Pinnock, *Flame of Love: A Theology of the Holy Spirit* (Downers Grove, Ill.: IVP Academic, 1999), 55. Jonathan Edwards also noted that God has "a disposition to abundant self-communication" (quoted in Migliore, *Faith Seeking Understanding*, 85).

9 Migliore, *Faith Seeking Understanding*, 108.

10 Creativity is a natural product of the interactions among highly intelligent, complex beings such as the Trinitarian persons.

11 *Kenosis* (self-emptying) is intrinsic to God's agapeic love; God takes a risk of self-openness and vulnerability to embrace others.

12 Reflecting the active nature of God's character and reign, there are many actional languages and metaphors in Scripture, in particular in the pneumatological images of wind, fire, light, and water. See Jürgen Moltmann, *The Spirit of Life: A Universal Affirmation* (Minneapolis: Fortress, 1992), 269–84.

13 The work of the three persons of the Trinity is never separate or confused; it is done always in the perfect unity and distinctiveness of the three persons.

14 Gerald L. Bray, "Out of the Box: The Christian Experience of God in Trinity," in *God the Holy Trinity: Reflections on Christian Faith and Practice*, ed. Timothy George (Grand Rapids: Baker Academic, 2006), 49.

15 Colossians 1:20 reads: "Through him God was pleased to reconcile to himself all things, whether on earth or in heaven, by making peace through the blood of his cross."

16 Migliore, *Faith Seeking Understanding*, 80

17 Colin Gunton, *The One, The Three, The Many* (New York: Cambridge University Press, 1993), 184.

18 Walter Brueggemann, *A Social Reading of the Old Testament: Prophetic Approaches to Israel's Communal Life*, ed. Patrick D. Miller (Minneapolis: Fortress, 1994), 56.

19 Migliore, *Faith Seeking Understanding*, 89.

20 Covenant is the metaphor that runs across the OT and the NT, maintaining the canonical unity and theological and ethical coherence between the OT and the NT, which many Christians still struggle to comprehend.

21 Kevin Vanhoozer, *Remythologizing Theology: Divine Action, Passion, and Authorship* (New York: Cambridge University Press, 2012), 68.

22 Max L. Stackhouse, *Covenant and Commitments: Faith, Family, and Economic Life* (Louisville, Ky.: Westminster John Knox, 1997), 140.

23 "Old Testament divine covenants were essentially royal arrangements. Kingdom and covenants go hand in hand because covenants were the means by which God ruled over his kingdom. They were God's kingdom administrations, leading the kingdom of God toward its destiny of expanding to the ends of the earth." Kingdom, Covenants, and Canon of the Old Testament, http://btsfreeccm.org/local/lmp/lessons.php?lesson=KOT3text.

24 The exile is another important motif related to covenant in the Bible, which describes a negative human condition (like chaos or slavery) in contrast to a covenanted life.

25 Gerhard Lohfink, *Jesus and Community: The Social Dimension of Christian Faith* (Philadelphia: Fortress, 1984), 27.

26 Brueggemann, *Social Reading of the Old Testament*, 60.

27 David Novak, *Covenantal Rights: A Study in Jewish Political Theory* (Princeton: Princeton University Press, 2000), 88.

28 Migliore, *Faith Seeking Understanding*, 332.

29 Daniel J. Elazar, *Covenant and Polity in Biblical Israel: Biblical Foundations and Jewish Expressions*, vol. 1 of *The Covenant Tradition in Politics* (New Brunswick, N.J.: Transaction, 1995), 98.

30 Ingrid Esther Lilly, "Developing a Moral Vision for Climate Change," *Sojourners*, June 9, 2014. http://sojo.net/blogs/2014/06/09/developing-moral-vision-climate-change.

31 Pinnock, *Flame of Love*, 57.

32 This brief observation indicates that the idea of God's covenant with Creation/Adam is not far-fetched at all: it is consistent with the other covenants in the Bible in terms of its pattern, logic, and moral characteristics. God uses covenant for the original organizing of God's creation as well as the reorganizing of it

after the Fall. See William Dumbrell, *Covenant and Creation: An Old Testament Covenant Theology* (Milton Keynes, UK: Paternoster, 2013), chap. 1.

33 Eglinton, *Trinity and Organism*, 200.

34 Peter J. Gentry and Stephen J. Wellum, *Kingdom through Covenant: A Biblical-Theological Understanding of the Covenants* (Wheaton, Ill.: Crossway, 2012), 595.

35 Michael Horton, *Covenant and Salvation* (Louisville, Ky.: Westminster John Knox, 2007), 154.

36 It is "both polis, a community that lives under the rule of God, and bride, a community that lives in covenant fellowship with God" (Vanhoozer, *Remythologizing Theology*, 497).

37 Migliore, *Faith Seeking Understanding*, 249.

38 Migliore, *Faith Seeking Understanding*, 248.

39 The eschaton describes the state where "[t]he completion and finalization of political order under the free and worshipping embrace of God's rule coincides with the completion and finalization of social order in complete and uncoerced fellowship with God" (Oliver O'Donovan, *The Ways of Judgment* [Grand Rapids: Eerdmans, 2005], 240).

40 Nicholas Wolterstorff, *Until Justice and Peace Embrace* (Grand Rapids: Eerdmans, 1983).

41 Not every divine covenant in the Bible exactly follows or displays this overarching pattern; yet, one may say, every covenant indirectly serves the same goal of restoring God's shalom. In the biblical canon, some covenants, such as the Abrahamic and Davidic covenants, serve as bridges between the two major covenants.

42 Judging or ruling (*krinein* in Greek) connotes God's deliverance, liberation, or redemption.

43 Richard A. Horsley, *Jesus and the Spiral of Violence* (Minneapolis: Fortress, 1993), 204.

44 Isaiah 28:17 (ESV) reads: "And I will make justice the line, and righteousness the plumb line; and hail will sweep away the refuge of lies, and waters will overwhelm the shelter."

45 Interdisciplinary in nature, a modern discipline of political economy in general studies the interrelationships of politics, markets, and civil society—how a political system interacts with economic system and various sociocultural forces in civil society (law, ideologies, religious and cultural traditions) in the shaping of a particular form of political economy.

46 Richard A. Horsley, *Jesus and Empire: The Kingdom of God and the New World Disorder* (Minneapolis: Fortress, 2003), 77.

47 Elazar, *Covenant and Polity in Biblical Israel*, 70.

48 Elazar, *Covenant and Polity in Biblical Israel*, 65.

49 Conversely, covenant indicates the structure of communication among participants by setting the boundary and channel for their exchanges and interactions.

Covenant does not alter the difference between God and humans as the creator and creatures. Nor are they mutually equal. However, through God's gracious and generous act of kenosis (self-emptying), God creates a functional condition of equality in entering the covenant and maintaining fellowship.

50 Hak Joon Lee, "Cutting, Binding, and Re-membering: *A Covenantal Approach to Christian Liturgy and Ethics*," in *Liturgy and Ethics*, ed. Pieter H. Vos (Leiden: Brill, 2017), 223–45.

51 Elazar, *Covenant and Polity in Biblical Israel*, 43.

52 "[C]reation was not merely an event of the remote past, but also concerned with the present; the cosmic order was not merely given; it had to be sustained" (Ernest W. Nicholson, *God and His People: Covenant and Theology in the Old Testament* [Oxford: Oxford University Press, 1986], 194).

53 The law has a coercive dimension, but it is not primary, as it is embedded in the relational structure of the covenant.

54 Life in covenant is guided externally by the law and internally by the desire to love God and others.

55 A divine-human covenant relationship is not based primarily on human merits but on God's initiating grace and deliverance. For example, a new community of Israel was formed when they responded to God's initiating grace in freedom. So gratitude characterized their lives.

56 Perry Miller notes that covenant "made possible a voluntary relation of man to God, even though man's will was considered impotent and God's grace irresistible" (Perry Miller, *The New England Mind: The Seventeenth Century* [Boston: Beacon, 1961], 382).

57 Brueggemann, *Social Reading of the Old Testament*, 56–57.

2   Exodus

1 Michael Walzer, *The Revolution of the Saints* (Cambridge, Mass.: Harvard University Press, 1965).

2 For further discussion of lament, see Soong Chan Rah, *Prophetic Lament: A Call for Justice in Troubled Times* (Downers Grove, Ill.: IVP Academic, 2015).

3 Walter Brueggemann, *The Prophetic Imagination*, 40th anniversary ed. (Minneapolis: Fortress, 2008), 12.

4 "Women's emotional attachments to their families affect their everyday community commitments and their priorities about what are appropriate targets for local social change efforts." Randy Stoecker and Susan Stall, "Community Organizing or Organizing Community? Gender and the Crafts of Empowerment," *University of Wisconsin COMM_ORG Papers Collection* 2 (1996), rev. November 1997, accessed August 15, 2018, https://comm-org.wisc.edu/papers96/gender2.html. Stoecker and Stall refer to Carol J. Colfer and Michael L. Colfer, "Bushler Bay: Lifeways in Counterpoint," *Rural Sociology* 43, no. 2 (1978): 204–20; Rosalie G. Genovese, "A Women's Self-Help Network as a Response to Service Needs in the Suburbs," supplement, *Signs: Journal of Women in Culture and Society* 5, no. 3 (1980): S248–S256; Linda Stoneall, "Cognitive Mapping:

Gender Differences in the Perception of Community," *Sociological Quarterly* 51, no. 2 (1981): 121–28. Furthermore, attention to women's "modest struggles" is necessary "to understand the more elusive process of resistance that takes place beneath the surface and outside of what have conventionally been defined as community organizing, social protest, or social movements." See Susan Stall and Randy Stoecker, "Toward a Gender Analysis of Community Organizing Models: Liminality and the Intersection of Spheres," in *Community Organizing and Community Building for Health*, ed. Meredith Minkler, 2nd ed. (New Brunswick, N.J.: Rutgers University Press, 2005), 209–10.

5 These Hebrew women embodied God's intention for creation—"life-giving, life-preserving and life-blessing" (Terence E. Fretheim, *Exodus* [Louisville, Ky.: Westminster John Knox, 2010], 13). That is, God's creational plan and blessing of every life is embedded in women's motherly instinct to protect life.

6 Fretheim, *Exodus*, 23.

7 Anthony R. Ceresko, *Introduction to Old Testament Wisdom: A Spirituality for Liberation* (Maryknoll, N.Y.: Orbis, 1999), 97.

8 Michael Walzer, *Exodus and Revolution* (New York: Basic Books, 1985), 21; emphasis original.

9 Fretheim, *Exodus*, 111.

10 Fretheim, *Exodus*, 111.

11 Fretheim, *Exodus*, 110.

12 Fretheim, *Exodus*, 110.

13 Fretheim, *Exodus*, 106.

14 Fretheim, *Exodus*, 106.

15 Walzer, *Exodus and Revolution*, 21.

16 This vision of a new society is given in the form of God's promise, not just a human imaginary construction, a counterfactual utopia. God's promise saves the Hebrew slaves from fatalism and hopelessness, and instills a sense of hope and possibility.

17 Paul D. Hanson, *The People Called: The Growth of Community in the Bible* (Louisville, Ky.: Westminster John Knox, 2001), 22–23.

18 Norbert Lohfink, *Option for the Poor: The Basic Principle of Liberation Theology in the Light of the Bible* (Berkeley: BIBAL Press, 1987), 45; cited in Christopher Wright, *Old Testament Ethics for the People of God* (Downers Grove, Ill: IVP, 2004), 61.

19 Ross Kinsler and Gloria Kinsler, *The Biblical Jubilee and the Struggle for Life: An Invitation to Personal, Ecclesial, and Social Transformation* (Maryknoll, N.Y.: Orbis, 1999), 34.

20 Daniel J. Elazar, *Covenant and Polity in Biblical Israel: Biblical Foundations and Jewish Expressions*, vol. 1 of *The Covenant Tradition in Politics* (New Brunswick, N.J.: Transaction, 1995), 98.

21 "It was the *Edah* that God led directly and to which he spoke through the *Eved Adonai*. Within the limits of God's constitution the *Edah* acted autonomously" (Elazar, *Covenant and Polity in Biblical Israel*, 189).

22 God took the initiative for relationship through the Exodus event, and the people responded to God's initiative by consenting to God's offer. Covenant is the scaffold of this divine initiative and human response.

23 Hemchand Gossai, *Justice, Righteousness and the Social Critique of the Eighth-Century Prophets*, American University Studies, Series 7: Theology and Religion, vol. 141 (New York: Peter Lang, 1993), 55–56; cited in Wright, *Old Testament Ethics*, 256.

24 Some Bible versions translate justice (*mishpat*) as rights (e.g., Jer 5:28). Though not as fully developed as the contemporary idea of human rights, a deep concern for the dignity of strangers and aliens in the Old Testament points to a seminal form of human rights. See Wright, *Old Testament Ethics*, 257.

25 For example, the Torah stipulated in great detail the protection of aliens, strangers, and sojourners from abuse and discrimination, fair treatment for them in legal cases, the guarantee of timely and fair payment, rest on the Sabbath, and special care to receive a portion of special tithes that were collected every three years for the poor (Deut 14:28-29, 26:12-13; Lev 19:9-10, 33; Deut 24:19-22; Ruth 2). The law was based on the awareness that aliens and sojourners were vulnerable to the whims and abuses of the hosting society because of their lack of full membership, and their unfamiliarity with customs, laws, language, and topography. See Wright, *Old Testament Ethics*, 262–65.

26 Johannes Althusius, *Politica: An Abridged Translation of Politics Methodically Set Forth and Illustrated with Sacred and Profane Examples*, ed. and trans. Frederick S. Carney (Indianapolis: Liberty Fund, 1995), 142.

27 Fretheim, *Exodus*, 203–4.

28 "And I will make justice the line, and righteousness the plummet; hail will sweep away the refuge of lies, and waters will overwhelm the shelter" (Isa 28:17).

29 Elazar, *Covenant and Polity in Biblical Israel*, 209.

30 Elazar, *Covenant and Polity in Biblical Israel*, 209.

31 Daniel J. Elazar, "Althusius and Federalism as Grand Design," Jerusalem Center for Public Affairs, Daniel Elazar Papers Index, http://www.jcpa.org/dje/articles2/althus-fed.htm.

32 Elazar, *Covenant and Polity in Biblical Israel*, 188.

33 Kinsler, *The Biblical Jubilee*, 34.

34 Kinsler, *The Biblical Jubilee*, 35.

35 Alicia Winters, "El Goel en el Antiguo Israel," *RIBLA* 18 (1994): 3; cited in Kinsler, *The Biblical Jubilee*, 35.

36 Johannes Hoekendijk, "Mission—A Celebration of Freedom," *USQR* 21 (1966): 141; cited in John Howard Yoder, *The Politics of Jesus*, 2nd ed. (Grand Rapids: Eerdmans, 1994), 32.

37 Walter Brueggemann, *Worship in Ancient Israel: An Essential Guide* (Nashville: Abingdon, 2005), 8–9.

38 Sociologically, religious worship has a community-building effect that strengthens and expands a communal bond, as it regularly offers the occasion for assembly and common practices. In a monotheistic religion, serving the one same God has the organizing effect among participants of instilling a sense of identity, affection, and solidarity.

39 For the covenantal basis of worship and its communicative-transformative power, see Hak Joon Lee, "Cutting, Binding, and Re-membering: A Covenantal Approach to Christian Liturgy and Ethics," in *Liturgy and Ethics*, ed. Pieter H. Vos (Leiden: Brill, 2017).

40 Fretheim, *Exodus*, 139.

41 A ritual is a visible, performative form of the liberative narrative; in fact, Augustine of Hippo defined a sacrament as "a visible sign of invisible grace."

42 Walter Brueggemann, *Ice Axes for Frozen Seas: A Biblical Theology of Provocation* (Waco, Tex.: Baylor University Press, 2014), 272.

43 Alexia Salvatierra and Peter Heltzel, *Faith-Rooted Organizing: Mobilizing the Church in Service to the World* (Downers Grove, Ill.: IVP Academic, 2014), 36.

44 Elazar, *Covenant and Polity in Biblical Israel*, 193.

45 Daniel J. Elazar, "Deuteronomy as Ancient Israel's Constitution: Some Preliminary Reflections," Jerusalem Center for Public Affairs, https://www.jcpa.org/dje/articles2/deut-const.htm.

46 John Wright, "Spirit and Wilderness: The Interplay of Two Motifs Within the Hebrew Bible as a Background to Mark 1:2-13," in *Perspectives on Language and Text: Essays and Poems in Honor of Francis I. Andersen's Sixtieth Birthday, July 28, 1985*, ed. Edgar W. Conrad and Edward G. Newing (Winona Lake, Ind.: Eisenbrauns, 1987), 289; cited in Bryan D. Estelle, *Echoes of Exodus: Tracing a Biblical Motif* (Downers Grove, Ill.: IVP Academic, 2018), 9.

47 The rise of the prophetic office should be historically accounted for in relation to the consolidation of kingship and its abusive danger in monarchy. The development of the prophetic office was in part to counterbalance the royal rule, to check and balance the king's power. See William Dumbrell, *Covenant and Creation: An Old Testament Covenant Theology* (Milton Keynes, UK: Paternoster, 2013), 208–11.

48 In their social criticism, the Hebrew prophets relied on the election traditions (Amos 2:9-11; 3:2), certain Mosaic laws (Amos 2:7-8; cf. Lev 18:8, 15; 20:11-12; Deut 24:12-13), and the covenantal curses (Amos 4:6-10; cf. Deut 28:21-22, 24).

49 Estelle, *Echoes of Exodus*, 3.

50 Walter Brueggemann, *A Social Reading of the Old Testament: Prophetic Approaches to Israel's Communal Life*, ed. Patrick D. Miller (Minneapolis: Fortress, 1994), 57.

51 Brueggemann, *Social Reading of the Old Testament*, 56.

52 Hanson, *The People Called*, 21.

53 For a study of the Decalogue as the most reasonable paradigm for a well-ordered society in the West, see Paul Grimley Kuntz, *The Ten Commandments in History: Mosaic Paradigms for a Well-Ordered Society* (Grand Rapids: Eerdmans, 2004). The forgiveness of debt has been an exception, but in recent decades, explicitly drawing from the Exodus story, it has newly emerged as an important moral category in international relationships between rich and poor nations (e.g., Jubilee 2000, Drop the Debt).

3   Jesus

1 Gerhard Lohfink, *Jesus and Community: The Social Dimension of Christian Faith* (Philadelphia: Fortress, 1984), 26.

2 See J. Kameron Carter, *Race: A Theological Account* (New York: Oxford University Press, 2008).

3 My study of Jesus' Covenant in this chapter focuses more on its social-political meaning rather than its soteriology, although the two are never separate. My analysis is primarily based on the synoptic gospels, in particular Matthew. For a soteriological meaning of Jesus' Covenant, see Michael J. Gorman, *The Death of the Messiah and the Birth of the New Covenant* (Eugene, Ore.: Cascade Books, 2014).

4 "The covenant structure of biblical history was already clearly seen in Judaism prior to the dawn of the Christian era." See Scott Hahn, "Covenant in the Old and New Testaments: Some Current Research (1994–2004)," *Currents in Research* 3, no. 2 (2005): 278. The Qumran and early Christian communities believed that they were participating in the "new covenant" that Jeremiah and Ezekiel had promised.

5 Marcus J. Borg, *Conflict, Holiness, and Politics in the Teachings of Jesus* (New York: Trinity Press International, 1998), 11–12.

6 Richard A. Horsley, *Jesus and Empire: The Kingdom of God and the New World Disorder* (Minneapolis: Fortress, 2003), 85.

7 John Dominic Crossan, "Jesus and the Kingdom: Itinerants and Householders in Earliest Christianity," in *Jesus at 2000*, ed. Marcus Borg (Boulder, Colo.: Westview, 1997), 23–24.

8 Borg, *Conflict, Holiness, and Politics*, 13.

9 Obery M. Hendricks Jr., *The Politics of Jesus: Rediscovering the True Revolutionary Nature of Jesus' Teachings and How They Have Been Corrupted* (New York: Doubleday, 2006), 52.

10 Similarly, the Beatitudes (Matt 5:3-10) reveal the desperate social and economic conditions of Jews in Jesus' time.

11 John Yoder says that debt in the prayer genuinely refers to a financial debt, in its most "material sense." See John Howard Yoder, *The Politics of Jesus*, 2nd ed. (Grand Rapids: Eerdmans, 1994), 62.

12 "The anguished longing of Israel for her covenant god to come in his power and rule the world in the way he had always intended." See N. T. Wright, *Jesus and the Victory of God* (Minneapolis: Fortress, 1996), 203.

13 "Retelling, or re-enacting the story of the exodus, then, was a classic and obvious way of pre-telling, or pre-enacting, the great liberation, the great 'return from exile', for which Israel longed" (Wright, *Jesus and the Victory of God*, 155).

14 The motif of "return from the exile" in the Bible is inseparable from the narrative of the covenant because in Israel's imagination, since the exile is the result of breaking the covenant (sin and disobedience), then the return indicates its restoration, typically entailing the renewal of the covenant. In the case of Jesus, unlike previous covenant renewals, the expectation was deeply eschatological, just as hope was messianic: Israel's God was returning not only to restore Israel, but also to bring God's reign to the entire creation through the messiah, and through him, history would reach its consummation.

15 Lohfink, *Jesus and Community*, 27.

16 Hendricks, *The Politics of Jesus*, 55.

17 Horsley, *Jesus and Empire*, 78.

18 For example, the gospel stories, especially Matthew, have strong anti-imperial edges. Matthew contextualized and expanded the story of the Exodus in describing the birth of Jesus. Matthew introduces Jesus as a new Moses; he views and interprets his actions in parallel to the latter. For example, the nativity story of Matthew is in parallel to Exodus 1, which any Jew will immediately recognize—the genocide of all male children in Matthew and the Hebrew male children in Exodus. Both Jesus and Moses barely escaped an early death. The implication is that Herod is the new Pharaoh. See Warren Carter, *Matthew and the Margins: A Sociopolitical and Religious Reading* (Maryknoll, N.Y.: Orbis, 2000).

19 Wright, *Jesus and the Victory of God*, 251.

20 From a canonical perspective, it is important to recognize that the NT begins with the Gospel of Matthew because it most explicitly shows the historical ties between the OT (the history of the Jewish people) and Jesus and his community, and it unequivocally relies on the Exodus-Sinai paradigm.

21 N. T. Wright claims, "For a Jew, the context of behavior was of course the covenant. For Jesus, I suggest, the context of behavior was the renewal of the covenant" (Wright, *Jesus and the Victory of God*, 280).

22 This is distinctive evidence of covenantal renewal, which we discussed in the last chapter.

23 Hak Joon Lee, "Covenant as a Historical Drama for Incarnational Discipleship," in *Justice and the Way of Jesus: Christian Ethics and the Incarnational Discipleship of Glen Stassen*, ed. David Gushee and Reggie Williams (Maryknoll, N.Y.: Orbis, 2020), chap. 6.

24 Lohfink, *Jesus and Community*, 26.

25 Richard A. Horsley, *Covenant Economics: A Biblical Vision of Justice for All* (Louisville, Ky.: Westminster John Knox, 2009), 107.

26 Sean Freyne, *Jesus, a Jewish Galilean: A New Reading of the Jesus Story* (London: T&T Clark, 2004), 39.

27 Freyne, *Jesus, a Jewish Galilean*, 40.

28 Freyne, *Jesus, a Jewish Galilean*, 40.

29 Horsley, *Jesus and Empire*, 111–12.

30 John Dominic Crossan claims that Jesus' "open commensality," along with "free healing," were two central activities of Jesus. See John Dominic Crossan, *Jesus: A Revolutionary Biography* (New York: HarperOne, 2009).

31 Borg, *Conflict, Holiness, and Politics*, 94–96.

32 Borg, *Conflict, Holiness, and Politics*, 107.

33 Crossan, *Jesus*, 118–19.

34 His common meal was the practice of "religious and economic egalitarianism that negated alike and at once the hierarchical and patronal normalcies of Jewish religion and Roman power" (Crossan, *Jesus*, 198).

35 Crossan, *Jesus*, 79.

36 Walter Wink, *Engaging the Powers: Discernment and Resistance in a World of Domination* (Minneapolis: Fortress, 1992), 176.

37 Wink, *Engaging the Powers*, 182.

38 Wink, *Engaging the Powers*, 184. Jesus' organizing tactics, through Gandhi, inspired Martin Luther King Jr., who adopted this method for the Civil Rights Movement starting with the Montgomery Bus Boycott. Both Gandhi and King discovered the spiritual as well as political meaning of Jesus' teaching; power used in nonviolent resistance does not have to be political or economic, but moral and spiritual. In fact, people who are oppressed are typically lacking the former means, with only the latter dimension enabling people to look to themselves as available sources of power.

39 Wright, *Jesus and the Victory of God*, 297.

40 Paul Hanson says that the radical redefinition of membership in God's people was one of the most revolutionary aspects in Jesus' teaching. See Paul D. Hanson, *The People Called: The Growth of Community in the Bible* (Louisville, Ky.: Westminster John Knox, 2001), 400.

41 Chapter 5 of David Gushee and Glen Stassen, *Kingdom Ethics*, 2nd ed. (Grand Rapids: Eerdmans, 2016) offers a helpful discussion of this ethical renewal.

42 In Matthew, the Sermon on the Mount serves as the covenantal charter for Jesus and his community.

43 Hanson, *The People Called*, 426.

44 Wright, *Jesus and the Victory of God*, 296.

45 Wink, *Engaging the Powers*, 183.

46 It is very instructive that Jesus' announcement of forgiveness immediately effected the healing or infirmities of persons suffering from a crooked hand, paralysis, or personal stigma (e.g., the woman who anointed him).

47 Horsley, *Jesus and Empire*, 128.

4   Puritans

1 H. R. Niebuhr, "The Idea of Covenant and American Democracy," *Church History* 23, no. 2 (1954): 129.

2 Max L. Stackhouse, *Creeds, Society, and Human Rights: A Study in Three Cultures* (Grand Rapids: Eerdmans, 1984), 57.

3 William Klempa, "The Concept of Covenant in Sixteenth- and Seventeenth-Century Continental and British Reformed Theology," in *Major Themes in the Reformed Tradition*, ed. D. K. McKim (Grand Rapids: Eerdmans, 1992), 94.

4 Daniel J. Elazar, *Covenant and Commonwealth: From Christian Separation through the Protestant Reformation*, vol. 2 of *The Covenant Tradition in Politics* (New Brunswick, N.J.: Transaction, 1996), 156.

5 It is a mistake to identify Puritanism solely with Calvin and his theology. Reformed Protestantism is bigger than Calvin and Calvinism. Likewise, covenant theology is not exhausted by Calvinism alone. Puritans, while influenced by Calvin, were not blindly loyal to him. Calvin is identified as the father of the Reformed tradition, and Calvinism is the label attached to the movement. However, Zwingli and Bullinger, historically preceding Calvin, developed a more sophisticated and extensive theology of covenant. Often, their covenant theology, which is distinct from Calvin's, is unfairly subsumed under Calvinism, thus marginalizing its theological specificity, the result being that the Reformed emphasis on covenant is associated with Calvin alone. Elazar's comment is apt: "[S]cholars have usually regarded the Puritans, for example, as dour Calvinists when they were really more federalist in the Bullinger pattern. The principal influences on the formation of the Puritans' covenant theology came not from Geneva [Calvin], but from Zurich, Basel, and Strassburg. While Calvin was regarded by the most as the leader of the Reformed tradition, his teachings were not always followed exactly, enabling the several schools of federal theology to develop within this general tradition" (Elazar, *Covenant and Commonwealth*, 177).

6 James Hastings Nichols, *Democracy and the Churches* (Philadelphia: Westminster, 1951), 10.

7 For David Weir, early modern and Puritan literature treats "covenant as a formal theological principle that is used as the organizing motif for confessional theology and for Christian evangelism" (David A. Weir, *Early New England: A Covenanted Society* [Grand Rapids: Eerdmans, 2005], 5).

8 Elazar, *Covenant and Commonwealth*, 312.

9 Donald S. Lutz, "Introductory Essay," in *Colonial Origins of the American Constitution: A Documentary*, ed. Donald S. Lutz (Indianapolis: Liberty Fund, 1998), xx–xl, http://oll.libertyfund.org/pages/colonial-origins-of-the-american-constitution#lf0013_footnote_nt_009.

10 Michael Walzer, *The Revolution of the Saints: A Study in the Origins of Radical Politics* (New York: Atheneum, 1970), 161. Calvinists rejected the traditional, medieval hierarchal understanding of the social system and morality that was based on the idea of a chain of being, a natural inevitability of hierarchy, hereditary loyalty, and organic connection. According to Walzer, the Calvinist idea of covenant changed "the chains of being" to the chains of command and office,

and social relationships from status to mutual agreement (Walzer, *The Revolution of the Saints*, 166).

11 Weir, *Early New England*, 223.

12 With the Exodus at the center of their religious worldview, Puritans interwove various other themes and motifs of the Bible. For example, apocalyptic interpretations of history, inspired by the books of Daniel and Revelation, cast a vision of the end of history, the millennium, providence, prophecy, Jerusalem, the body of Christ, exile, etc., in order to create a plausibility structure for themselves and their followers.

13 As we discuss later, it should be acknowledged that this political analogy also led to a grave misuse of the biblical idea of covenant against Native Americans, treating them as "Canaanites" under God's judgment. This misuse is closely associated with supersessionism.

14 Avihu Zakai, *Exile and Kingdom: History and Apocalypse in the Puritan Migration to America* (Cambridge: Cambridge University Press, 1992), 65.

15 Zakai, *Exile and Kingdom*, 59.

16 Specifically, migration to the colony was prompted by the persecution of Puritans by Charles I, known as the Eleven Years' Tyranny (1629–1640).

17 Lutz, "Introductory Essay."

18 "Mayflower and Mayflower Compact," Plymouth Plantation, accessed September 5, 2018, http://www.plimoth.org/learn/just-kids/homework-help/mayflower -and-mayflower-compact.

19 The Exodus paradigm continued to shape the political imagination of the colony. Revolutionaries later compared King George III to the Pharaoh and George Washington to Moses.

20 Cited in Nathaniel Philbrick, *Mayflower* (New York: Viking Penguin, 2006), 352.

21 "People and Ideas: The Puritans," PBS Frontline and American Experience, PBS, accessed September 5, 2018, http://www.pbs.org/godinamerica/people/ puritans.html.

22 John Winthrop, *A Modell of Christian Charity* (1630), Hanover College Historical Texts Collection, accessed September 5, 2018, https://history.hanover .edu/texts/winthmod.html.

23 Elazar, *Covenant and Commonwealth*, 157.

24 Following Luther, these Puritans believed that individuals had the God-given right to freely worship God according to their own conscience and the teachings of Scripture.

25 This insight provided the ground for the idea of religious freedom.

26 Stackhouse, *Creeds, Society, and Human Rights*, 51.

27 Glen Stassen, *A Thicker Jesus: Incarnational Discipleship in a Secular Age* (Louisville, Ky.: Westminster John Knox, 2012), 67; William Lee Miller, *The First Liberty: Religion and the American Republic* (New York: Paragon, 1985).

28 Robert Bellah, "Is There a Common American Culture?" *Journal of the American Academy of Religion* 66, no. 3 (1998): 613–26.

29 Stackhouse, *Creeds, Society, and Human Rights*, 57.

30 Stackhouse, *Creeds, Society, and Human Rights*, 51.

31 Stackhouse, *Creeds, Society, and Human Rights*, 64.

32 Weir, *Early New England*, 229.

33 Stackhouse, *Creeds, Society, and Human Rights*, 51–52.

34 Stassen, *Thicker Jesus*, 75–76.

35 Stassen, *Thicker Jesus*, 75.

36 James E. Bradley, *Religion, Revolution, and English Radicalism: Nonconformity in Eighteenth-Century Politics and Society* (Cambridge: Cambridge University Press, 2002), 134.

37 Walzer, *The Revolution of the Saints*, 318. Despite his excellent study on the positive role that Puritanism played in the rise of modern democracy, Walzer has been criticized for his omission of the distinctive contribution of the Levellers and free church advocates to the development of modern democracy and human rights (Stassen, *A Thicker Jesus*, 66).

38 John Witte, *The Reformation of Rights: Law, Religion and Human Rights in Early Modern Calvinism* (Cambridge: Cambridge University Press, 2007), 6.

39 Quentin Skinner, *The Foundations of Modern Political Thought*, vol. 2, *The Age of Reformation* (Cambridge: Cambridge University Press, 1978), 335.

40 Daniel J. Elazar, *Covenant and Constitutionalism: The Great Frontier and the Matrix of Federal Democracy*, vol. 3 of *The Covenant Tradition in Politics* (New Brunswick, N.J.: Transaction, 1997), 38.

41 Weir, *Early New England*, 4.

42 Weir, *Early New England*, 9.

43 "There are four distinct foundation elements, and any document can contain one, all, or any combination of these elements: (1) the founding or creation of a people; (2) the founding or creation of a government; (3) the self-definition of the people in terms of shared values and goals so that the founded people may cross generations; and (4) the specification of a form of government through the creation of institutions for collective decision making" (Lutz, "Introductory Essay").

44 Donald S. Lutz, ed. *Documents of Political Foundation Written by Colonial Americans from Covenant to Constitution* (Philadelphia: Institute for the Study of Human Issues, 1986), 9–21; cited in Elazar, *Covenant and Constitutionalism*, 38–39.

45 Elazar, *Covenant and Constitutionalism*, 33, 37.

46 Weir, *Early New England*, 5.

47 Max L. Stackhouse, *Covenant and Commitments: Faith, Family, and Economic Life* (Louisville, Ky.: Westminster John Knox, 1997), 155.

48 Stackhouse, *Covenant and Commitments*, 25–26. Sphere sovereignty implies the requirement of God for a distinctive institution or relationship.

49 In some important aspects, Calvinist and Puritan theology continued the tradition of Augustinian political realism (i.e., that the state was a consequence of

the Fall, arising from the necessity to check and curb destructive human lust, greed, and violence).

50 Stephen J. Grabill, *Rediscovering the Natural Law in Reformed Theological Ethics* (Grand Rapids: Eerdmans, 2006).

51 Cf. Walzer, *Revolution of the Saints*, 12–13.

52 Walzer, *Revolution of the Saints*, 2.

53 William F. May, *Testing the National Covenant: Fears and Appetites in American Politics* (Washington D.C.: Georgetown University Press, 2011), 89–90.

54 Elazar, *Covenant and Commonwealth*, 312.

55 Stackhouse states, "It is likely, in this regard, that the much-celebrated idea of 'contract' as developed by the Enlightenment tradition deriving from such figures as Hobbes, Locke, Rousseau, and Immanuel Kant, is fundamentally dependent on interpretations of the covenant idea (Davidic, Mosaic federalist, and Adamic) as these theorists attempted to state it in terms drawn from the traditions of Roman legal theory" (Stackhouse, *Covenant and Commitments*, 151).

56 Elazar, *Covenant and Constitutionalism*, 32.

57 Elazar, *Covenant and Constitutionalism*, 38.

58 Elazar, *Covenant and Constitutionalism*, 48.

59 Elazar, *Covenant and Constitutionalism*, 50. One sees a similar influence of covenant in the motto on the Great Seal of the United States: *E Pluribus Unum*, or "Out of Many, One." The motto precisely speaks of the federal principle (unity in diversity) of covenant.

60 "We hold these truths to be self-evident; that all men are created equal; that they are endowed by their Creator with certain inalienable rights; that among these are life, liberty and the pursuit of happiness; that to secure these rights, governments are instituted among men, deriving their just powers from the consent of the governed."

61 Elazar, *Covenant and Constitutionalism*, 51.

62 Elazar, *Covenant and Constitutionalism*, 169.

63 Stackhouse, *Creeds, Society, and Human Rights*, 64.

64 The historical strength of covenant in the United States is also found in the popular usage of the word "commonwealth" in social and political life. The word describes the vision of a good society based on a covenantal worldview. First invoked by the Puritans to express their covenantal social vision, a commonwealth refers to "a self-governing community of equals concerned about the general welfare—a republican or democratic government, where citizens remained active throughout the year" (Harry Boyte, *CommonWealth* [New York: Free Press, 1989], 4). It is the community where personal freedom and rights are harmonized with solidarity and the common good.

65 Robert N. Bellah, *Beyond Belief: Essays on Religion in a Post-Traditionalist World* (Berkeley: University of California Press, 1991), 168–86.

66 Niebuhr, "The Idea of Covenant," 135.

5   Martin Luther King Jr.

1 Martin Luther King Jr., cited in Donald T. Phillips, *Martin Luther King, Jr., on Leadership: Inspiration and Wisdom for Challenging Times* (New York: Warner Books, 1998), 174.

2 Daniel J. Elazar notes that the Civil Rights Movement was "the most recent comprehensive public expression of the covenantal tradition in a proactive way" in the United States (Daniel J. Elazar, *Covenant and Constitutionalism: The Great Frontier and the Matrix of Federal Democracy*, vol. 3 of *The Covenant Tradition in Politics* [New Brunswick, N.J.: Transaction, 1998], 167).

3 Consequently, his public ministry combined the "Social-gospel Christianity," "democratic idealism," and "resolute advocacy of nonviolent protest" (Martin Luther King Jr., *The Papers of Martin Luther King, Jr.*, vol. 3: *Birth of a New Age, December 1955–December 1956*, ed. Stewart Burns et al. [Berkeley: University of California Press, 1997], 6).

4 See Peter J. Paris, *The Social Teaching of the Black Churches* (Philadelphia: Fortress, 1985).

5 Lorraine M. Gutierrez and Edith A. Lewis, "A Feminist Perspective on Organizing with Women of Color," in *Community Organizing in a Diverse Society*, ed. Felix G. Rivera and John L. Erlich (Boston: Allyn & Bacon, 1998), 104.

6 Aldon Morris argues for the crucial role of indigenous African American organizations for the Civil Rights Movement, as they served as locally organized "movement centers" which planned campaigns in their own cities. These organizations not only participated in collective activities such as filing lawsuits and organizing sit–ins, boycotts, and marches, but also helped to expand communication channels and to mobilize resources through the social networks, professional ties, kinships, friendships, and common residences built around them. See Aldon Morris, *The Origin of the Civil Rights Movement: Black Communities Organizing for Change* (New York: Free Press, 1984).

7 Hak Joon Lee, *We Will Get to the Promised Land: The Communal-Political Spirituality of Martin Luther King, Jr.* (Eugene, Ore.: Wipf and Stock, 2016), 43.

8 William D. Watley, *Roots of Resistance: The Nonviolent Ethic of Martin Luther King, Jr.* (Valley Forge, Pa.: Judson, 1985), 25.

9 "[I]n slave religion the figural vision of the emancipation as a type of biblical 'exodus' provides the paradigm for subsequent strategies and acts of political imagination" (Theophus H. Smith, *Conjuring Culture: Biblical Formations of Black America* [Oxford: Oxford University Press, 1994], 63). See also Herbert Robinson Marbury, *Pillars of Cloud and Fire: The Politics of Exodus in African American Biblical Interpretation* (New York: NYU Press, 2015).

10 In addition, the affinity between covenant and the liberation movement of African Americans is found in the historical synthesis of the slaves' penchant for justice and the African quest for community, which gave rise to a unique form of a politico-communal spirituality that upheld freedom, justice, and love, which covenant stipulates.

11 See Howard Thurman's *Jesus and the Disinherited* (Boston: Beacon, 1996) for the spiritual-psychological organizing effects of Jesus' life and ministry on African Americans.

12 James Cone, *The Cross and the Lynching Tree* (Maryknoll, N.Y.: Orbis, 2011), 156.

13 M. Shawn Copeland, "Wading through Many Sorrows," in *A Troubling in My Soul*, ed. Emilie M. Townes (Maryknoll, N.Y.: Orbis, 1993), 109–29; cited in Cone, *Lynching Tree*, 151.

14 Martin Luther King Jr., "Civil Right No. 1: The Right to Vote," in *A Testament of Hope*, ed. James M. Washington (1991; repr., New York: HarperOne, 2003), 184.

15 Martin Luther King Jr., *Where Do We Go from Here, Chaos or Community?* (1967; repr., Boston: Beacon, 2010), 167.

16 King, *Where Do We Go from Here*, 170.

17 Among many of his speeches and sermons, see especially Martin Luther King Jr., "The Death of Evil upon the Seashore," in *The Papers of Martin Luther King, Jr.*, vol. 3, *Birth of a New Age, December 1955–December 1956*, ed. Stewart Burns et al. (Berkeley: University of California Press, 1997), 256–62.

18 King, "The Death of Evil upon the Seashore," *Papers*, 3:261–62.

19 Barbara Allen, "Martin Luther King's Civil Disobedience and the American Covenant Tradition," *Publius* 30, no. 4 (Autumn 2000): 72.

20 Martin Luther King Jr., *Strength to Love* (1963; repr., Philadelphia: Fortress, 2010), 163.

21 Martin Luther King Jr., *Stride toward Freedom: The Montgomery Story* (1958; repr., Boston: Beacon, 2010), 94.

22 In a narrow scope, King's idea of desegregation and integration also follows a covenantal pattern of judgment and restoration, resistance and alternative. Desegregation meant abolishing the legal system that justified segregation of races, while integration indicated a new community based on the unity and harmony among different races that reflects "true intergroup, interpersonal living" (King, *Where Do We Go from Here*, 62). If integration is the goal of the struggle, desegregation is a necessary step toward it, just as the Exodus is a necessary step toward the promised land.

23 Hak Joon Lee, *The Great World House: Martin Luther King, Jr., and Global Ethics* (Cleveland: Pilgrim, 2011), 51.

24 Martin Luther King Jr., "MIA Mass Meeting at Holt Street Baptist Church," in *The Papers of Martin Luther King, Jr.*, 3:73.

25 Lewis V. Baldwin, *There Is a Balm in Gilead: The Cultural Roots of Martin Luther King, Jr.* (Minneapolis: Fortress, 1991), 255.

26 Martin Luther King Jr., *The Trumpet of Conscience* (New York: Harper & Row, 1967), 68.

27 Intellectually, King's idea of unity in diversity has its affinity with Personalist philosophy. See Rufus Burrow Jr., *God and Human Dignity: The Personalism,*

Theology, and Ethics of Martin Luther King, Jr. (Notre Dame: University of Notre Dame Press, 2006).

28 His sermon "The Distinction in God's Creation" addressed this issue.

29 Martin Luther King Jr., "The Distinction in God's Creation," in *The Papers of Martin Luther King, Jr.*, vol. 6, *Advocate of the Social Gospel, September 1948–March 1963*, ed. Tenisha Hart Armstrong et al. (Berkeley: University of California Press, 2007), 579.

30 Phillips, *Leadership*, 175.

31 King, *Stride Toward Freedom*, 94.

32 King's usage of "militant love" and "weapon of love" reveals the intimate connection between love and power.

33 One may add that love at its consummation is finally fulfilled when the power used for the service of others fulfills every demand of justice (King, *Where Do We Go from Here?* 38).

34 King's belief in the natural law has several combined sources, including the Bible, Western philosophy, the American democratic tradition, and the African cosmological tradition.

35 King, "Rediscovering Lost Values," in *The Papers of Martin Luther King, Jr.*, vol. 2, *Rediscovering Precious Values, July 1951–November 1955*, ed. Clayborne Carson et al. (Berkeley: University of California Press, 1994), 251.

36 Martin Luther King Jr., "Letter from Birmingham City Jail," in *A Testament of Hope*, ed. James M. Washington (1991; repr., New York: HarperOne, 2003), 293.

37 Allen, "Martin Luther King's Civil Disobedience," 99.

38 King, "Letter from Birmingham City Jail," in *A Testament of Hope*, 294.

39 Martin Luther King Jr., "I Have a Dream," in *A Testament of Hope*, 217.

40 King, cited in Phillips, *Leadership*, 153.

41 King, *Where Do We Go from Here*, 164.

42 King's idea of nonviolence is more than political practice; it theologically embodies the triad of love, justice, and power.

43 Martin Luther King Jr., "An Experiment in Love," in *A Testament of Hope*, 17.

44 King's sermon "Tough Mind, Soft Heart" reveals his sophisticated idea of this tension between idealism and realism in the Christian life.

45 The code name of his Birmingham campaign was "Project C," "C" standing for confrontation.

46 King, *Trumpet of Conscience*, 5.

47 King, *Where Do We Go from Here*, 96.

48 King highlighted a constructive function of social conflict for moral progress. He believed that nonviolent direct action is instrumental in bringing suppressed, or disguised, social tensions and collective injustices to the surface so that the members of a society may see and confront them (King, *Where Do We Go from Here*, 96).

49 King, *Where Do We Go from Here*, 55.

50 King, *Where Do We Go from Here*, 51.

51 King, *Where Do We Go from Here*, 49.

52 Martin Luther King Jr., "My Trip to the Land of Gandhi," in *A Testament of Hope*, 24.

53 King, *Where Do We Go from Here*, 139.

54 King, *Where Do We Go from Here*, 144.

55 King was critical of LBJ's War on Poverty that followed a corporate model; it was paternalistic and elite-controlled, thus bureaucratic and undermining local grassroots power and their self-organizing potential.

56 King, *Where Do We Go from Here*, 139.

57 Harry Belafonte and Stanley Levison, "Eulogy"; cited in Coretta King, *My Life with Martin Luther King, Jr.* (New York: Holt, Rinehart and Winston, 1969), 310.

58 Allen, "Martin Luther King's Civil Disobedience," 72.

6   *Saul Alinsky's Community Organizing*

1 Saul D. Alinsky, *Rules for Radicals: A Practical Primer for Realistic Radicals* (New York: Random House, 1971), 113.

2 No single political system is stipulated by the covenant. Covenant could take various political forms, such as presidency, parliamentary, or plural executive. It could also apply to local as well as national politics. What is more important is whether a political system reflects the foundational vision and values of the covenant.

3 "Essay: Radical Saul Alinsky: Prophet of Power to the People," *Time*, March 2, 1970.

4 In developing his method of community organizing, he gleaned insights from various intellectual sources such as the Judeo-Christian traditions, American democratic tradition (Jeffersonian democracy, Federalist Papers), Marxism, the labor movement, etc. While learning from diverse sources, Alinsky refused to identify with any single ideology (e.g., Marxism) or political movement. If there was one thing that was consistent throughout his life, however, it was his passion for radical democracy.

5 Community organizing has evolved, becoming further sophisticated in the post-Alinsky era, through the contribution of his coworkers and disciples such as Ernie Cortez, Ed Chambers, Mike Gecan, Arnie Graf, Fred Ross, and Christine Stephens. Alinsky's vision for grassroots democracy, power analysis, and organizing methods, however, is cherished as the backbone of community organizing.

6 Despite their suspicion and criticism of Saul Alinsky and his community organizing, Tea Party members adopted his controversial tactics in opposing the policies and legislative agendas of Obama, for example, in their disruptive actions at town hall meetings.

7 Saul D. Alinsky, *Reveille for Radicals* (Chicago: University of Chicago Press, 1946), 81.

8 Luke Bretherton notes that "the practices of organizing mediate a common life between different traditions" (Luke Bretherton, *Resurrecting Democracy* [New York: Cambridge University Press, 2015], 181).

9 Alinsky, *Reveille*, 111.

10 Saul D. Alinsky, "Is There Life after Birth?" Speech to the Centennial Meeting of the Episcopal Theological School. Cambridge, Mass., June 7, 1967 (Chicago: IAF Reprint), 60; cited in Bretherton, *Resurrecting Democracy*, 38.

11 It is a similar insight to that of a Chinese proverb: "Give a man a fish, and you feed him for a day; teach a man to fish, and you feed him for a lifetime." In a sense, to build an organization means to develop the capacity of people to speak and act for themselves.

12 Alinsky, *Reveille*, 196.

13 Alinsky, *Rules for Radicals*, xix.

14 Alinsky, *Reveille*, 99.

15 Alinsky, *Reveille*, 172.

16 Aaron Schutz and Mike Miller, eds., *People Power: The Community Organizing Tradition of Saul Alinsky* (Nashville: Vanderbilt University Press, 2015), 14.

17 Alinsky, *Reveille*, 46.

18 Alinsky, *Rules for Radicals*, 3.

19 This is David Moberg's description of "traditional Chicago style-community organizing." David Moberg, "New Rules for Radicals," In These Times, February 12, 2014, http://inthesetimes.com/article/16144/new_rules_for_radicals.

20 Edward T. Chambers, *Roots for Radicals: Organizing for Power, Action, and Justice* (New York: Continuum, 2003), 77.

21 Alinsky, *Reveille*, 47.

22 Jeffrey Stout, *Blessed Are the Organized: Grassroots Democracy in America* (Princeton: Princeton University Press, 2010), 7.

23 Alinsky notes,

> A People's Organization actually is built upon all of these diverse loyalties—to the church, to the labor union, to the social groups, to the nationality groups, to the myriads of other groups and institutions which comprise the constellation of the American way of life. These loyalties combine to effect an abiding faith in, and a profound loyalty to, the democratic way of life. (Alinsky, *Reveille*, 111)

24 Alinsky accepted democratic norms. His correspondence with Jacques Maritain reveals his support for human rights (the Universal Declaration of HR). See Bernard E. Doering, ed., *The Philosopher and the Provocateur: The Correspondence of Jacques Maritain and Saul Alinsky* (Notre Dame: University of Notre Dame Press, 1994).

25 Alinsky, *Reveille*, 79.

26 Alinsky, *Rules for Radicals*, 113.

27 Webster Dictionary, "interest," https://www.webster-dictionary.org/definition/interest.

28 Dennis A. Jacobsen, *Doing Justice: Congregations and Community Organizing* (Minneapolis: Fortress, 2001), 51. This understanding of self-interest points to a covenantal nature of community organizing, as we discuss later.

29 Boyte notes:

> [P]eople's basic concerns are not only for themselves in an immediate, short-term sense. When people think about what they care about in the longer term they evidence a strong interest in the intangibles of their lives—their families' well-being, their own sense of contribution and dignity, their core beliefs, their friends and closest associates, and their sense of efficacy in the world. (Harry Boyte, *CommonWealth* [New York: Free Press, 1989], 89)

30 Mike Miller, "Alinsky for the Left: The Politics of Community Organizing," *Dissent: Democracy and Barbarism*, Winter 2010, https://www.dissentmagazine.org/article/alinsky-for-the-left-the-politics-of-community-organizing.

31 Industrial Area Foundation, "Standing for the Whole," in Aaron Schutz and Mike Miller, eds., *People Power: The Community Organizing Tradition of Saul Alinsky* (Nashville: Vanderbilt University Press, 2015), 241–42.

32 Industrial Area Foundation, "Standing for the Whole," in Schutz and Miller, *People Power*, 241.

33 This approach is similar to Paulo Freire's pedagogy of the oppressed and conscientization. See Paulo Freire, *The Pedagogy of the Oppressed*, 30th anniversary ed. (New York: Bloomsbury, 2000).

34 Alinsky, *Reveille*, 183.

35 Alinsky, *Reveille*, 86.

36 Alinsky, *Reveille*, 110.

37 Alinsky, *Reveille*, 109.

38 Alinsky, *Reveille*, 153.

39 Alinsky, *Rules for Radicals*, 116.

40 For examples of tactics of agitation and confrontation, see Alinsky, *Rules for Radicals*, 125–64.

41 Alinsky, *Rules for Radicals*, 154.

42 Alinsky, *Rules for Radicals*, 127.

43 Alinsky, *Rules for Radicals*, 129.

44 Alinsky, *Rules for Radicals*, 116.

45 Miller, "Alinsky for the Left."

46 Alinsky, *Rules for Radicals*, 24.

47 http://infed.org/mobi/saul-alinsky-community-organizing-and-rules-for-radicals/.

48 Alinsky, *Rules for Radicals*, 36. In a similarly militant vein, he said, "A war is not an intellectual debate, and in the war against social evils there are no rules of fair play. In this sense all wars are the same" (Alinsky, *Reveille*, 154).

49 Doering, *The Philosopher and the Provocateur*, 89.

50 The following statement exhibits succinctly the connection between power and democracy in Alinsky's thought.

> In this book we are concerned with how to create mass organizations to seize power and give it to the people; to realize the democratic dream of equality, justice, peace, cooperation, equal and full opportunities for education, full and useful employment, health, and the creation of those circumstances in which man can have the chance to live by values that give meaning to life. We are talking about a mass power organization which will change the world into a place where all men and women walk erect, in the spirit of that credo of the Spanish Civil War, "Better to die on your feet than to live on your knees." This means revolution. (Alinsky, *Rules for Radicals*, 3)

51 Bretherton makes a helpful observation on this balancing act.

> If there is too much emphasis on generating a sense of crisis, then organizers burn out the relationships and the institutions. Yet if there is too much emphasis on training and relationship building, then no change is generated and organizers simply accommodate people to the status quo. (Bretherton, *Resurrecting Democracy*, 191)

52 Schutz and Miller, *People Power*, 312.

7   Covenantal Organizing and Community Organizing

1 Yuval Noah Harari, *Sapiens: A Brief History of Humankind* (New York: HarperCollins, 2015), 118.

2 Harari, *Sapiens*, 26–27.

3 An organizing structure of a society is closely associated with its notion of justice.

4 "The paradox entails using conflict and cunning not to reject one's opponent, but to reweave or convert the situation and enmesh a more powerful adversary into a transformed relationship" (Luke Bretherton, *Resurrecting Democracy* [New York: Cambridge University Press, 2015], 194).

5 Bretherton, *Resurrecting Democracy*, 192.

6 One sees different approaches in resolving these tensions in the Puritans and Martin Luther King Jr. English Puritans did not hesitate to use military means to confront and undo monarchical power, while King was adamant in using nonviolence as the means of his organizing work and movement.

7 Paulo Freire, *The Pedagogy of the Oppressed*, 30th anniversary ed. (New York: Bloomsbury, 2000), chap. 2.

8 Harry Boyte, "Community Organizing and the Next Stage of Democracy," *Huffington Post*, October 18, 2018, http://www.huffingtonpost.com/harry -boyte/community-organizing-and-_1_b_7200280.html.

9 Cf. Edward T. Chambers, *Roots for Radicals: Organizing for Power, Action, and Justice* (New York: Continuum, 2003), 34.

10 Alinsky's friendship with Jacques Maritain offers a hint of his eager embrace of the Catholic subsidiarity principle. A covenantal view of subsidiarity has been best elaborated by Johannes Althusius and Abraham Kuyper. For a comparison of the Catholic and Reformed Christian views, see Paul E. Sigmund, "Subsidiarity, Solidarity, and Liberation: Alternative Approaches in Catholic Social Thought,"

in *Religion, Pluralism, and Public Life: Abraham Kuyper's Legacy for the Twenty-First Century*, ed. Luis E. Lugo (Grand Rapids: Eerdmans, 2000), 205–20.

11 Max L. Stackhouse, *Covenant and Commitments: Faith, Family, and Economic Life* (Louisville, Ky.: Westminster John Knox, 1997), 142.

12 See Jürgen Habermas, *The Theory of Communicative Action*, 2 vols. (Boston: Beacon, 1984–1985).

13 The idea of self-interest may sound somewhat alienating to many Christians; more familiar language for self-interest might be self-care, self-love, or respect of one's basic rights. The Bible acknowledges the necessity of proper self-care and self-love in a social life. A healthy self-love is the precondition for other-love. Jesus taught love of others, but not at the annihilation of the self; for example, his command, "Love your neighbor as yourself," presupposes self-love.

14 "[C]ovenanting (and spirituality) consists in learning the skills and sensitivities that include both the courage to assert self and the grace to abandon self to another. Such covenanting recognizes that both parties have claims to make, and that one must learn the right time in which to pursue and honor each claim, and then have the confident, unencumbered freedom to move in both directions" (Walter Brueggemann, *The Covenanted Self* [Minneapolis: Fortress, 1999], 8). Covenant operates in the alternating modes of trust and yield. Trust without self-assertion is blind, just as self-assertion without trust is graceless and self-indulgent.

15 The Christian identity in the covenant is *ipso* identity rather than *idem* identity. See Kevin Vanhoozer, *Faith Speaking Understanding* (Louisville, Ky.: Westminster John Knox, 2014). The Reformed theological motto, *semper reformanda*, captures the deep sensibility and contextual ethos of the ongoing organizing (reformative) effort of the Church in its covenantal relationship with God and others.

16 Aaron Schutz and Mike Miller, "Editors' Introduction," in Aaron Schutz and Mike Miller, eds., *People Power: The Community Organizing Tradition of Saul Alinsky* (Nashville: Vanderbilt University Press, 2015)

17 Puritans developed a highly sophisticated view of associational pluralism, federalism, and the corollary of the church-state relationship inspired by covenant theology.

18 One finds similar universalistic moral insights in Logos theology, biblical wisdom literature, and the Reformed theological understanding of common grace.

19 Bretherton, *Resurrecting Democracy*, 241.

20 However, despite this striking similarity in describing community organizing via covenantal motifs and ideas, Bretherton fails to identify covenant as the basis of community organizing for Christians, as well as the historical covenantal origin of civil society and community organizing.

21 Harry Boyte, *CommonWealth* (New York: Free Press, 1989), 129.

22 Cf. Hans-Georg Gadamer, *Truth and Method* (New York: Continuum, 2004).

23 It is not completely dissonant with the Aristotelian, inductive, and empirical idea of politics that emphasizes historicity, community customs, and practical judgment.

24 Daniel J. Elazar, *Covenant and Constitutionalism: The Great Frontier and the Matrix of Federal Democracy*, vol. 3 of *The Covenant Tradition in Politics* (New Brunswick, N.J.: Transaction, 1998), 43.

25 For Puritans, the idea of covenant was "a theory of society . . . In the Puritan formulation it held that a body politic could be constituted only out of the consent of the governed, yet also out of an agreement not to terms of the people's own devising but only to the pre-stated terms of God's eternal law of justice" (Perry Miller, quoted in Elazar, *Covenant and Constitutionalism*, 20).

26 The bond is strong to the extent of giving rise to a new collective (group) identity for the participants as in the case of marriage and in God's covenant with Israel and the Church.

27 Boyte, *CommonWealth*, 61.

28 Boyte, *CommonWealth*, 12.

29 In this context, redemption means the restoration of just and loving relationships among God, humanity, the earth, and its creatures.

30 Larry L. Rasmussen, *Earth-Honoring Faith: Religious Ethics in a New Key* (New York: Oxford University Press, 2013), 17.

31 For a discussion of these dimensions cf. Randy Stoecker and Susan Stall, "Community Organizing or Organizing Community? Gender and the Crafts of Empowerment," *University of Wisconsin COMM_ORG Papers Collection* 2 (1996), rev. November 1997, accessed August 15, 2018, https://comm-org.wisc.edu/papers96/gender2.html.

32 Stout resonates with Alinsky's concern: "Utopian visions have an uplifting role to play in some forms of religion but become dangerous when they interfere with legitimate attempts to constrain what lions are now doing to lambs. Caring about the vulnerable means little if one fails to name and prevent violence being done to the vulnerable" (Jeffrey Stout, *Blessed Are the Organized: Grassroots Democracy in America* [Princeton: Princeton University Press, 2010], 42).

33 However, Alinsky was aware of this necessary tension and balance between protest and compromise: while protest is necessary, it alone is overly conflictual and thus unproductive; in certain situations, compromise and negotiation are inevitable.

34 Alinsky's writings are often intentionally provocative to get people's attention; such provocation is part of the tactics of community organizing.

35 The Truth and Reconciliation Commission in South Africa is an example.

36 Boyte, *CommonWealth*, 82.

37 Cf. Eboni Marshall Turman, *Toward a Womanist Ethic of Incarnation: Black Bodies, the Black Church, the Council of Chalcedon* (New York: Palgrave Macmillan, 2013).

38 Hak Joon Lee, *We Will Get to the Promised Land: The Communal-Political Spirituality of Martin Luther King, Jr.* (Eugene, Ore.: Wipf and Stock, 2016), 44–45.

39 Zygmunt Bauman, *Liquid Modernity* (Cambridge, UK: Polity, 2000).

40 Boyte, *CommonWealth*, 61.

41 Kevin Vanhoozer, *Remythologizing Theology: Divine Action, Passion, and Authorship* (New York: Cambridge University Press, 2012), 333–34.

42 Boyte, *CommonWealth*, 89.

43 Boyte, *CommonWealth*, 95.

44 Donald Lutz says that covenantal organizing of a society has two stages: the founding of a people and the founding of a governing arrangement for them. See Elazar, *Covenant and Constitutionalism*, 33.

45 Covenant has multiple dimensions: judicial (the law), transactional (agreement), activist (confronting injustices), ideological (social philosophy of organizing), and ritualistic (worship). Among these, community organizing pertains to an activist expression of covenantal politics.

46 Sheila Greeve Davaney, et al., "Funding and Teaching Challenges Facing Faith-Based Organizing," in *Yours the Power*, ed. Katie Day, Esther McIntosh, and William Storrar (Leiden: Brill, 2013), 105.

8   Covenantal Organizing Today

1 Karl Marx, *Economic and Philosophic Manuscripts of 1844* (Amherst, N.Y.: Prometheus Books, 1988), 138.

2 Daniel J. Elazar, "What Happened to Covenant in the Nineteenth Century?" http://www.jcpa.org/dje/articles/cov-19thcent.htm; Max L. Stackhouse, *Covenant and Commitments: Faith, Family, and Economic Life* (Louisville, Ky.: Westminster John Knox, 1997); William F. May, *Testing the National Covenant: Fears and Appetites in American Politics* (Washington, D.C.: Georgetown University Press, 2011).

3 I am preparing a sequel to this book that studies the reconstruction of ecclesiology and pastoral leadership based on covenantal organizing while addressing the interlocked four crises. This chapter offers some of these insights.

4 My analysis in this section is modest, far from being comprehensive or exhaustive; such a task deserves another book-length discussion. My focus in this section is primarily how Christians can approach these crises in their own contexts.

5 David Harvey, *A Brief History of Neoliberalism* (Oxford: Oxford University Press, 2005), 2.

6 Edward Herman and Robert McChesney, "The Global Media," in *The Global Transformations Reader: An Introduction to the Globalization Debate*, ed. David Helder and Anthony McGrew (Cambridge, UK: Polity, 2000), 222.

7 Peter Dreier, quoted in Mike Miller, "Alinsky for the Left: The Politics of Community Organizing," *Dissent: Democracy and Barbarism*, Winter 2010, https://www.dissentmagazine.org/article/alinsky-for-the-left-the-politics-of-community-organizing.

8 See Chris Hedges, *Death of the Liberal Class* (New York: Nation Books, 2010).

9 Michael Walzer, "Gulf Crisis," *The New Republic* 215 (1996): 25.

10 Hak Joon Lee, *The Great World House: Martin Luther King, Jr., and Global Ethics* (Cleveland: Pilgrim, 2011), 152–53.

11 Jeffrey Stout, *Blessed Are the Organized: Grassroots Democracy in America* (Princeton: Princeton University Press, 2010), 18–19.

12 Richard A. Horsley, *Covenant Economics: A Biblical Vision of Justice for All* (Louisville, Ky.: Westminster John Knox, 2009), 142.

13 Daniel J. Elazar, *Covenant and Polity in Biblical Israel: Biblical Foundations and Jewish Expressions*, vol. 1 of *The Covenant Tradition in Politics* (New Brunswick, N.J.: Transaction, 1995), 7.

14 David Fitch, *Faithful Presence: Seven Disciplines that Shape the Church for Mission* (Downers Grove, Ill.: IVP, 2016), 50.

15 Covenant organizing advocates contemplative activism that balances mysticism and political engagements.

16 Richard G. Wilkinson and Kate Pickett, *The Spirit Level: Why Greater Equality Makes Societies Strong* (New York: Bloomsbury, 2010).

17 Lisa Sowle Cahill, *Sex, Gender, and Christian Ethics* (Cambridge: Cambridge University Press, 1996), 137, 155.

18 Luke Bretherton, *Resurrecting Democracy* (New York: Cambridge University Press, 2015), 211.

19 Stout, *Blessed Are the Organized*, 18.

20 Nathan Gardels, "Renovating democracy from the bottom up," *Washington Post*, October 5, 2018, https://www.washingtonpost.com/news/theworldpost/wp/2018/10/05/direct-democracy-2/?utm_term=.57a6d6d88d60.

21 Covenant was at the center of Israel's understanding of cosmic order. The well-being of the cosmos depends on upholding it. Religious festivals played a crucial role in the renewal of covenant, celebrating the triumph of the will of the creator over chaotic powers.

22 The prophet Micah's eschatological vision (2:1-5) points toward such a direction.

23 Stackhouse's observation is notable: "The presence of covenant-like possibilities in many, perhaps all, cultures suggests that in the very structure of human relationships we find traces of what God has graciously revealed to humanity in the fabric of creation." See Max L. Stackhouse, "The Moral Meanings of Covenant," *The Annual of the Society of Christian Ethics* 16 (1996): 253.

24 Daniel L. Migliore, *Faith Seeking Understanding: An Introduction to Christian Theology* (Grand Rapids: Eerdmans, 2014), 285.

25 Migliore, *Faith Seeking Understanding*, 286.

26 Walter Brueggemann, *A Social Reading of the Old Testament: Prophetic Approaches to Israel's Communal Life*, ed. Patrick D. Miller (Minneapolis: Fortress, 1994), 43.

Conclusion

1 Francis Fukuyama, *The End of History and the Last Man* (New York: Free Press, 1992).

2 I take nativism/white nationalism as a form of identity politics with a populist thrust.

3 In many ways, cosmopolitanism is the extension of liberal democracy to the global level.

4 Another dangerous development, opposed to technocracy, is the rise of authoritarian or charismatic leadership in politics and senior leadership of government

under an authoritarian leader that ridicules expertise and professionalism. See Michael Lewis' *The Fifth Risk* (W. W. Norton, 2018).

5   Steven Levitsky and Daniel Ziblatt, interview by Dave Davies, *Fresh Air*, January 22, 2018, https://www.npr.org/2018/01/22/579670528/how-democracies -die-authors-say-trump-is-a-symptom-of-deeper-problems.

6   Arthur Schlesinger Jr., "The Runaway Presidency," *The Atlantic*, November 1973.

7   Harry Boyte, "Educational Change, Cultural Organizing and Citizen Politics," *The Huffington Post*, November 9, 2015, http://www.huffingtonpost.com/harry -boyte/educational-change-and-ci_b_8499348.html

8   Contemporary communitarian scholars include Alasdair MacIntyre, Amitai Etzioni, Michael Sandel, and Stanley Hauerwas.

9   *Encyclopedia Britannica*, s.v. "Postmodernism," accessed October 30, 2018, https://www.britannica.com/topic/postmodernism-philosophy.

10 See David Harvey, *The Condition of Postmodernity: An Inquiry into the Origins of Cultural Change* (Oxford: Blackwell, 1990) for a material basis of the rise and progress of postmodernism. He offers a critical analysis of the close historical tie between postmodern philosophy and capitalism.

11 H. R. Niebuhr, "The Idea of Covenant and American Democracy," *Church History* 23, no. 2 (June 1954): 134.

12 Zygmunt Bauman, *Liquid Modernity* (Cambridge, UK: Polity, 2000), 21.

13 Richard Sennett, *The Corrosion of Character* (New York: W. W. Norton, 1998), 43.

14 Bill Bishop, "Americans have lost faith in institutions. That's not because of Trump or 'fake news,'" *Washington Post*, March 3, 2017, https://www .washingtonpost.com/posteverything/wp/2017/03/03/americans-have-lost -faith-in-institutions-thats-not-because-of-trump-or-fake-news/?hpid=hp_no -name_opinion-card-e%3Ahomepage%2Fstory&utm_term=.bf92e43694c0.

15 Luke Bretherton, "Exorcising Democracy: The Theopolitical Meaning of Black Power," *Journal of the Society of Christian Ethics*, 38, no. 1 (2018): 15.

16 Martin Luther King Jr., "An Experiment in Love," in *A Testament of Hope*, ed. James M. Washington (1991; repr., New York: HarperOne, 2003), 17.

17 This is God's primary intention since the Exodus. The Davidic covenant, which justifies royal theology and the monarchy, seems to run counter to this observation. However, it should be noticed that kingship was not God's intention but a reluctant accommodation to Israel's request in 1 Samuel 8.

18 Walter Brueggemann, *A Social Reading of the Old Testament: Prophetic Approaches to Israel's Communal Life*, ed. Patrick D. Miller (Minneapolis: Fortress, 1994), 51.

19 Brueggemann, *A Social Reading of the Old Testament*, 50.

20 Daniel J. Elazar, *Covenant and Constitutionalism: The Great Frontier and the Matrix of Federal Democracy*, vol. 3 of *The Covenant Tradition in Politics* (New Brunswick, N.J.: Transaction, 1997), 181.

21 Elazar, Daniel J. Elazar, *Covenant and Polity in Biblical Israel: Biblical Foundations and Jewish Expressions*, vol. 1 of *The Covenant Tradition in Politics* (New Brunswick, N.J.: Transaction, 1995), 43.

Bibliography

Alinsky, Saul D. "Is There Life after Birth?" Speech to the Centennial Meeting of the Episcopal Theological School. Cambridge, Mass., June 7, 1967. Chicago: IAF Reprint.

———. *Reveille for Radicals*. Chicago: University of Chicago Press, 1946.

———. *Rules for Radicals: A Practical Primer for Realistic Radicals*. New York: Random House, 1971.

Allen, Barbara. "Martin Luther King's Civil Disobedience and the American Covenant Tradition." *Publius* 30, no. 4 (2000): 71–113.

Althusius, Johannes. *Politica: An Abridged Translation of Politics Methodically Set Forth and Illustrated with Sacred and Profane Examples*. Edited and translated by Frederick S. Carney. Indianapolis: Liberty Fund, 1995.

Baldwin, Lewis V. *There Is a Balm in Gilead: The Cultural Roots of Martin Luther King, Jr.* Minneapolis: Fortress, 1991.

Bauman, Zygmunt. *Liquid Modernity*. Cambridge, UK: Polity, 2000.

Bellah, Robert N. *Beyond Belief: Essays on Religion in a Post-Traditionalist World*. Berkeley: University of California Press, 1991.

———. *The Broken Covenant: American Civil Religion in Time of Trial*. Chicago: University of Chicago Press, 1998.

———. "Is There a Common American Culture?" *Journal of the American Academy of Religion* 66, no. 3 (1998): 613–26.

Bishop, Bill. "Americans have lost faith in institutions. That's not because of Trump or 'fake news.'" *Washington Post*. March 3, 2017. https://www.washingtonpost .com/posteverything/wp/2017/03/03/americans-have-lost-faith-in-institutions

-thats-not-because-of-trump-or-fake-news/?hpid=hp_no-name_opinion-card-e
%3Ahomepage%2Fstory&utm_term=.bf92e43694c0.

Borg, Marcus J. *Conflict, Holiness, and Politics in the Teachings of Jesus*. New York: Trinity Press International, 1998.

Boyte, Harry. *CommonWealth*. New York: Free Press, 1989.

———. "Community Organizing and the Next Stage of Democracy." *Huffington Post*. Last modified October 18, 2018. http://www.huffingtonpost.com/harry-boyte/community-organizing-and-_1_b_7200280.html.

———. "Educational Change, Cultural Organizing and Citizen Politics." *Huffington Post*. November 9, 2015. http://www.huffingtonpost.com/harry-boyte/educational-change-and-ci_b_8499348.html.

Bradley, James E. *Religion, Revolution, and English Radicalism: Nonconformity in Eighteenth-Century Politics and Society*. Cambridge: Cambridge University Press, 2002.

Bray, Gerald L. "Out of the Box: The Christian Experience of God in Trinity." In *God the Holy Trinity: Reflections on Christian Faith and Practice*, edited by Timothy George, 37–56. Grand Rapids: Baker Academic, 2006.

Bretherton, Luke. "Exorcising Democracy: The Theopolitical Meaning of Black Power." *Journal of the Society of Christian Ethics* 38, no. 1 (2018): 3–24.

———. *Resurrecting Democracy*. New York: Cambridge University Press, 2015.

Brueggemann, Walter. *The Covenanted Self*. Minneapolis: Fortress, 1999.

———. *Ice Axes for Frozen Seas: A Biblical Theology of Provocation*. Waco, Tex.: Baylor University Press, 2014.

———. *The Prophetic Imagination*. 40th anniversary ed. Minneapolis: Fortress, 2008.

———. *A Social Reading of the Old Testament: Prophetic Approaches to Israel's Communal Life*. Edited by Patrick D. Miller. Minneapolis: Fortress, 1994.

———. *Worship in Ancient Israel: An Essential Guide*. Nashville: Abingdon, 2005.

Burrow, Rufus, Jr. *God and Human Dignity: The Personalism, Theology, and Ethics of Martin Luther King, Jr.* Notre Dame: University of Notre Dame Press, 2006.

Cahill, Lisa Sowle. *Sex, Gender, and Christian Ethics*. New York: Cambridge University Press, 1996.

Carter, J. Kameron. *Race: A Theological Account*. New York: Oxford University Press, 2008.

Carter, Warren. *Matthew and the Margins: A Sociopolitical and Religious Reading*. Maryknoll, N.Y.: Orbis, 2000.

Ceresko, Anthony R. *Introduction to Old Testament Wisdom: A Spirituality for Liberation*. Maryknoll, N.Y.: Orbis, 1999.

Chambers, Edward T. *Roots for Radicals: Organizing for Power, Action, and Justice*. New York: Continuum, 2003.

Colfer, Carol J., and Michael L. Colfer. "Bushler Bay: Lifeways in Counterpoint." *Rural Sociology* 43, no. 2 (1978): 204–20.

Cone, James. *The Cross and the Lynching Tree*. Maryknoll, N.Y.: Orbis, 2011.

Copeland, M. Shawn. "Wading through Many Sorrows." In *A Troubling in My Soul*, edited by Emilie M. Townes, 109–29. Maryknoll, N.Y.: Orbis, 1993.

Crossan, John Dominic. "Jesus and the Kingdom: Itinerants and Householders in Earliest Christianity." In *Jesus at 2000*, edited by Marcus Borg, 21–54. Boulder, Colo.: Westview, 1997.

———. *Jesus: A Revolutionary Biography*. New York: HarperOne, 2009.

Davaney, Sheila Greeve, John Bowlin, Jarrett Kerbel, and Elizabeth Valdez. "Funding and Teaching Challenges Facing Faith-Based Organizing." In *Yours the Power*, edited by Katie Day, Esther McIntosh, and William Storrar, 99–106. Leiden: Brill, 2013.

Doering, Bernard E., ed. *The Philosopher and the Provocateur: The Correspondence of Jacques Maritain and Saul Alinsky*. Notre Dame: University of Notre Dame Press, 1994.

Dumbrell, William J. *Covenant and Creation: An Old Testament Covenant Theology*. Milton Keynes, UK: Paternoster, 2013.

———. *Covenant and Creation: A Theology of the Old Testament Covenants*. Eugene, Ore.: Wipf and Stock, 2009.

Eglinton, James Perman. *Trinity and Organism: Toward a New Reading of Herman Bavinck's Organic Motif*. New York: T&T Clark, 2012.

Elazar, Daniel J. "Althusius and Federalism as Grand Design," Jerusalem Center for Public Affairs, Daniel Elazar Papers Index. http://www.jcpa.org/dje/articles2/althus-fed.htm.

———. *Covenant and Commonwealth: From Christian Separation through the Protestant Reformation*. Vol. 2 of *The Covenant Tradition in Politics*. New Brunswick, N.J.: Transaction, 1996.

———. *Covenant and Constitutionalism: The Great Frontier and the Matrix of Federal Democracy*. Vol. 3 of *The Covenant Tradition in Politics*. New Brunswick, N.J.: Transaction, 1998.

———. *Covenant and Polity in Biblical Israel: Biblical Foundations and Jewish Expressions*. Vol. 1 of *The Covenant Tradition in Politics*. New Brunswick, N.J.: Transaction, 1995.

———. "Deuteronomy as Ancient Israel's Constitution: Some Preliminary Reflections," Jerusalem Center for Public Affairs, Daniel Elazar Papers Index. https://www.jcpa.org/dje/articles2/deut-const.htm.

———. "What Happened to Covenant in the Nineteenth Century?" Jerusalem Center for Public Affairs, Daniel Elazar Papers Index. http://www.jcpa.org/dje/articles/cov-19thcent.htm.

"Essay: Radical Saul Alinsky: Prophet of Power to the People." *Time*. March 2, 1970.

Estelle, Bryan D. *Echoes of Exodus: Tracing a Biblical Motif*. Downers Grove, Ill.: IVP Academic, 2018.

Fitch, David. *Faithful Presence: Seven Disciplines that Shape the Church for Mission*. Downers Grove, Ill.: IVP, 2016.

Freire, Paulo. *The Pedagogy of the Oppressed*. 30th anniversary ed. New York: Blooms-bury, 2000.

Fretheim, Terence E. *Exodus*. Louisville, Ky.: Westminster John Knox, 2010.

Freyne, Sean. *Jesus, a Jewish Galilean: A New Reading of the Jesus Story*. London: T&T Clark, 2004.

Fukuyama, Francis. *The End of History and the Last Man*. New York: Free Press, 1992.

Gadamer, Hans-Georg. *Truth and Method*. New York: Continuum, 2004.

Gardels, Nathan. "Renovating democracy from the bottom up," *Washington Post*, October 5, 2018. https://www.washingtonpost.com/news/theworldpost/wp/2018/10/05/direct-democracy-2/?utm_term=.57a6d6d88d60.

Genovese, Rosalie G. "A Women's Self-Help Network as a Response to Service Needs in the Suburbs." Supplement, *Signs: Journal of Women in Culture and Society* 5, no. 3 (1980): S248–56.

Gentry, Peter J., and Stephen J. Wellum. *Kingdom through Covenant: A Biblical-Theological Understanding of the Covenants*. Wheaton, Ill.: Crossway, 2012.

Giddens, Anthony. *Runaway World: How Globalization Is Reshaping Our Lives*. New York: Routledge, 2003.

Gorman, Michael J. *The Death of the Messiah and the Birth of the New Covenant*. Eugene, Ore.: Cascade Books, 2014.

Gossai, Hemchand. *Justice, Righteousness and the Social Critique of the Eighth-Century Prophets*. American University Studies, Series 7: Theology and Religion, vol. 141. New York: Peter Lang, 1993.

Grabill, Stephen J. *Rediscovering the Natural Law in Reformed Theological Ethics*. Grand Rapids: Eerdmans, 2006.

Gresham, John L., Jr. "The Social Model of the Trinity and its Critics." *Scottish Journal of Theology* 46, no. 3 (1993): 325–43.

Gunton, Colin. *The One, The Three, The Many*. New York: Cambridge University Press, 1993.

Gushee, David, and Glen Stassen. *Kingdom Ethics*. 2nd ed. Grand Rapids: Eerdmans, 2016.

Gutierrez, Lorraine M., and Edith A. Lewis. "A Feminist Perspective on Organizing with Women of Color." In *Community Organizing in a Diverse Society*, edited by Felix G. Rivera and John L. Erlich, 97–116. Boston.: Allyn & Bacon, 1998.

Habermas, Jürgen. *The Theory of Communicative Action*. 2 vols. Boston: Beacon, 1984–1985.

Hahn, Scott. "Covenant in the Old and New Testaments: Some Current Research (1994–2004)." *Currents in Research* 3, no. 2 (2005): 263–92.

Hanson, Paul D. *The People Called: The Growth of Community in the Bible*. Louisville, Ky.: Westminster John Knox, 2001.

Harari, Yuval Noah. *Sapiens: A Brief History of Humankind*. New York: HarperCol-lins, 2015.

Harvey, David. *A Brief History of Neoliberalism.* Oxford: Oxford University Press, 2005.

———. *The Condition of Postmodernity: An Inquiry into the Origins of Cultural Change.* Oxford: Blackwell, 1990.

Hedges, Chris. *Death of the Liberal Class.* New York: Nation Books, 2010.

Hendricks, Obery M., Jr. *The Politics of Jesus: Rediscovering the True Revolutionary Nature of Jesus' Teachings and How They Have Been Corrupted.* New York: Doubleday, 2006.

Herman, Edward, and Robert McChesney. "The Global Media." In *The Global Transformations Reader: An Introduction to the Globalization Debate,* edited by David Helder and Anthony McGrew, 216–29. Cambridge, UK: Polity, 2000.

Hoekendijk, Johannes. "Mission—A Celebration of Freedom." *USQR* 21 (1966): 135–44.

Horsley, Richard A. *Covenant Economics: A Biblical Vision of Justice for All.* Louisville, Ky.: Westminster John Knox, 2009.

———. *Jesus and Empire: The Kingdom of God and the New World Disorder.* Minneapolis: Fortress, 2003.

———. *Jesus and the Spiral of Violence.* Minneapolis: Fortress, 1993.

Horton, Michael. *Covenant and Salvation.* Louisville, Ky.: Westminster John Knox, 2007.

Industrial Area Foundation. "Standing for the Whole." In *People Power: The Community Organizing Tradition of Saul Alinsky,* edited by Aaron Schutz and Mike Miller, 239–44. Nashville: Vanderbilt University Press, 2015.

Jacobsen, Dennis A. *Doing Justice: Congregations and Community Organizing.* Minneapolis: Fortress, 2001.

King, Coretta Scott. *My Life with Martin Luther King, Jr.* New York: Holt, Rinehart and Winston, 1969.

King, Martin Luther, Jr. *The Papers of Martin Luther King, Jr.* Vol. 2, *Rediscovering Precious Values, July 1951–November 1955.* Edited by Ralph E. Luker, Penny A. Russell, Peter Holloran, and Louis R. Harlan. Berkeley: University of California Press, 1997.

———. *The Papers of Martin Luther King, Jr.* Vol. 3, *Birth of a New Age, December 1955–December 1956.* Edited by Stewart Burns, Susan Carson, Pete Holloran, and Dana L. Powel. Berkeley: University of California Press, 1997.

———. *The Papers of Martin Luther King, Jr.* Vol. 6, *Advocate of the Social Gospel, September 1948–March 1963.* Edited by Tenisha Hart Armstrong, Susan Englander, Susan Carson, Troy Jackson, Gerald L. Smith. Berkeley: University of California Press, 1997.

———. *Strength to Love.* 1963. Reprint, Philadelphia: Fortress, 2010.

———. *Stride toward Freedom: The Montgomery Story.* 1958. Reprint, Boston: Beacon, 2010.

———. *A Testament of Hope.* Edited by James M. Washington. 1991. Reprint, New York: HarperOne, 2003.

————. *The Trumpet of Conscience*. New York: Harper & Row, 1967.

————. *Where Do We Go From Here, Chaos or Community?* 1967. Reprint, Boston: Beacon, 2010.

Kinnaman, David. *unChristian: What a New Generation Really Thinks about Christianity . . . and Why It Matters*. Grand Rapids: Baker, 2007.

Kinsler, Ross, and Gloria Kinsler. *The Biblical Jubilee and the Struggle for Life: An Invitation to Personal, Ecclesial, and Social Transformation*. Maryknoll, N.Y.: Orbis, 1999.

Klempa, William. "The Concept of Covenant in Sixteenth- and Seventeenth-Century Continental and British Reformed Theology." In *Major Themes in the Reformed Tradition*, edited by D. K. McKim, 94–107. Grand Rapids: Eerdmans, 1992.

Kuntz, Paul Grimley. *The Ten Commandments in History: Mosaic Paradigms for a Well-Ordered Society*. Grand Rapids: Eerdmans, 2004.

Lee, Hak Joon. "Covenant as a Historical Drama for Incarnational Discipleship." In *Justice and the Way of Jesus: Christian Ethics and the Incarnational Discipleship of Glen Stassen*, edited by David Gushee and Reggie Williams, 86–104. Maryknoll, N.Y.: Orbis, 2020.

————. "Cutting, Binding, and Re-membering: A Covenantal Approach to Christian Liturgy and Ethics." In *Liturgy and Ethics*, edited by Pieter H. Vos, 223–45. Leiden: Brill, 2017.

————. *The Great World House: Martin Luther King, Jr., and Global Ethics*. Cleveland: Pilgrim, 2011.

————. "Public Theology." In *The Cambridge Companion to Christian Political Theology*, edited by Craig Hovey and Elizabeth Phillips, 44–65. New York: Cambridge University Press, 2016.

————. *We Will Get to the Promised Land: The Communal-Political Spirituality of Martin Luther King, Jr.* Eugene, Ore.: Wipf and Stock, 2016.

Levitsky, Steven, and Daniel Ziblatt. Interview by Dave Davies. *Fresh Air*, January 22, 2018, https://www.npr.org/2018/01/22/579670528/how-democracies-die-authors-say-trump-is-a-symptom-of-deeper-problems.

Lewis, Michael. *The Fifth Risk*. New York: W. W. Norton, 2018.

Lilly, Ingrid Esther. "Developing a Moral Vision for Climate Change." *Sojourners*. June 9, 2014. http://sojo.net/blogs/2014/06/09/developing-moral-vision-climate-change.

Lohfink, Gerhard. *Jesus and Community: The Social Dimension of Christian Faith*. Philadelphia: Fortress, 1984.

Lohfink, Norbert. *Option for the Poor: The Basic Principle of Liberation Theology in the Light of the Bible*. Berkeley: BIBAL Press, 1987.

Lutz, Donald S., ed. *Documents of Political Foundation Written by Colonial Americans from Covenant to Constitution*. Philadelphia: Institute for the Study of Human Issues, 1986.

————. "Introductory Essay." In *Colonial Origin of the American Constitution: A Documentary*, edited by Donald S. Lutz, xx–xl. Indianapolis: Liberty Fund, 1998. https://oll.libertyfund.org/pages/colonial-origins-of-the-american-constitution.

————. *The Origin of American Constitutionalism*. Baton Rouge: Louisiana State University Press, 1988.

Marbury, Herbert Robinson. *Pillars of Cloud and Fire: The Politics of Exodus in African American Biblical Interpretation*. New York: NYU Press, 2015.

Marx, Karl. *Economic and Philosophic Manuscripts of 1844*. Amherst, N.Y.: Prometheus Books, 1988.

May, William F. *Testing the National Covenant: Fears and Appetites in American Politics*. Washington, D.C.: Georgetown University Press, 2011.

Migliore, Daniel L. *Faith Seeking Understanding: An Introduction to Christian Theology*. Grand Rapids: Eerdmans, 2014.

Miller, Mike. "Alinsky for the Left: The Politics of Community Organizing." *Dissent: Democracy and Barbarism*, Winter 2010. https://www.dissentmagazine.org/article/alinsky-for-the-left-the-politics-of-community-organizing.

Miller, Perry. *The New England Mind: The Seventeenth Century*. Boston: Beacon, 1961.

Miller, William Lee. *The First Liberty: Religion and the American Republic*. New York: Paragon, 1985.

Moltmann, Jürgen. *The Spirit of Life: A Universal Affirmation*. Minneapolis: Fortress, 1992.

Morris, Aldon. *The Origin of the Civil Rights Movement: Black Communities Organizing for Change*. New York: Free Press, 1984.

Nichols, James Hastings, *Democracy and the Churches*. Philadelphia: Westminster, 1951.

Nicholson, Ernest W. *God and His People: Covenant and Theology in the Old Testament*. Oxford: Oxford University Press, 1986.

Niebuhr, H. R. "The Idea of Covenant and American Democracy." *Church History* 23, no. 2 (1954): 126–35.

Novak, David. *Covenantal Rights: A Study in Jewish Political Theory*. Princeton: Princeton University Press, 2000.

O'Donovan, Oliver. *The Ways of Judgment*. Grand Rapids: Eerdmans, 2005.

Paris, Peter J. *The Social Teaching of the Black Churches*. Philadelphia: Fortress, 1985.

PBS. "People and Ideas: The Puritans." PBS Frontline and American Experience. Accessed September 5, 2018. http://www.pbs.org/godinamerica/people/puritans.html.

Philbrick, Nathaniel. *Mayflower*. New York: Viking Penguin, 2006.

Phillips, Donald T. *Martin Luther King, Jr., on Leadership: Inspiration and Wisdom for Challenging Times*. New York: Warner Books, 1998.

Pinnock, Clark. *Flame of Love: A Theology of the Holy Spirit*. Downers Grove, Ill.: IVP Academic, 1999.

Rah, Soong Chan. *Prophetic Lament: A Call for Justice in Troubled Times*. Downers Grove, Ill.: IVP Academic, 2015.

Rasmussen, Larry L. *Earth-Honoring Faith: Religious Ethics in a New Key*. New York: Oxford University Press, 2013.

————. *Moral Fragments and Moral Community: A Proposal for Church in Society.* Minneapolis: Fortress, 1993.

Salvatierra, Alexia, and Peter Heltzel. *Faith-Rooted Organizing: Mobilizing the Church in Service to the World.* Downers Grove, Ill.: IVP Academic, 2014.

Schlesinger, Arthur, Jr. "The Runaway Presidency." *The Atlantic,* November 1973.

Schutz, Aaron, and Mike Miller, eds. *People Power: The Community Organizing Tradition of Saul Alinsky.* Nashville: Vanderbilt University Press, 2015.

Sennett, Richard. *The Corrosion of Character.* New York: W. W. Norton, 1998.

Sigmund, Paul E. "Subsidiarity, Solidarity, and Liberation: Alternative Approaches in Catholic Social Thought." In *Religion, Pluralism, and Public Life: Abraham Kuyper's Legacy for the Twenty-First Century,* edited by Luis E. Lugo, 205–20. Grand Rapids: Eerdmans, 2000.

Skinner, Quentin. *The Foundations of Modern Political Thought, Vol. 2: The Age of Reformation.* Cambridge: Cambridge University Press, 1978.

Smith, Theophus H. *Conjuring Culture: Biblical Formations of Black America.* Oxford: Oxford University Press, 1994.

Stackhouse, Max L. *Covenant and Commitments: Faith, Family, and Economic Life.* Louisville, Ky.: Westminster John Knox: 1997.

————. *Creeds, Society, and Human Rights: A Study in Three Cultures.* Grand Rapids: Eerdmans, 1984.

————. "The Moral Meanings of Covenant." *The Annual of the Society of Christian Ethics* 16 (1996): 249–64.

Stall, Susan, and Randy Stoecker. "Toward a Gender Analysis of Community Organizing Models: Liminality and the Intersection of Spheres." In *Community Organizing and Community Building for Health,* edited by Meredith Minkler. 2nd ed. New Brunswick, N.J.: Rutgers University Press, 2005.

Stassen, Glen. *A Thicker Jesus: Incarnational Discipleship in a Secular Age.* Louisville, Ky.: Westminster John Knox, 2012.

Stoecker, Randy, and Susan Stall. "Community Organizing or Organizing Community? Gender and the Crafts of Empowerment." *University of Wisconsin COMM_ORG Papers Collection* 2 (1996): 729–56. Revised November 1997. Accessed August 15, 2018. https://comm-org.wisc.edu/papers96/gender2.html.

Stoneall, Linda. "Cognitive Mapping: Gender Differences in the Perception of Community." *Sociological Inquiry* 51, no. 2 (1981): 121–28.

Stout, Jeffrey. *Blessed Are the Organized: Grassroots Democracy in America.* Princeton: Princeton University Press, 2010.

Thurman, Howard. *Jesus and the Disinherited.* Boston: Beacon, 1996.

Turman, Eboni Marshall. *Toward a Womanist Ethic of Incarnation: Black Bodies, the Black Church, the Council of Chalcedon.* New York: Palgrave Macmillan, 2013.

Tillich, Paul. *Systematic Theology.* Vol. 1. Chicago: University of Chicago Press, 1951.

Vanhoozer, Kevin. *Faith Speaking Understanding.* Louisville, Ky.: Westminster John Knox, 2014.

————. *Remythologizing Theology: Divine Action, Passion, and Authorship*. New York: Cambridge University Press, 2012.

Walzer, Michael. *Exodus and Revolution*. New York: Basic Books, 1985.

————. "Gulf Crisis." *The New Republic* 215 (1996): 25.

————. *The Revolution of the Saints: A Study in the Origins of Radical Politics*. Cambridge: Harvard University Press, 1965.

Watley, William D. *Roots of Resistance: The Nonviolent Ethic of Martin Luther King, Jr.* Valley Forge, Pa.: Judson, 1985.

Weir, David A. *Early New England: A Covenanted Society*. Grand Rapids: Eerdmans, 2005.

Wilkinson, Richard G., and Kate Pickett. *The Spirit Level: Why Greater Equality Makes Societies Strong*. New York: Bloomsbury, 2010.

Wink, Walter. *Engaging the Powers: Discernment and Resistance in a World of Domination*. Minneapolis: Fortress, 1992.

Winters, Alicia. "El Goel en el Antiguo Israel." *RIBLA* 18 (1994): 19–29.

Winthrop, John. *A Modell of Christian Charity*. 1630. Hanover College Historical Texts Collection. Accessed September 5, 2018. https://history.hanover.edu/texts/winthmod.html.

Witte, John. *The Reformation of Rights: Law, Religion and Human Rights in Early Modern Calvinism*. Cambridge: Cambridge University Press, 2007.

Wolterstorff, Nicholas. *Until Justice and Peace Embrace*. Grand Rapids: Eerdmans, 1983.

Wright, Christopher. *Old Testament Ethics for the People of God*. Downers Grove, Ill.: IVP, 2004.

Wright, John. "Spirit and Wilderness: The Interplay of Two Motifs Within the Hebrew Bible as a Background to Mark 1:2–13." In *Perspectives on Language and Text: Essays and Poems in Honor of Francis I. Andersen's Sixtieth Birthday, July 28, 1985*, edited by Edgar W. Conrad and Edward G. Newing, 269–98. Winona Lake, Ind.: Eisenbrauns, 1987.

Wright, N. T. *Jesus and the Victory of God*. Minneapolis: Fortress, 1996.

Yoder, John Howard. *The Politics of Jesus*. 2nd ed. Grand Rapids: Eerdmans, 1994.

Zakai, Avihu. *Exile and Kingdom: History and Apocalypse in the Puritan Migration to America*. Cambridge: Cambridge University Press, 1992.

Zizioulas, John D. *Communion and Otherness: Further Studies in Personhood and the Church*. New York: T&T Clark, 2006.

Index